pages suggests a comprehensive pluralistic strategy. It deals in detail with steps that must be taken in employment programs, in federal taxation, in social security, in health programs, and in welfare to redistribute well over $100 billion a year now being spent in transfer programs. The proposals have the advantage of remaining within the limits of commonly accepted principles of liberal reform and can be achieved in increments. In this way the country can move deliberately to achieve redistribution, correcting or modifying programs as dislocations appear.

From the analysis of employment and income transfer programs, the book derives lessons for moving forward toward a sense of community based on a more just allocation of income in which everyone—the privileged as well as the less privileged—stands to benefit. *Jubilee* is an agenda for forward-looking legislators and ‧ administrators and a text for policy students.

Alvin L. Schorr is general director of the Community Service Society of New York. Formerly an official at the Department of Health, Education, and Welfare and the Office of Economic Opportunity, he has also been a teacher, researcher, and practicing social worker. John Gardner has said of him that "both his heart and his mind are in good working order."

Jubilee for Our Times

Jubilee for Our Times

A Practical Program for Income Equality

EDITED BY ALVIN L. SCHORR

COLUMBIA UNIVERSITY PRESS NEW YORK 1977

Copyright © 1977 Columbia University Press
All rights reserved

Columbia University Press
New York   Guildford, Surrey

Library of Congress Cataloging in Publication Data
Main entry under title:
Jubilee for our times.

Includes bibliographical references and index.
    1. Income distribution—United States.   I. Schorr,
Alvin Louis, 1921–
HC110.I5J8   339.2′0973   76-41824
ISBN 0-231-04056-3

THE LAW OF THE FIFTIETH YEAR OF JUBILEE

And thou shalt sound the trumpet. . . . And thou shalt sanctify the fiftieth year, and shalt proclaim remission to all the inhabitants of thy land: for it is the year of jubilee. . . . If thy brother being impoverished sell his little possession, and his kinsman will, he may redeem what he had sold. . . . But if his hands find not the means to repay the price, the buyer shall have what he bought until the year of jubilee. For in that year all that is sold shall return to the owner, and to the ancient possessor.

—Leviticus 25

DEDICATION

This book is dedicated to those who
enter into the passion of our time
and remain engaged,
whether like my friends Mitchell Ginsberg
and Bernard Shiffman they have made
it their vocation,
or like Louise Bogan they struggle through
pleasure and pain to a reality and compassion
that her poetry perfectly expresses,
or as many young adults must now be doing
move inside for a moment to some
sandy lee and interior task
to sort out confusion without
taking the escape of cynicism
and to study an idealism that does
not require romanticism.

Preface

The title of this book may be regarded as an elaboration of R. H. Tawney's more economical *Equality,* published almost fifty years ago. It seems fitting to quote from that book our first disclaimer:

To criticize inequality and to desire equality is not, as is sometimes suggested, to cherish the romantic illusion that men are equal in character and intelligence. It is to hold that, while their natural endowments differ profoundly, it is the mark of a civilized society to aim at eliminating such inequalities as have their source . . . in its own organization, and that individual differences, which are a source of social energy, are more likely to ripen and find expression if social inequalities are, as far as practicable, diminished.

That is, we declare that we understand all men to have been created equal with individual differences.

This book is the result of a collaboration of economists and social workers, three of each. All speak with different competences and, the reader may occasionally be unsettled to find, jargons. A conscientious effort has been made to eliminate jargon, but a certain shifting of mind set may be required from chapter to chapter. Yet the collaboration seemed useful in an attempt to fuse social values eschewed by most economists with analytic hardheadedness not sufficiently widespread among social workers. Also, the subject matter of transfer payments tends, for some reason, to be divided between the two fields.

Much of the work reported in these chapters was supported at the School of Social Work of New York University by The Milbank Memorial Fund, The Rockefeller Brothers Fund, and The Rockefeller Foundation. They were generous in their trust that useful results might emerge, and we are grateful.

We make a small apology for using 1972, 1973, 1974, and 1975 data variously. Computers may be quick, but analysis and publication take agonizing periods of time. Data bearing on the distribution of income is not the first to emerge from official sources, and we used the latest that was available on each particular matter. As will be seen, however, income distribution has a gyroscopic stability and it is unlikely that a difference of a year or two in data would alter an argument.

A number of people were helpful at various stages of this endeavor. The chapter on employment draws substantially on material developed by Helen Ginsburg. Dennis Bushe provided research assistance for the chapter on AFDC, and John S. Stockton for the chapter on health. Jean T. D. Bandler and Sar Levitan provided helpful comments on the first and second chapters, respectively. Bertrand Russell Seidman also commented on the second chapter and, moreover, insisted that a book like this was required long before it had been thought of.

Stanley Surrey offered constructive advice on the chapter on taxation. Philip Booth, Ida C. Merriam, Daniel L. Price, and James H. Schulz provided useful advice on the chapter on social insurance. Saul J. Blaustein did the same and, in addition, provided technical assistance in writing the part of the chapter related to unemployment insurance. Eveline Burns, Patricia Bauman, and Frank Van Dyke offered useful comments on the chapter on health.

And Borge Varmer and Robert Lampman were of considerable assistance with the chapter on AFDC. These people are not responsible for conclusions or remaining errors, but there would have been more errors and less clarity without their generous help.

Perhaps this preface should also end with a quotation, this one from Diderot's article on "Society" in the eighteenth-century *Encyclopédie:*

There is no more inequality between the different stations in life than there is among the different characters in a comedy: the end of the play finds all the players once again in the same position, and the brief period for which their play lasted did not and could not convince any two of them that one was really above or below the other.

Such a quotation risks the judgment that in the end the matter signifies nothing. On the other hand, some recognition of our common mortality may help in surmounting rough spots, whether of intellect or feeling.

ALVIN L. SCHORR

March 1976

Contents

THE CONTRIBUTORS   *xv*

CHAPTER 1.   **FAIR SHARES**
Alvin L. Schorr   *1*

CHAPTER 2.   **WORK AND SHARES**
Charlotte Muller   *25*

CHAPTER 3.   **TAXATION**
David Gayer   *73*

CHAPTER 4.   **SOCIAL INSURANCE AND REDISTRIBUTION**
Martha N. Ozawa   *123*

CHAPTER 5.   **FAIR SHARE IN HEALTH CARE**
Rachel Floersheim Boaz   *179*

CHAPTER 6.   **AFDC: SYMPTOM AND POTENTIAL**
Winifred Bell   *221*

CHAPTER 7.   **THE STRATEGY AND HOPE**
Alvin L. Schorr   *265*

NOTES   *189*

INDEX   *315*

THE CONTRIBUTORS

WINIFRED BELL is Associate Director of Research of the Comision Sobre Sistema de Seguridad Social Integral, Puerto Rico.

RACHEL FLOERSHEIM BOAZ is a Service Fellow, National Center for Health Services Research, U.S. Department of Health, Education, and Welfare.

DAVID GAYER is a staff economist at the Regional Planning Association, New York City.

CHARLOTTE MULLER is a professor of economics at the Graduate Center, City University of New York.

MARTHA OZAWA is a professor of social work at the George Warren Brown School of Social Work, Washington University, St. Louis.

ALVIN L. SCHORR is General Director of the Community Service Society of New York.

1

Fair Shares

ALVIN L. SCHORR

This book deals with privilege, especially financial privilege, and how to modify it. In particular, we deal with government payments to families and individuals, so-called income transfers.

One tends to think about money in terms of established relationships—a carpenter is worth so much an hour, a piece of land so much a year, a sum of money so much in interest rates—as if these values had intrinsic meaning. Yet, viewed another way, wages, rent, and interest merely serve to divide up the goods and services produced in the country over a period of time. The division that results always seems imperfect. In the end, we apply correctives like preferences and graduated rates to the tax system, and pay out money through cash transfers such as social security and public assistance. Taxes and transfers have other objectives as well, but correcting the division of national income is one.

Income shares may be measured in a number of ways, some of them quite technical. Here, on the whole, we will deal with shares of personal income secured by the poorest fifth (or quintile) of the population, the next fifth, and so on to the richest fifth. Some regard such a measure as misleading. It does not necessarily reflect possessions, access to credit, expense accounts and other perquisites, or what people actually consume. And it does not focus on the sources of inequality that we might want to alter—wealth, wages, and so forth. Still, income shares are highly correlated with possessions, credit, and consumption, and are readily visualized. Moreover, income shares have been charted statistically over a period of time, and other measures have not.

Income Transfers— A Limited Approach

Distribution of income depends on the state of the economy, the structure of wages, the distribution of wealth, tax and transfer policies, and considerations even harder to define and discipline— power, discrimination, shifting demographic and geographic patterns. One can approach these issues fundamentally, with a utopian critique and strategy. There are times for such an approach, but we have chosen not to use it here. Recent utopians have sought fundamental change without having a clear idea of what the outcome might be. When nothing happens, they take the psychic credit and let the cash go. Some have programs, but the programs do not develop momentum. One has to wonder whether inertia is now built into our system in manners so complex and subtle that major systematic, directed change is not possible.[1] We adopt a pragmatic and incremental strategy here because there is too much pain and danger abroad in our country to fail to do what we can. Too much is being settled about income shares while the argument about fundamentals remains unsettled. Moreover, we value our political system. It is vital to that system—and a test of it—to outline liberal reform and set out to achieve it.

The strategy here focuses on income transfers in particular.

Limiting the subject to income transfers permits us to explore a major element of the distributional system with care. Income transfers are a directly manageable instrument of government policy. In 1972 they comprised $71 billion in cash transfers; $11 billion in food stamps, housing subsidies, and similar programs; $25 billion in medical care; and $63 billion in money spent on education—$170 billion in all. Plainly income transfers in themselves can have considerable effect on income shares.

Income-transfer policy is linked to policies governing the economy and employment. For example, it is thought that one cost of the 1975 recession (i.e., of the actual 8.7 percent rather than a moderate 4 percent unemployment rate) was an increase in the number of poor people by 3.2 million.[2] The nation compensates for a net reduction in jobs through income transfers, if at all. The matter may be illustrated in this way: in 1972, 18 million people would have been poor but for income transfers. After transfers, only 10 million were poor.[3] Transfer policy is linked to overall economic and employment policy in other ways we shall explore. The two sets of policies interact; yet one set does not replace or make the other unnecessary. Income transfers are or can be of particular significance to the poorest. We take up income-transfer policy as one strategy, understanding that it does not stand alone.

In the remainder of this chapter, we will set forth our view of income shares, make clear the values that lead us to want to change them, offer an objective, and explain how the book is organized.

The Unequal Fifths

It should provoke reflection that income shares have been more stable over the decades than absolute wages or family income. For example, real family income has about doubled in the last generation. Yet, between 1947 and 1972 variation in the income share of the lowest quintile, before taxes, was confined between 4.5 and 5.5 percent of national income. The share of the top quintile varied only between 41.4 and 43.0 percent. Before 1947, the depression had brought down the share of the top quintile markedly; these people were the ones who had it to lose. Full employment and government controls in World War II brought up the share of the bottom quintile modestly. Those are the notable fluctuations in half a century.

They seem small as one recalls affluence, recession, inflation, wars (cold, hot, and antipoverty), and movements. They seem even smaller if one brings to mind the

staggering changes in the size and composition and geographic location of the population; . . . the decline of the three-generation extended family; . . . men starting to work later and returning earlier and more women working away from home; the decline of farming and self-employment and the rise of service industries, government employment, and professional and technical occupations. . . .[4]

We will return shortly to the question of stability. Table 1.1 sets forth the top income of the lowest, second, middle, and fourth

Table 1.1 Income at the Upper Limit of Each Quintile and Bottom of Top 5 Percent of Incomes, for Families and Unrelated Individuals, 1972

	Families	Unrelated Individuals
Lowest Fifth	$ 5,612	$ 1,596
Second Fifth	9,300	2,689
Middle Fifth	12,855	4,660
Fourth Fifth	17,760	8,000
Top 5 Percent	27,836	13,500

Source: U. S. Bureau of the Census, *Money Income in 1973 of Families and Persons in the United States,* Current Population Reports, ser. P-60, no. 97, table 22.

quintiles, and the cut-off income at which in 1972 one entered the top 5 percent of incomes. Because families and unrelated individuals represent quite different situations, the Census Bureau handles them separately and they are reported here separately. It is apparent that the top of the lowest fifth hovers just above the poverty line, and the highest fifth is a figure not so large as one might imagine. Income from wealth is not fully reflected in the latter figure, as the Census Bureau counts it. For example, money received from the sale of property such as stocks and bonds is not included.

Table 1.2 reports the distribution of income in 1972, before and after federal taxes and transfer payments.

Income-share tables are put together in a variety of ways (for example, table 1.2 forgoes the complications of state and local taxes); nevertheless, the relationships are generally familiar. The

Table 1.2 Distribution of Income, 1972, before and after Federal Taxes and Transfer Payments (Percent)

Population Quintile	Income before Taxes and Transfers [a]	Income after Federal Taxes	Income after Federal Taxes and Transfers	Income after Transfers and before Taxes
Lowest Fifth	1.7	1.8	6.3	5.4
Second Fifth	6.6	7.0	9.1	11.9
Middle Fifth	14.5	14.8	14.6	17.5
Fourth Fifth	24.1	24.4	22.8	23.9
Highest Fifth	53.1	51.9	47.1	41.4

Sources: Edward R. Fried, et al., *Setting National Priorities—The 1974 Budget* (Washington, D.C.: The Brookings Institution, 1973), p. 50; and U.S. Bureau of the Census, *Money Income in 1972 of Families and Persons in the United States,* Current Population Reports, ser. P-60, no. 90.

[a] The first three columns of figures are based on the Brookings MERGE file projected to calendar 1972 levels. They combine incomes of families and individuals into a single set of figures and include capital gains as income. The final column, based on census data, deals with the income of families only and does not include capital gains in income. It can only grossly be compared to the other columns and is therefore set off from them.

poorest fifth of families wound up with 5.4 percent of personal income before taxes, the richest fifth with almost eight times as much. Federal taxes turn out to have relatively little effect on the overall distribution of income. That is because social-security taxes are regressive, and the progressive income-tax system is as laden with favors for those who have the keys as a harem. (No deeply buried secret is revealed there; more will be said in the chapter on taxes.) Transfer payments make rather a greater difference: the two bottom quintiles gain in shares at the expense, in particular, of the fifth of the population with the largest incomes. (The $71 billion in cash-transfer payments in fiscal 1972 included $53 billion in social security and related programs, $12 billion in public assistance, and $6 billion in veterans' pensions and compensation.) [5]

The table gathers together people of all sorts, noting only their income. Particular groups show somewhat different distributions. The distribution of income among the aged is more unequal than is the case overall. The same is true for nonwhites. Distribution is more unequal in cities than in towns. [6] Groups that might be regarded as vulnerable or discriminated against are especially important to us. With variations, to be sure, their incomes tend to reflect the stability of the overall pattern, but at a lower level. That is, the incomes of those who are discriminated against improve over time as a stable fraction of overall improvement. For many years, for example, the median income of black families was 50 to 55 percent of the income of white families. In the virtually revolutionary civil rights situation of the 1960s, the ratio climbed to 61 percent—only to start a steady decline in 1971.

Women earn less than men. In 1971, a woman employed full time earned three-fifths as much as a man. Youths earn less than older people, of course. (Income has tended to peak for men around the age of 40 and for women around 50.) But the income of youths has shown a tendency to decline *relative to* the income of older people, a tendency arising from a mixture of more and less cheerful developments. That is, they have lost out relatively both because they have stayed longer in school and because they have been unable to find work when they sought it.[7] The income of the aged, though still substantially lower than average, has been improving relatively over the last decades, reflecting improvement in social-insurance programs.[8] Other special groups also consistently occupy the lower reaches of income distribution—families headed by women, the less educated, farm workers, and other special occupational groups.

One perceives that the distribution of income is a broad and imprecise index of the fates of various disadvantaged (and advantaged) groups. As disadvantaged groups are defined—and especially when they define themselves—one may read portents for the future in the very stability of disadvantage. The cases of blacks and of women are well understood but, as another example: "The increasingly unfavorable income position of the younger age groups points to a danger that inequalities in the income distribution will be perpetuated over the next twenty years as these cohorts age. . . ."[9] That is to say, youths today who are confronting inequality are perforce establishing poor work records and habits. Years from now, they will have trouble finding and keeping good jobs, which will no doubt be attributed to a culture of poverty.

Why Is the Distribution Stable?

These examples of the fate of special groups compound the question that was raised about the stability of income distribution over time. Special efforts have been applied to improve the position of these groups; yet they seem barely to move in relative terms. In some cases the efforts succeed (for example, trade unionism has markedly improved the income share of salaried employees); nevertheless, others take their places in the 20 percent of families that manage on 5 percent of total personal income. If one views our distributive system as a vast homeostatic mechanism, the elements that produce stasis may suggest themselves.

Wealth is one factor; it is more unevenly distributed than income. The richest 10 percent of the population receive 29 percent of personal income but own 56 percent of national wealth.[10] And that wealth is largely income producing, while the 44 percent in the hands of others who are less wealthy more heavily represents homes, cars, and appliances. As a result, income from wealth would tend to stabilize income distribution in the face of opposing tendencies affecting wages or income transfers. Peter Barnes illustrated the matter in this fashion. In 1970, owners of wealth received $82 billion in interest, dividends, and rent. (Capital gains are not included in the figure.) The total amount spent for public assistance and other noncontributory welfare programs was $16 billion.[11] So the distribution, setting wages and salaries apart, ran five to one in favor of advantaged people.

Discrimination is another factor in the stability of income shares. Because it is circular and pervasive, discrimination is difficult to quantify. Groups that are discriminated against are, on the whole, less well educated and therefore less qualified for jobs that pay well. Disadvantage must be distributed in tie-in sales. For example, a family that is black is more likely to be headed by a woman and to have other characteristics associated with poor capacity to earn. It is difficult to isolate the single factor of blackness and know that it—which is to say discrimination—accounts for income differences. Nevertheless, the task has been undertaken with steadily increasing sophistication.

Reporting a Princeton University study, Charles B. Markham, a government official, said that educational level "accounts for only about one-third of the difference in occupational ranking between Negro men and majority group men; the inevitable conclusion is that the other two-thirds must be attributed to discrimination. . . ."[12] Other studies adjust for age, education, occupation, industry, region, years of work experience, and differences in family composition. Although the results are reported in varying terms, the fundamental conclusion is the same: nonwhite unemployment rates are still 50 percent higher than white rates.[13] Comparing people with equivalent education and experience, blacks earn from $624 to $5,477 less than whites annually.[14] Manipulating 1974 census data, one finds that "an income gap of approximately 20 percent remains for which there is no reasonable explanation other than discrimination." [15]

When color, sex, accent, age, or similar factors not readily changed or hidden can bar people from work or lead them to work for less, we are dealing with caste rather than class. Caste is a classic device for maintaining a static and unequal income distribution.

In discussing wealth and discrimination, we deal with instruments that maintain stability, but obviously the motive force is political. Otherwise, citizens could redistribute wealth itself, diminish discrimination, or improve and create instruments for redistributing income. The evolution of the tax system may give a clue to what happens here. Federal income-tax rates have declined more or less steadily since World War II, even when there seemed some danger of inflation or a desperate need for public rather than private expenditure. Although they approached the matter quite differently, both Joseph Pechman and Tibor Scitovsky have suggested that as people move into income brackets in which they are more heavily taxed they join an effort to reduce tax rates.[16] In other words, effective tax rates are a result of a balance in which a shifting majority draws the line about the burden it will bear. It has been argued that that balance was typically an alliance of the middle classes with the rich, and that the middle classes would now shift to an alliance with the poor.[17] But that prediction was made at the close of the 1960s.

One might indeed suppose that the middle classes, or lower middle classes, would join in an alliance with the poor to redistribute income more effectively toward themselves, but often they do not seem to grasp their economic self-interest. The issues involved are extensive, technical, and complex. The issues in the tax system alone defy the understanding of a reasonably intelligent but inexpert layman. As an example, it is fairly well established that federal tax deductions for interest payments and local taxes on one's home "provide largest benefits to recipients of larger than average income whose experience with wealth is typically not limited to their own houses. They provide negligible aid to low income households. . . ."[18] It would be to the advantage of those who are less than wealthy to wipe out deductions for home ownership, but practically no one who would profit believes that. A candidate could lose an election on no other grounds than trying to explain this matter.

In the example of home ownership, poor information is probably mixed with ideology ("a decent home for every American family"). The triumph of ideology over apparent self-interest was clearly seen in the defeat in the early 1970s of President Nixon's proposed welfare reform. Much else might be said about that proposal, but substantially it would have benefited southern states and their populations, black and white. Yet southern senators provided the core of opposition to the bill. Why? Prejudice, the work ethic, simple lack of information?[19] The nature of a public debate and the grip—not to say manipulation—of ideology, prejudice, and sentiment represent a considerable qualification on the operation of economic self-interest. That brings us to a deeper impediment to change in the distribution of income.

The United States is not a town-meeting democracy but a representative one, and that turns out to mean an interest-group democracy. We hardly ever get a plebiscite on a clear issue; we get broadly instructed representatives, besieged with advice and influence, who can in any event be effective only on issues selected from a long and confusing menu. In that circumstance, interest groups require power, competence, a wide-angle lens for locating issues, and continuity. Robert Heilbroner observed that "it is not the institutional framework that is static. It is the social core of the system, its structure of privilege." [20] In other words, our institutions allow for change, but economic privilege provides tools for political effectiveness, and political effectiveness supports economic privilege. Populist movements which carry the day, or some days, may make only narrow and sporadic changes.

Obviously, we have not touched on the whole wide range of supports of a stable income distribution. But we glimpse the essential elements of homeostasis: economic anchors, such as unequal distribution of wealth; socioeconomic stabilizers, such as discrimination; and the near identity of economic and political power, supported by the increasing extent and complexity of real issues of self-interest. Given these elements, occasional concentration of reformist or egalitarian interest on some single issue, *to the exclusion of all others,* serves stability rather than change. One example will close this section.

In 1970, social-security payments were raised by 15 percent for all beneficiaries. The poorest beneficiaries had $7 or $8 added to the $55 a month they were already receiving, but $30 was added to the benefits of those who were already receiving $200 a month. Nothing much for redistribution! At the same time, Congress rejected a provision that would have raised the minimum payment for any beneficiary from \$55 to \$100 a month. The matter was disposed of in a congressional committee virtually in passing when a technician said the money would go to people who did not need it. That measure would have cost \$2 billion, and two-thirds of the money would have gone to poor people.[21] It was dealt with in minutes—undebated and practically unnoticed.

At the very moment that the committee was acting, in a White House conference across the city several hundred reformers carried on a heated argument about whether welfare reform should guarantee minimum income at \$3,600 or \$5,600. They and many others were to invest a good deal of energy for three years. That they seem to have lost in the end is not the point. Even if they had won the prize would have been \$5 billion, in a period when upwards of \$25 billion was being divided up in social-security increases and tax reductions alone—without their attention.

Why Alter Shares?

It is now widely accepted "that the existence of inequality is a legitimate provocation to social criticism. Every inequality is on the defensive, must prove itself against the imputation of injustice and unnaturalness." [22] The most widely cited recent justification for this point of view was offered by John Rawls. "All goods," he argued, "are to be distributed equally unless an unequal distribution of any or all of these goods is to the advantage of the least favored." [23]

The contemporary counterargument relies on the need of an industrial society for hierarchy. In economists' terms, social justice is pitted against efficiency, that is, against the capacity of greed and the private market to provide the most production when least interfered with. "For over a century [this presumption] has survived on theoretical speculation rather than sound empirical evidence"; [24] nevertheless the presumption holds sway among economists. In the end they, like most people, find a pragmatic position somewhere between pure social justice and pure greed. [25] The difficulty is that arguments from social justice and from efficiency, while they oppose each other, do not meet, and there is no way of settling how much equality or how much efficiency. The compromise is itself worked out in the free market, which is to say it is a shifting (but in its result, not far shifting) vector of conscience, unrest, and economic and political power.

Efficiency is not, strictly speaking, an ideology or principle of social justice. The principle that has come to undergird efficiency and support inequality is—to put it unceremoniously—equal opportunity. Those who wish less equality of result typically call for more equality of opportunity. It was R. H. Tawney who recalled the primary purpose and achievement of the idea of equal opportunity. That idea helped to bring down feudalism's structure of inherited legal privilege, and fostered the industrial revolution and the development of a solid middle class. Equal opportunity, Tawney added,

is right in attaching a high significance to social mobility; it is wrong in implying that effective mobility can be secured merely through absence of legal restraints, or that, if it could, economic liberty would be a sufficient prophylactic against the evils produced by social stratification. [26]

The demand of the civil-rights movement for compensatory justice adds overtones to that caution that simple removal of restraints will not correct evils produced by stratification.

We have learned more generally, in any case, and over and over again, that underprivilege interferes with advancement and, indeed, ambition in a thousand ways. While some of the underprivileged manage to seize and use equal opportunity, it has to be acknowledged that far more of the privileged manage to do so. It is not feudalism or inherited legal privilege about which our society now struggles; it is rather the undesirable aspects—in particular the degree of inequality—of our free-enterprise system. Dealing with that requires not simply absence of legal restraints but deliberate and systematic alteration of the affirmative policies that determine income distribution.

In recent years, a newly sophisticated appreciation of the limits of social policy has tended to undermine the egalitarian impulse, where it exists. It has become clear that we can spend large amounts of money without diminishing the problems we address. This has been attributed to the inertia, not to say inner-directedness, of expanding bureaucracies; to the possibility that our character as a people creates our problems as much as what we fail to spend on or do about them; and to the tendency for solutions to lead to new and sometimes more serious problems.[27] These reflective and often conservative and pessimistic views join curiously with environmentalist and humanitarian views about the limits of economic growth. The latter see production and economic growth as undesirably materialistic and destructive. The logic of neither set of views is necessarily inegalitarian, but they unite in tending to regard the distribution of goods or resources as secondary or, in any case, beyond systematic control. Little helps a homeostatic mechanism as much as being left to its own devices.

As a rational matter, then, considerations of social justice have been opposed by arguments of efficiency in production, an ideology of equal opportunity, and a pessimistic view of policy. Where philosophy confronts ideology and resistable reasoning, one comes out where he likes. It must be evident that the authors write here from an egalitarian point of view. That arises from an assessment of the arguments already offered, and two additional considerations. These have to do, first, with the elimination or reduction of poverty and, second, with the need for a sense of community.

Poverty and Community

One ordinarily assumes that poverty is an objectively defined level of living related to basic bodily needs and social decency. But it is evident that, viewed across countries or across time in our own country, the poverty level is defined in relation to national wealth and, in particular, to average family income. Victor Fuchs explored definitions of poverty over an extended period of time to conclude that "any family [is poor] whose income is less than one-half the median family income." [28] By that definition, a more or less stable 20 percent of the population has proved to be poor since 1947. One can press the point over a longer period of time. Preparing for the war against poverty in 1964, the Council of Economic Advisers accepted a standard of living of $3,000 as the poverty level for a family of four and judged 20 percent of the population to be poor.[29] By that standard of living, practically everyone should have been called poor sixty years earlier. But looking around himself in 1904, Robert Hunter estimated that 12 to 24 percent of the population lived in poverty.[30]

What technicians have lately learned is only the simplest common sense, after all. The blacks who rioted in the Watts section of Los Angeles in 1965 felt poor in relation to the style of living they saw on television screens every day. That they may have been wealthy by the standards of people living in shacks in Argentina or, for that matter, Mississippi helped them not at all. As the Economic Council of Canada phrased it, poverty is not sheer lack of essentials, but feeling oneself an "unwilling outsider" at the banquet table where everyone else feeds.[31] Because the United States government uses a dollar definition of poverty, adjusted for changes in the cost of living but not for general improvement in real income, its statistics show a decline in poverty from 20 to 10 percent of the population over the past decade. But by 1975 the dollar figure it was using, $5,000 for an urban family of four, strained credulity. It takes little imagination to predict newly refined studies of poverty, emerging with new definitions in a few years, and the conclusion that 20 percent of the population is poor.

The stability of the poor as a proportion of the total population is, a moment's reflection will suggest, a consequence of the stability of the distribution of income. If families are poor that have less than half of median income, with exquisite management the poorest fifth of the population might be kept from poverty with about one-tenth of national income—that is, with half their strictly proportional share. But if their share is only one-twentieth, the task is hopeless.[32] Arithmetic makes it so, and the dollar figure that defines poverty, taken alone, whether $3,000 or $5,000 or more, is not really determining. In other words, reducing poverty in any substantial way requires redistribution.

To turn to the second additional consideration, it has been remarked quite widely that we suffer in this country from lack of community. We are said to be a classless society; in principle we do not ascribe nor accept fixed class positions. Nevertheless, groups regard themselves as subordinated and typically believe that progress can be made only at the expense of other groups. Blacks, Spanish-speaking Americans, and Indians seem to have been the declared objects of public policy in the mid-1960s, the so-called blue-collar groups at the turn of the decade, and the middle classes when they felt the recession in the mid-1970s. That such groups may riot or, if they get themselves together, overturn an administration through the electoral process is one face of the problem. The

other face, termed anomie, is characterized by a sense of out-
sideness, cynicism, and disconnection from the central purposes
and actors of our society. Anomie is a reservoir for unrest, but is
even apart from that a deeply troubling phenomenon.

A nationwide British study suggests two conditions that
may, in particular, lead to a sense of relative deprivation or grievance. One is a person's position relative to others: How far does he
perceive himself as removed from people with whom he compares
himself? Second is a person's state of expectation: What does he
think is the chance or likelihood that he may improve himself? [33] A
larger gap in relative positions and higher expectations tend to
magnify a sense of grievance. American ideology leads to the most
ambitious and hopeful comparisons, and so—with positions actually disparate and relatively fixed—the sense of grievance is great.
The National Commission on the Causes and Prevention of Violence saw this problem as one of the major causes of an increasing
crime rate. [34] Sociologists see it as the reason that poverty seems so
much more destructive psychologically in the United States than in
poorer countries. [35]

Despite our ideology to the contrary, there have been warnings in the last decade or two that we are developing a "permanent" or "undifferentiated underclass." [36] These are people with
chronically inferior incomes, set off from the majority of the population by a characteristic employment pattern and minority status or
other cultural differences. Gunnar Myrdal warned in 1960 that such
a development would retard our economy. [37] Since that time, a
school of economists has argued that we already have two distinct
pools of labor, one of them essentially low paid, nonunion, and
dead end. Government policy has, in recent years, expanded programs like Medicaid and food stamps that deal with the poor separately—reinforcing other forces that make for a "duplex society." [38] That the underclass turns out to be constituted of the most

aggrieved minorities makes the development entirely dangerous. Even if not dangerous, an underclass would stand as an abiding insult to the spirit and mood of the nation.

Deprivation may be made to feel worse by the fact that, however stable the income distribution, no one stakes out a defense of a desirable degree of inequality. The argument is conducted like a tug-of-war, as if it must end categorically in the kingdom of equality or of inequality. The very rulelessness, or free-market character, of the struggle for increased relative income has been identified by Barbara Wootton and John H. Goldthorpe as the crux of the problem of anomie.[39] Contending groups have no criterion of success. Critical national situations of inflation or deflation promote conflict rather than cohesion, for there is no understanding on which to base an incomes policy. John Goldthorpe put the matter as follows:

> If the problem of ''anomie'' in economic life is to be attacked effectively, then the problem of social inequality must be attacked simultaneously. It can be argued as a matter of sociology rather than ideology, that in a society that is both industrial and democratic a *relatively* stable order in economic life can *only* be created through some minimum degree of consensus. . . . And such consensus in turn cannot be achieved without the distribution of economic resources and rewards becoming in some degree principled; that is, more capable of rational and moral justification [his emphasis].[40]

In sum, the stability of inequality in the face of an ideology of classlessness fosters alienation. The development of an underclass, promoted by a dual labor market if that has in fact been developing, by government policies that increasingly deal separately with the poor, and by historic factors that encourage ethnic identification of the underclass, destroys community. In other countries and other times, such separation has been supported and explicitly justified. The rulelessness of income distribution in the United States exacerbates alienation and conflict.

We conclude that some increased measure of equality is necessary to reduce poverty and increase community, let alone for reasons of social justice. Then how much more equality?

How Much More Equality?

Few would seek literal equality. The shape of such a society would be difficult to imagine and, in any event, unlikely of achievement. On the other hand, no rationale exists for the degree of inequality reflected in table 1.2. The stability of the income distribution does not, in any demonstrable way, reflect internal necessity. At its upper and lower reaches, the income distribution was in fact different early in the century. And at least some of the countries with which we might compare ourselves have less inequality.

A United Nations expert group found the United States to have substantially more inequality than most European countries and Canada.[41] Another study found that "in terms of either comparative dispersion or aggregate income, there was apparently a greater inequality in income distribution in the United States than in the other countries [Germany, Sweden, and the United Kingdom]." [42] This is not to suggest that we pattern ourselves on one or another of these countries, but only that there appears to be room for a more nearly equal distribution within the general framework of western industrial democracies.

A numerical objective will help to frame the issues. It is selected here particularly in relation to the reasoning that has been offered about reducing poverty and enhancing community. *The distribution of income should be shifted sufficiently to double the share of the bottom quintile, that is, to increase its share from roughly 5 to a little over 10 percent of personal income.* (That is after transfers and before taxes; taxes would also be adapted to interfere as little as possible with the income of the lowest quintile.) In the process, the share of the next to the lowest quintile would also have to improve by, say, 2 percent. The changeover share, 7 percent, would come from the fourth and highest quintiles. The sum to be shifted works out to $55 to $60 billion.

A hypothetical distribution is shown in table 1.3 and compared with the 1972 distribution. Obviously, fractions might be passed around differently, particularly in the highest quintiles. The share proposed for the lowest quintile is the only objective. The precise nature of adjustments that are set off in the rest of the income distribution would work themselves out in the marketplace.

Table 1.3 Family Income after Transfers and before Taxes, in 1972 and as a Hypothetical Objective (Percent) [a]

	Lowest Fifth	Second Fifth	Middle Fifth	Fourth Fifth	Highest Fifth
1972	5.4	11.9	17.5	23.9	41.4
Hypothetical	10.4	13.9	17.5	21.9	36.4

[a] Rounding produces a slight discrepancy

Substantial political and economic problems are involved; it is particularly necessary that they not be exaggerated. It will become apparent that no grand scheme is proposed that requires two-fifths of the population to hand over large and small sums of money. Precisely the kind of political and economic negotiation that has gone on for years would continue, with the interest of the poorer quintiles more carefully defined and a clearer government position on their side. In the nature of our political system, a shift would take place in the ways that are least painful and, undoubtedly, out of national growth rather than out of income already in people's hands. At an annual growth rate of 3 or 4 percent, it seems reasonable to suppose that a 7 percent shift could be accomplished in five to seven years—without excessive trauma and leaving the larger part of national growth for other purposes.

The proposed changes are cast within the context of our current system but they are substantial; the point should not be glossed over. They would almost double the income of the lowest quintile. The ratio between the aggregate income of the highest and lowest quintiles is now 7.5 to 1; it would wind up 3.5 to 1.

Other kinds of changes are implied that must be more speculative. One wonders whether certain kinds of unpleasant or stigmatized work would be performed. Would we pay more for help with housework or do without it? Even more speculative, the very structure of our families might respond, on one hand, to women's increased earning capacity and, on the other hand, to the increased financial security of poorer women if they stayed at home. In recent years, such questions have possibly borne more weight of speculation than evidence will support, one way or another.[43] Here we observe only that matters like the role of women are the very stuff of current social movements and are affected by a variety of powerful forces. Where a shift in income shares might have more than marginal effect (on the link between low income and minority status, for example), the effect is naturally also likely to be egalitarian. But a movement of income shares in the manner explored here would be by degrees, providing opportunity for testing and compensatory measures when the citizenry desired them.

A Pluralistic Strategy

The strategy that is pursued here, an attempt to change the overall impact of all income transfers, has been out of style. In the last decade, a number of scholars and reformers have pressed a seemingly simpler strategy that would divide cash transfers into two reoriented systems.[44] Social security would become rather more like private insurance; public assistance would be converted into a negative income tax [45] or "income supplement." This approach contains difficulties of logic and arithmetic, which ultimately led some early proponents to express reservations about it.[46] Moreover, it contains difficulties of basic political strategy which were alluded to in the illustration earlier of the 1970 social-security changes. A few observations about the difficulties of this simpler approach may be useful.

First, the design of a negative income tax requires that some amount of earned income (say, 50 percent) be disregarded for purposes of a government payment. Unfortunately, that means that the payment to people without earnings would be very low or that families with good incomes would receive payments. For example, a 1969 presidential commission recommended income supplements that, as they guaranteed poverty-level payments, would have enrolled 4 out of 10 families in the country.[47] As legislatures deal with this dilemma and face giving a payment for poor people to almost half the country, the so-called income guarantee at the bottom winds up very low indeed.[48]

A second problem arises from our terribly complex, overlapping system of benefits.[49] Every proposal for restructuring these programs reduces benefits to a great many people or, to avoid that, sets benefit levels so high that costs are prohibitive. Either way, a standing jump into a new system has proved not to be feasible politically. We require a way to negotiate ourselves step by step into a better version of the system we have. It was for such underlying reasons, as well as because of the betrayals charged to liberals, conservatives, and the president himself, that Nixon's welfare reform—a version of a negative income tax—was rejected by Congress.[50]

The "divide and reform" approach contains a third and

deeper difficulty. If social security were set free from its obligations to poor people, undoubtedly it (and those who were not poor) would flourish in payment levels and expansion of entitlements. At the same time, the quality of public assistance or of a negative income tax would be tied directly to the political power of poor people—as now. Within a few years, the income share of the bottom quintile might be expected to deteriorate.

Reviewing welfare developments in Great Britain and the United States, Norman Furniss put this conclusion directly:

The lesson of both countries is that selectivity from below launches the poor into a contest they cannot win. Benefits may be raised at the outset in an ad hoc manner; headlines may be made; but in the long run relative positions are at best maintained. Indeed, it is hard to imagine how the outcome could be otherwise. . . .[51]

The distinction in points of view may, perhaps, be put as follows: Proposals for a simpler or divided system include a reformed welfare program for poor people that may, within its own narrow confines, be an improvement. It is, at best, a small improvement relative to all income transfers. And if by inattention or design its effect is to cut them out of other programs, it will reduce their overall share in the end.

Here, we are interested in net redistribution over the years, not in a particular redistributive program at a particular moment. Our strategy is concerned with the manner in which major current programs, as well as new programs within current American ideology, may serve to produce fairer shares. The reader will find the pattern that is examined not neat, and the recommendations not readily summed up in a single plan. That makes more demands on the attention and understanding of scholars and reformers. But all the nooks and crannies of the transfer system are where money is likely to lodge. Those who wish to affect shares have to grasp that.

We begin with a chapter on employment, because it is related to and frames issues of income distribution. We go then to the tax structure that provides the money for transfers. Chapters on social insurance and public assistance deal with cash transfers, and another chapter with health insurance. There are a number of omissions—for example, food stamps and subsidies for housing. In general, they are less significant in magnitude than programs that are covered; a little will be said about them in the closing chapter. Education, which contains its own complex set of issues relating to fair shares, and which is basically a state and local rather than federal matter, is also excluded.

The effort of these chapters is to suggest a series of disparate changes which, taken together, would produce a shift of $55 to $60 billion, or 7 percent of the national income. If all the suggestions were to be implemented, the change would be even larger, but one hardly expects that. It is not an all-or-nothing game (one of its advantages), and the net change desired may be secured by pursuing these changes discretely, where opportunity permits. If this statement is read as permission for inattention or faint effort, the point will have been missed. The range of relevant issues is set forth in some detail in order to indicate the scope necessary for producing change.

The concluding chapter will review and take special note of major trends and policies.

2

Work and Shares

CHARLOTTE MULLER

The redistribution of income cannot come about through transfer payments alone. It is simply too big a problem. Furthermore, people want to receive their income from work. If annual earnings levels were adequate for all who now work, and if opportunities to work were equal to the number of those who desire to work, a more equal income distribution would result.

The life cycle of the "ideal" labor-market participant would be made up of a series of successes as the person passed through various stages. Each success would improve the worker's chances of attaining adequate, secure, and increased earnings at future stages and of avoiding negative outcomes. Initial preparation for the labor market would impart a good foundation of basic skills and some special competence. Continuous employment—year round, full time, year in, year out—would provide a stable work record in a given job and avoid costly job searches, inopportunely timed, and dependence on transfer payments. The industry in which the person worked would shelter its workers against exposure to unemployment of all kinds, accidents, and illness, and would protect them from what could not be avoided by financial benefit schemes. The wage level, job security, and fringe benefits would be guarded by a successful union. Finally, the worker, on retiring, would have attained rights to an adequate income.

For many, this ideal is out of reach from day one. For others, the cycle may have begun auspiciously, but the person encountered setbacks that could not be overcome—such as a disabling illness or attachment to an industry that was permanently displaced. Women are at risk of a particular version of labor-market troubles when they enter with poor skills, several children, and a starring role as primary breadwinner. In many cases this occurs because of the adversities befalling a male primary earner; in others, because of premature family formation.

This chapter will begin by exploring the dimensions of earnings-related inequality. Closed doors to certain superior labor markets (reflected in part in occupational and industrial variations) and the number of earners in the household are economic correlates of earnings inequality. The personal and demographic correlates include age, race, sex, and disability. Recent trends in inequality and the gap in unemployment rates between favored and unfavored groups indicate persistent and in some ways mounting problems.

The second part of the chapter reviews the policy options available for amelioration of low wages, unemployment, and subemployment. Each policy choice is addressed to some particular component of the total problem. Certain policies focus on improving individual capacity to work, availability for work, and access to relevant information within a broad manpower program. Creation of jobs in the public sector is useful when private employment is inadequate. Improved wage bargains can remedy another cause of poverty. And the stabilization of the general economy (along with certain modifications of the autonomy of corporations in the market) would provide a better setting for the more specific manpower and employment policies. While there is a limit to what each approach can do, once a commitment is made, the power that can be wielded by a broad battery of remedies is great. So is the need.

The Problem: An Earnings Strategy

In our society, work is a major source of personal identity. Most Americans work, have worked, or will work some day. And for most, work is the primary source of income. More than 75 percent of income comes from earnings.[1] In 1971, 9 out of 10 families received some income from earnings.[2] Hence earnings have a profound influence on income distribution.

However, earnings alone do not determine income distribution. Income from capital, because its ownership is so concentrated, is distributed much more unevenly than earned income. The richest 19 percent of families own 76 percent of all privately held assets; the poorest 25 percent have no net assets.[3] Nonearned income is most significant at the extremes: the rich rely heavily on income from wealth, and the poor on income transfers. For the large majority in between, earnings tell the story.

Less than half of income is from wages and salaries among those with incomes under $5,000, who account for almost 17 percent of families. (Most of the rest of their income comes from transfer payments.) For the 49 percent of families between $10,000 and $25,000, 86 percent of income comes from wages and salaries. For the 7 percent of families at or over $25,000, income from wages and salaries drops to 71 percent of total income, reflecting the importance of property income.[4]

Earnings also come, though less so than in the past, from self-employment. In October 1974, 78.2 million of the nation's 86.5 million employed persons worked for wages and salaries; 7.4

million were self-employed; and 872,000 worked without pay for family-run businesses.[5] In agriculture, the majority are still self-employed. But in the rest of the economy, employees outnumber the self-employed by about 14 to 1.[6]

Vital though earnings are to most persons, the American economy has been unable to solve the problem of providing adequate jobs (although the job market allegedly has been sustained in the last decades by policies favorable to corporate growth, to extension of markets of multinational corporations, and to military involvement). A commitment to guarantee full employment was avoided when proposed legislation was watered down after World War II. The 1946 law that was actually passed set "maximum" rather than full employment as the policy goal.

In successive epochs, the measurement of employment and of the labor supply reflected shifting concerns of the economy of the day. Progressively, attention moved from the size of the general labor supply to occupational specialization and then to the level of employment. In the current period the definition of the labor force has become a controversial matter because it affects policy. That is, the level of unemployment that is considered "normal" is only one part of the task of defining the total national problem. Also involved is whether part-timers, discouraged job-seekers, women with children, and handicapped persons are to be included when the total number of jobs needed for full employment is reckoned. The Bureau of Labor Statistics (BLS), according to Commissioner Shiskin, is not planning to issue a combined "subemployment rate" that would combine low earners with the unemployed.[7] The bureau states that it would be difficult to specify a low-earnings criterion applicable to all employed workers, and that earnings distributions and unemployment measures represent different universes, so that *different policy measures* are needed for low-paying jobs and no jobs. However, the bureau does measure combined manhours lost by the totally and partially unemployed. One consequence of conceiving of chronic low wages as part of the employment problem by defining a group "unable to find work at standard wages" is that a limit is set to how much we can count on wage reductions to increase the number of jobs. Measurement of the numbers affected by low wages has drawn heavily on the poverty-level concept developed by Mollie Orshansky of the Social Security Administration and applied to families of different size. Because the poverty line is set at an absolute subsistence level, it has lagged seriously behind living standards. For this reason, a more satisfactory count of those who receive inadequate wages can be made on the basis of Bureau of Labor Statistics price surveys for low-cost and moderate-cost family budgets in different locations. The component items are based on family-expenditure studies updated from time to time, and minimum social as well as physical needs are represented.

The measurement of low wages is perhaps less controversial than the measurement of unemployment, but the choice and achievement of appropriate policies to deal with low wages are no less a challenge.

The causes of low wages and of unemployment need to be considered together. This is true also of the policy options for solving these problems. Low-wage industries and occupations often have more inherent risk of joblessness. And when unemployment occurs, the low-wage worker is poorly protected. He or she is less likely to qualify for public unemployment benefits or to receive maximum amounts, and has fewer private assets. The chances of finding another job are less for the unskilled or for people who are kept out of high-wage employment by discrimination based on ethnicity or sex.

If the earnings share *can* be modified, the need for other redistribution policies that arises from the workings of the labor market will, of course, be reduced.

EARNINGS INEQUALITIES AND THEIR CORRELATES

A strategy to improve the level and distribution of work-related income is essential to a broad program against poverty and inequality. Adequate earnings reduce the burdens that must otherwise be taken up by income-transfer programs such as welfare and social security, and make it possible for such programs to do more for groups that cannot turn to the labor market. The wage relationship provides the basis for private group protection against unemployment, medical expense, disability, and retirement, and thus against the need for income maintenance. Entitlement to public benefits protecting against various risks is also dependent on wage level and stability of employment (which determine whether the applicant meets a base-period requirement and which establish size of benefits).

In the absence of improvement in work-related income, a large part of income-maintenance transfer payments may be used to sustain a low-wage pool of workers, shifting costs of production from certain employers and consumers to society.

The two basic components of earnings for the individual are wage level or rate and continuity of employment. For the family, there is an additional factor of the number of workers contributing to household income.

The actual value of earnings as a resource for households depends also on family size (number of dependents), and thus on fertility, and on tax policy, which determines net disposable income. For interperiod comparisons, correction for consumer price changes must be made.

The general level of the economy, of course, basically determines the number of jobs and the aggregate wage pool in a given time period. In fact, the employment rate is used as a general economic indicator. Fiscal and monetary policies, direct public employment, and public commitment to economic development and investment are the major factors that will influence the jobs/earnings situation for the economy as a whole and facilitate or restrict programs directed to specific labor-market problems.

Security of employment and the level of wages both vary by occupation and industry. Stable employment ideally means employment that is not affected by seasonal fluctuation in markets based on weather (agriculture) and on social custom (school year, holidays), not dependent on lumpy large-scale expenditures by businesses (construction), and not affected by the business cycle. The individual whose skills have several uses is more protected against variations in demand for particular products and against technological changes.

The native endowment of individuals insofar as physical stamina, manual dexterity, and special talents are concerned is a component in wage returns for work. Given a normal distribution of these characteristics in a large population, differences in the level of human capital formed by education and training (which, representing economic resources, are not evenly distributed) contribute to an unequal distribution of earned income and of opportunities for the most stable jobs. Moreover, since human capacities for work at adulthood are influenced by nutrition, childhood environment, and even prenatal care, personal investment in human capital by richer and poorer households may be directed so as to intensify rather than compensating for this tendency toward inequality.

This does not mean that human-capital programs can be counted on to overcome the employment/earnings problems of the poor; we shall see the issues involved in the discussion on training later on in the chapter.

EARNINGS INEQUALITIES

The wage system under a completely free market is not egalitarian in intent. In an unrestrained market, supply and demand determine wages.

In a market economy the living wage is largely a moral rather than an economic concept. It is theoretically true that a subsistence wage must be paid in order to assure survival and replacement of the labor force in the long run. However, historical experience shows that populations endure very low wages for long periods and that employers use migration and employment of families to augment the low-wage labor supply. The living wage as a moral concept, based on the primacy of the human being, is at odds with the traditional justification for wage variations—allocative efficiency. Labor is said to be directed where it is scarce by high wages and repelled where it is redundant by low wages. Large wage differences are simply market signals distributing resources throughout the economy. In the absence of discrimination, skill and occupational differences are thought to reflect mainly differences in ability and in learning costs, embodied in wages.

But of course, the wage system does not operate in this idealized manner. Cairnes's theory of noncompeting groups, expressed in the nineteenth century, records a simple observation: barriers to entry in the form of well-defined individual limitations of ability and skills effectively inhibit perfect competition across occupations. The extent of these bounds varies among labor-market entrants, but in no case will individual choice extend over the entire spectrum of occupations. "The barrier [of the agricultural, i.e., unskilled worker] is his social position and circumstances, which render his education defective while his means are too narrow to allow of his repairing the defect. . . ." [8]

For each person social circumstances limit participation

beyond a certain set of occupations, however high the rates of remuneration may be outside this range.

The dual labor-market theory, which has been used in recent years to explain, among other things, the use of a casual labor pool to augment manpower supply in periods of peak demand,[9] is derived from recognition of limits on worker mobility. In this approach, the labor market is seen as divided into primary and secondary sectors. (In the extreme version of this theory there is a complete dichotomy of sectors.) Jobs in the primary market are distinguished by superior pay, fringe benefits, working conditions, employment stability, and chances for advancement relative to positions in the secondary market. Parallel differences exist between the workers in these two sectors; specifically, workers in the primary market exhibit relatively stable work behavior, i.e., less absenteeism and lateness, fewer people quitting, etc.

According to the theory, secondary workers, because of poor work histories and inadequate skills, find it impossible to enter the primary sector. (The role of discrimination in recent years as a screening device limiting the access of minorities to primary positions has been checked by changes in the law.) When all primary jobs are filled, the theory suggests, there no longer exists a demand for such workers; jobs are then transformed into secondary-sector positions. The secondary labor market is perfectly competitive, i.e., all labor is homogeneous, as are demanders of labor. Hence even marginal wage changes will result in the worker leaving his job, as experience is not valued, and the employer is disinclined to invest in training. A pattern of high job turnover tends to be self-perpetuating.

A study conducted by the New York City Human Resources Administration [10] contradicts the notion of two labor markets but indicates strong differences among individuals as to opportunities to compete for high-wage jobs. Education, training, and work experience—that is, aspects of human capital—were found to affect upward mobility and chances of initial employment in high-wage jobs. The effectiveness of training in raising wages of women was nil, and this was explained in part by discrimination. Another effect of ethnic and sex discrimination was very low starting wages that could not be overcome by education and training.

High- and low-wage markets were not found to be entirely separate, as 25 percent of workers moved downward between "first" and "last year" jobs—and 30 percent moved upward. Nor is the secondary labor market less stable insofar as employment is concerned. Employers in the latter market appear to be responsive to productivity as well as to personal characteristics.

The study concludes that education and training are effective in advancing workers along the line for high-wage jobs but need reinforcement by antidiscrimination efforts. Evaluation of the superior effects of certain types of training programs is also needed, to establish whether the training itself or differential personal characteristics of entrants is responsible for improved wage levels. Finally, neither investment in human capital nor correction of market discrimination can do much for low earners if the overall economy fails to supply enough good jobs.

One can acknowledge the existence of permanent or deeply entrenched barriers to mobility without subscribing to a particular version of the dual-market theory. The general concept is a warning that improving the training or motivation of individual workers may not solve the problem of low wages.

In the nineteenth century, working conditions were so oppressive and wages so low that state intervention and unionization eventually became controlling forces. As Karl Polanyi pointed out, these methods *aimed* at interference with the market:

To argue that social legislation, factory laws, unemployment insurance, and above all trade unions have not interfered with the mobility of labor and the flexibility of wages, as is sometimes done, is to imply that these institutions have entirely failed in their purpose, which was exactly that of interfering with the laws of supply and demand in respect to human labor and removing it from the orbit of the market.[11]

How much inequality remains after this history of intervention?

CORRELATES OF INEQUALITY OF EARNINGS

Inequality of earned income is revealed by national statistics on male workers. The highest-paid fifth received 40 percent of all wage and salary income, whereas the lowest fifth received only 5 percent. Lack of year-round, full-time work is one of the important factors in inequality. When only those males with a year-round work history are compared, the share of the poorest quintile is almost doubled.

Low earnings also go with certain occupations.[12] For both white and nonwhite males, for example, the farm worker, laborer, service worker, and operative were worse off in 1970 than the professional and manager, for obvious reasons. Some occupational groups encompass a broad structure within which further ranking, which may be steep, occurs. For instance, a medical specialist and a grade-school teacher are both professionals.

Wage rates are lower too in certain industries. For production workers, earnings are less in wholesale and retail trade, service, finance, and manufacture of nondurable goods than in other industries.[13]

So far we have talked about individuals. For households, low earnings go with having only one family member employed. For white families the average earnings are $10,750 if the husband only is employed and $14,095 if both spouses are.[14]

In 1972, 4.2 percent of families with two or more earners had incomes below the official poverty line, compared to 11 percent of those with only one earner.[15] (This is one reason why families headed by women are disadvantaged, for in general there can be only one wage earner.)

The proportion of wives in the labor force rose rapidly between 1960 and 1972, from 3 to more than 4 out of 10.[16] Employment of wives has tended to equalize family income somewhat. With more than one person working, a family's income relative to other families is less dependent on the earnings of the chief breadwinner. The extra contribution if the wife works is greater for black families; indeed, 54 percent of wives in black families work, compared to 41 percent in white families.[17] (See table 2.1.)

Table 2.1 Distribution of Wage and Salary Income of Male Workers, 1970 (Percent)

Share of Each Quintile	All Workers	Year Round Full-Time
Total Income	100.0	100.0
Lowest Fifth	4.6	8.7
Second Fifth	12.8	13.8
Middle Fifth	18.0	17.5
Fourth Fifth	24.0	22.8
Highest Fifth	40.7	37.2
Top 5 percent	15.0	13.3

Source: Peter Henle, "Exploring the Distribution of Earned Income," *Monthly Labor Review,* December 1972, tables 18 and 19.

The association of low wages with major demographic features—age, race, and sex—and with disability has important consequences for policy. It means that economic betterment is intertwined with movements for social justice for different groups and elimination of discriminatory practices in the labor market, housing, and schools. It also means that policy must address particular problems such as prevention or remediation of disability and adaptation of child-care and job arrangements to women's nonmarket responsibilities. Finally, it calls attention to the overlapping of disadvantages in job seeking, placement, turnover, and promotion.

One of these demographic associations is that the average earnings of full-time female workers were only three-fifths of those of males in 1973 for ages 25 and over, and the gap was wider for younger females (16–24).[18] Women workers generally have higher unemployment rates (5 percent in 1973 compared with 3 percent for males, counting those looking for full-time work only).[19] Females have far lower job tenure in the same job than males, especially between ages 25 and 54,[20] largely because of withdrawal from the labor force for family reasons. One in every 8 families is headed by a woman, and 53 percent of the female heads are in the labor force. They are at more risk of long-term unemployment if they lose their jobs than male heads.[21]

Wages are lowest for youth of both sexes, and fall off again after middle years of life. But in general the age profile of earnings (that is, the age at which earnings rise to a peak) varies by industry and occupation.

Poor earnings opportunities cause many workers to withdraw from the labor force as they experience disability in middle age, and lead many others to retire. For both males and females, nonparticipation in the labor market owing to disability is higher for blacks than for whites.[22]

The race differential in earnings is substantial.[23] Occupation for occupation, such differences are consistent for males. However, it is interesting that for females there are a number of occupations in which median earnings of blacks exceeded those of whites in 1970.[24] It is possible that more of the white females were working part time. Fewer black families have a head who is a full-time worker,[25] and black families are more likely to have a female head.

Repeated convergence of several factors of disadvantage is observed in figures on low wages. Looking at sex and color differences together, one sees a distinct pattern among full-time full-year workers: white men are top earners, followed by black men, white women, and black women.[26] Because the wages of all women are so low, the gap between earnings of blacks and whites is more pronounced for men than for women. In 1973, black men, despite their gains after 1955, still earned only 66 percent as much as white men, whereas black women earned 86 percent as much as white women.[27] Black women gained as a result of a large movement out of low-paying domestic work. By 1973 only 6 percent of employed black women were in that field.[28] White women hardly changed their position relative to men; in fact, they slipped slightly behind. (Blacks lost jobs heavily as unemployment rose, which explains why the ratio of black to white family income—a different figure from the ratio of the earnings of blacks and whites who were *employed*—began to slide.)

Disability in the primary earner is an important reason for dependency. This was reflected in 1971 figures for Aid to Families with Dependent Children (AFDC). Old Age, Survivors, and Disability Insurance (OASDI) data after 1972 show a similar pattern. In 1971 about 387,000 AFDC families, or one-fourth, had at least one parent incapacitated, and between 2 and 2.5 million persons were in such families. Of the 246,000 disabled fathers, 36 percent were unskilled laborers, 18 percent operatives, and 16 percent farm laborers. The figures indicate the convergence of disability and low skill in interrupting the flow of earnings, for the likelihood of an occupational relocation and avoidance of dependency following a disability would be low.[29]

Inflation reduced real earnings in 1972–73 for everyone and kept the average annual increase in real earnings between 1963 and 1972 to a modest 1.4 percent. The relative position of female family heads worsened, as measured in median after-tax income. Inflation and male-female differences were joint causes of the economic difficulties faced by female breadwinners.[30]

Part of the problem for blacks and women is that they are in different and lower-wage occupations and industries. "In 1972, the proportion of Negro and other races employed in the lower-paying, lower status occupational categories (service, farm, and nonfarm laborer jobs combined) was about double that of the comparable group of whites—40 percent compared with 20 percent." [31] Economist Barbara Bergmann points out that "about 70 percent of women work in occupations where women predominate." [32] Although differentials persist even within occupations and industries, Mary Stevenson has noted that:

by the time a researcher has focussed on men and women who work in the same narrowly defined occupation, a major source of the male-female wage difference for the labor market as a whole has already been eliminated; those differences in pay that arise when women do not have access to all occupations on an equal basis.[33]

The same might be said of blacks.

Trends in labor-market conditions have in some respects worsened the inequality related to earnings. More men are unable to work because of disability in the age group 45–64,[34] although some of the increase may be accounted for by the growth of disability coverage in the private sector in the period. Females with college educations are more likely to turn to unrelated jobs than in the 1960s, and the male-female differential in relation to this probability has widened.[35] The income advantage of two-earner families over one-earner families increased between 1962 and 1973 (from a 21 percent to a 29 percent gap). Weekly earnings of private household workers in constant dollars dropped between 1970 and 1973.[36]

Examining trends in the distribution of earned income

among men from 1958 to 1970, Peter Henle found a slow but persistent trend toward inequality. Various factors other than the
movement of earnings levels influence these changes. For instance,
a large influx of better-educated young workers into the labor force
alters the relative position of other workers. Moreover, better-paying industries and occupations generally had the highest rates of
increase in earnings, reflecting their faster growth but contributing
to overall inequality. Even within industries and occupations, there
was a trend toward inequality.[37] Achieving overall equality, or
greatly reducing inequality, is, therefore, a complex task.

With the growing number of female family heads, the male-
female earnings gap is an even more serious problem: it is almost
certain that a high proportion of these women will land in poverty.
Low earning power also makes it difficult for welfare mothers to
become self-supporting. In January 1973, mothers on AFDC who
worked full time (at least 35 hours per week) earned an average of
$399 for the month.[38] If one assumes no period of unemployment,
these women could have earned an average of only $4,068 a year,
out of which they would have had to pay for child care as well as
usual living expenses. The sex difference in wages has another
implication as well. If, in the husband-and-wife families that are
poor, the women earned as much as the men, the two-earner family
might more effectively equalize family income.

UNEMPLOYMENT AND INEQUALITY

During World War II, the United States did experience full employment. It took that war to end the Great Depression, a period in
which joblessness peaked at 25 percent. In the year that bombs
dropped on Pearl Harbor, unemployment still averaged 10 percent
(counting people on WPA as unemployed). But from 1943 to 1945
the rate stayed below 2 percent and in 1944 dipped to an all-time

low of 1.2 percent.[39] With labor shortages, the formerly unemployed, women, the young, the old, and the disabled became valuable workers. Black workers scored important employment breakthroughs in industry, though mostly as manual laborers. According to Robert M. Solow, as a consequence of full employment, earnings inequalities lessened during those years.[40] We will have more to say about this later.

Fear of a return of mass unemployment after the war was pervasive. Labor and liberal circles were determined that the nation could and should guarantee jobs for all in peacetime. In this spirit, the Full Employment Bill of 1945 declared it the federal government's responsibility to guarantee that "all Americans able to work and seeking work have the right to useful, remunerative, regular and full-time employment." [41] But the bill was defeated by conservatives in the House, and a weaker measure passed, the Employment Act of 1946. The concrete goal of the right to a job guaranteed by the federal government had been replaced by the vaguer one of "maximum employment" consistent with "other essential considerations of national policy," [42] and no provision was made to implement this vaguer promise.

Since 1946, although there has been no recurrence yet of the mass joblessness of the 1930s, unemployment has been substantial, persistent, and drifting upwards. There have been postwar recessions, including the one that started in 1974. Most disturbing is the fact that, since 1948, joblessness has not dipped below 4 percent except during the Korean and Vietnam wars.

From 1960 to 1970, joblessness averaged 4.8 percent in the United States compared to 0.6 percent in Germany, 1.3 percent in Japan, 1.7 percent in Sweden, 2.0 percent in France, and 3.1 percent in Great Britain.[43] In more recent years, the gap between the United States and most other industrial capitalist nations narrowed, but U.S. unemployment rates have remained higher. Unemploy-

ment rates considered extremely low by American standards are un-
acceptable in countries where labor and the political left play different roles, and cause political tensions to mount. In Sweden a 3
percent rate of unemployment nearly cost the Social Democratic
party the 1973 election.[44]

In 1973 urban areas had the worst unemployment. Standard
metropolitan statistical areas (SMSAs), with 39 percent of the labor
force, had 5.3 percent unemployment compared with a national
average of 4.9 percent. Central cities had 6.1 percent and suburbs
4.7 percent. Individuals SMSAs varied.[45]

Unemployment figures for the United States in December
1973 and December 1974 are shown in table 2.2. In December
1973, the national rate was 4.8 percent. About 4.4 million people
were officially and millions of others unofficially jobless. By December 1974, the recession had pushed up the official number of
jobless to 6.5 million. The distribution was similar in the two
years. Most of the unemployed were white and adults. But the rate
for blacks was about double that for whites, and the rate was higher
for adult women than for men. Teenage rates were the highest of
all. (See table 2.2.)

The unemployment rates of disadvantaged groups have dete-
riorated relative to others. The recent black-white ratio has been the
predominant pattern only since 1954. Between 1948 and 1953 the
ratio of black unemployment to white was 1.7 to 1. Then, as blacks
moved North, they were hit by recessions—three between 1954 and
1961 alone—and their relative unemployment rose each time. The
slow growth of manufacturing employment, increasing segregation
within metropolitan areas, and the persistence of long-standing discriminatory hiring practices in many firms all worked against them.

Although unemployment is relatively more severe for
teenagers as a group than it was two decades ago, most of the impact has been felt by black youths. Between 1954 and 1972, the

Table 2.2 The Number of Unemployed and the Rate of Unemployment, Selected Categories (Seasonally Adjusted)

Selected Categories	Number of Unemployed Persons (in Thousands)		Rate of Unemployment (Percent)	
	Dec. 1973	Dec. 1974	Dec. 1973	Dec. 1974
Total, 16 years and over	4,364	6,535	4.8	7.1
Males, 20 years and over	1,526	2,587	3.0	5.1
Females 20 years and over	1,573	2,330	5.0	7.2
Both sexes, 16–19 years	1,265	1,618	14.4	18.3
White, total	3,481	5,205	4.4	6.4
Males, 20 years and over	1,285	2,119	2.9	4.7
Females, 20 years and over	1,190	1,814	4.4	5.5
Both sexes, 16–19 years	1,006	1,272	12.8	16.0
Nonwhite, total	888	1,333	8.6	12.8
Males 20 years and over	255	495	4.9	9.5
Females 20 years and over	366	485	8.7	11.3
Both sexes, 16–19 years	267	353	28.7	37.8

Source: U.S. Department of Labor, Bureau of Labor Statistics, "The Unemployment Situation: December 1974," News Release (Washington, D.C.: Government Printing Office, January 3, 1975), table A-2.

rate rose for blacks from 17 percent to 34 percent but for whites from 12 to 14 percent.[46] The Council of Economic Advisers observed that "during the 1960s, the differential in reported unemployment between men and women widened." [47] Barbara Bergmann attributes this to the entrance of large numbers of women into the labor force during these years, combined with their virtual exclusion from many kinds of work,[48] a factor mentioned earlier in connection with earnings levels.

Unemployment rates, like earnings, vary with other factors besides color, sex, and age. For those with more education, unemployment rates are lower. Blue-collar and service workers experience more unemployment than white-collar workers. Rising on the occupational ladder usually makes a worker less vulnerable; and employment in some industries is more stable than in others. In December 1974, 2.5 percent of nonfarm managers and administrators but 13.0 percent of nonfarm laborers were out of work; 3.1 percent of government workers were jobless compared to 15.0 percent in construction and 8.6 percent in manufacturing. It is in the unemployment-prone blue-collar and service occupations that black workers tend to be clustered.

For youths aged 16–24, as national unemployment rose, the unemployment among those who dropped out of school without a high-school diploma rose from 22.2 percent to 28.3 percent. The increase was greater than for those who had graduated and entered the labor force—from 8.2 percent to 10.8 percent. The rate for black dropouts rose 1½ times, and for female dropouts it doubled. Inexperience as such, incomplete schooling, race, and sex all contributed to a severe problem of unemployment for this age group.[49]

Although national policies have been oriented toward requiring AFDC recipients to work, these people are affected quite like the rest of the poor by the absence of jobs. The percentage of AFDC clients awaiting job placement under the AFDC Work Incentive Program (WIN) rises by three percentage points with every percentage point rise in the national unemployment rate.[50] In 1973, 1.2 million women and men on AFDC were registered for their suitability in the WIN program. Half a million were appraised and 353,000 became participants, but only 39 percent of participants actually got jobs. That is, only 11 percent of registrants were employed—and only half that percentage were continuously employed for 90 days.[51]

In ghettos, the official unemployment is just the tip of the iceberg. A survey in 10 large urban slums counted the so-called subemployed—the unofficially unemployed, part-time workers desiring full-time jobs, household heads working full time for less than $60 a week (the poverty level at that time), men who had become discouraged and dropped out of the labor force, and a few similar groups. In January 1967, when national unemployment averaged 4 percent, official unemployment in these slums was 10 percent and subemployment ranged from 24 percent in Boston to 47 percent in San Antonio. Several years later, the staff of a Senate subcommittee found that subemployment averaged 30.5 percent in poverty areas of 51 cities. An alternate index found fully 61.2 percent of workers in slums to be subemployed.[52]

WORK ATTACHMENT, POVERTY, AND INCOME MAINTENANCE

Naturally, families are most likely to be poor when the head is not in the work force at all, and are least likely to be poor when the head works all year. The risk of poverty rises as the number of weeks worked falls. In 1972, 2.9 percent of families headed by full-time full-year workers, 5.9 percent of those whose heads worked 40 to 49 weeks, and more than 50 percent of those whose heads were unemployed for the whole year had poverty-level incomes. A family headed by someone who does not work at all because of illness or disability is also quite likely to be poor. About 1 out of 3 of these families had incomes under the poverty level. So did slightly over half of families headed by women who did not work at all because of housekeeping responsibilities.[53]

Not unexpectedly, a much lower proportion of poor than nonpoor families is headed by persons who worked most of the year. Nevertheless, most poor families have ties to the world of work. More than half of poor families had heads who worked sometime during the year, but relatively few of these family heads had steady work all year.

Some of the male heads of poor families who do not work at all during the year are ill or disabled: about 17 percent of all male heads with incomes below the poverty line, but only 3 percent of those with incomes above it. And proportionately more poor than nonpoor women are ill or disabled: 11 percent compared to 7 percent.[54]

This is the background of the need for income maintenance: it involves those who work and earn too little; those who cannot find work; those who cannot find steady work; and those who are ill, disabled, aged, or have housekeeping responsibilities.

Some persons would require income maintenance regardless of the state of the labor market. But many require it who would not if the labor market performed differently. This is readily apparent in the case of unemployment insurance. Rising unemployment causes an immediate increase in claims for jobless benefits, and falling unemployment causes a decrease. Though the relationship is less obvious, programs designed for the aged, for the disabled, and for families with dependent children are also affected by the labor market. A Brookings Institution study has shown that rising unemployment adds to the number of OASDI claims.[55] Many retirees have no choice but to seek income maintenance even if they would prefer to work. The situation of the disabled is similar. When jobs are scarce, severely disabled persons don't stand a chance, and even persons with minor disabilities may be screened out. As has been noted, part of the need for AFDC arises from high unemployment and inadequate earnings.

Even when jobs are more plentiful, a need for income maintenance may be created by working conditions. In 1968, some 14,000 were reported to have died in industrial accidents, 90,000 suffered permanent impairment, and more than 2 million were temporarily disabled. Exposure to industrial pollutants caused 1 million new cases of occupational disease.[56] In truth, the full extent of work-related death and disease is not known. For carcinogens and other substances, disease and death come years after exposure, and the relationship between work and the disease may not be recognized. Even members of workers' families can be inadvertently exposed to the hazards of the workplace.

Passage of the Occupational Safety and Health Act of 1970, with the aim of reversing the rising rate of job-related injuries and deaths, was helpful.[57] Funds spent to implement such laws may be considered as preventing the need for income maintenance. However, there have been obstacles in the setting of toxic-materials safety standards. Fines are low, and violations are not often classed as serious. Review of cases has tended to be unfavorable to workers. Public employees are excluded. Meanwhile, there are over 100,000 deaths yearly from occupational diseases. Early detection can prolong life: hence the need for medical surveillance. Under present law, doctors and hospitals have no legal obligations to report occupational health hazards.[58]

With 72.6 million persons employed full time in 1973, in an average work week around 66 million were covered by workmen's compensation. Low-wage workers in the most hazardous occupations are often unprotected. Agriculture ranks second only to construction in the number of job-related deaths; yet farm workers are largely excluded from coverage under state workmen's compensation laws.[59]

Income-maintenance programs, whether social insurance or related to income, are tied to labor markets through wage levels. As a matter of policy, payments are lower than earnings for unemployed workers, and previous wages determine the benefit levels of retired workers. For income-tested programs, the relationship is less clear: although the intent may be to set levels of payment below the lowest wages in the market, the intent may not be realized in the case of large families because welfare payments are tied to family size and wages are not.

One reason for these formulas is a long-standing fear that

paying more will break down the work ethic and leave society with no one to do the most onerous tasks. Another reason is financial constraints, and a third reason is that benefits tied to previous wages are viewed by many workers as a matter of right. Remedying substandard wages would raise the floor in a variety of income programs, and would have other consequences that are set forth at the conclusion of this chapter.

Policy Options

Based on our national experience, the major policy options for remedying substandard wages can be divided into the following groups.

First, there are policies that focus on the individual. Some relate to training and a cluster of associated services. Others develop availability for suitable work through health-service delivery, day care, and transport. Those services that center on referral, guidance, and information help improve the functioning of the labor market at the same time as they assist individuals in choice of jobs and training.

Another group of policies focuses on the creation of jobs through public employment, often conceived as temporary or transitional for the individual. A related policy is economic development on a regional basis to increase the number of jobs.

A third group of options has its focus on the employer-worker bargain. Strengthening unionism, minimum-wage legislation, wage supplements, and enactment and implementation of affirmative-action programs make up the policy toolkit.

Finally, there are policies that center on the larger economy, both quantitatively and qualitatively. In the former group are fiscal and monetary policies to sustain and stabilize aggregate demand. Qualitative macroeconomic policies include strategies for containing the power of corporations to pursue their goals without regard to the fate of individuals. In an ideal society, powers now exercised more or less autonomously by corporations, such as relocation of plants, introduction of new technology, and price decisions, would be subject to some form of social control. Our discussion does not attempt to outline the nature of such sweeping policy changes or the criteria for judging their merits. But it must be recognized that qualitative macropolicies are interconnected with the task of improving inadequate earnings.

It would be wrong to be sanguine about the effectiveness of these various types of remedy. One reason is that the economy is complex and changeable. For example, efforts directed to a particular cluster of jobs, whether through placement, training, or wage bargain, may be upset by a technological change or by international competition. Another reason involves institutional resistance to changes in, for example, civil-service employment or corporate autonomy. Particularly vital to a work-dependent economy is a set of beliefs about the ethics of an necessity for a gradient in compensation for work based on learned skills and on effort. Often these beliefs exist in jarring proximity to acceptance of high living standards and economic power that are unrelated to personal effort and even derived from activities that make life more difficult for society as a whole. Yet no society has completely freed itself from dependence on a system of differential rewards for the effort of training and of work. Achieving equality of opportunity would make the differences in rewards now accepted appear more just. And they would be less pronounced. But it does not seem wise to base present action on the expectation that wage inequality will disappear.

Despite the practical and theoretical difficulties of far-reaching change, the eradication of a chronic problem of low wages and underemployment should not be beyond our national capacities. The rate at which change is introduced should take into account the capacity of the economy to adjust to change. But advocacy of eradication of the problem as a goal does imply unwillingness to tolerate the perpetuation of low earnings. It also implies rejection of the use of welfare and other transfers as a disguised and inadequate supplementary wage.

TRAINING AND MANPOWER POLICY

Numerous issues are involved in designing training programs. To which groups should priority be given: disabled, women, blacks, youth? How should occupations be selected; how reliable are forecasts of relative labor shortage? In selecting occupations, should it be enough that a one-time improvement in job status would occur, or should the likelihood of further advancement be considered? What is the expected cost per trainee, allowing for attrition and the possibility of eventual failure of placement? Will trainees compete with unionized workers and cause unemployment or undercut wage scales, shifting the distribution of poverty?

To understand training as a strategy, one must consider manpower policy as a whole. The manpower programs that emerged in the 1960s were a response to chronic employment problems that lingered during economic recovery periods and showed up with great severity as aggregate demand weakened. The problems were attributed in part to the flow of surplus rural labor to urban settings at the very time that technology was increasingly based on formal education.

The initial target of manpower policy, embodied in the Manpower Development and Training Act of 1962 (MDTA), was the family head with years of labor-force participation whose skills were becoming obsolete. But other problem groups surfaced. As postwar babies came to adulthood, the pressure of their numbers drew attention to the converging problems of racial discrimination, depressed-area residence, poor basic education and training, and lack of suitable jobs. One way of meeting the problem was to provide work relief, which could be described in manpower terms as safe storage for young people. The Job Corps attempted remedial training for youth, and later Congress decided to attempt a massive move from welfare to jobs through the Work Incentive Program.[60]

Employer prejudice, discrimination, and child-care difficulties could not be overcome by training programs that merely processed individuals into candidates of increased employability. Moreover, individuals were often ignorant as to the available services, hampered by disbelief in the chance of improving their lot, and restricted in travel to job search or work by transport systems adapted to the travel patterns of suburbanites. Employers often imposed irrelevant job requirements that successfully shut out the inner-city candidate. Under the circumstances, it is not surprising that the results in terms of placement rates, duration of placement, and comparative wages were skimpy. This would have been true even with perfectly operated programs, and the real ones suffered from their novelty, piecemeal introduction, poor data systems, and interagency confusion. Despite all difficulties, however, graduates of the programs have increased their earning power. Meanwhile, it became obvious that remediation of accumulated deficiencies each year would be far outweighed by the flow of more individuals into the labor market.[61]

As problems were identified, a spectrum of manpower services began to take shape. In the *training* area, services included programs to seek out the discouraged and undermotivated, adult basic education, prevocational orientation to expose a person to alternatives, training for entry-level skills, training allowances, and residential facilities to make training feasible for rural dwellers and others in special circumstances. In the *employment* area, the services included work experience for those lacking it, job development to solicit opportunities that disadvantaged persons could use, subsidization of private employment, and job coaching to expedite supervisor-worker adjustments after a job was found. Relocation allowances and inducements to employers to bring jobs to depressed areas were to provide a lubricant for movement of persons and jobs; for those who could not be absorbed in the private market, or who needed time for transition, public-service jobs were an essential part of the service spectrum. Finally, *supportive* services such as health care and day care would help certain groups to improve their availability for training, job search, and work. Understanding of this service spectrum was a major and long-lasting contribution of the manpower programs of the 1960s.

Even experienced workers with acceptable work histories develop acute needs for manpower services. A widely cited example is the move of the Mack Truck Company in the 1960s from Plainfield, New Jersey, to Hagerstown, Maryland. Dorsey's analysis [62] shows that a company can influence the mobility of its workers by discouraging transfers; at any rate, a large number of men were left in Plainfield, out of work. Special efforts were made by the state employment services, but these were not well organized. Referrals were not always realistic, and workers refused jobs at inordinate distances from home. Moreover, ordinary placement efforts could not offset employer resistance to Mack workers, who were from a strong union. Most workers found new jobs at wages well below their previous rates. Those who searched longer did not get higher wages in the end; in fact, their wages were worse. The problem was acute for semiskilled workers. They had nontransferable skills, highly useful to a given employer but of little value elsewhere. Retraining would have been beneficial. Such an experience, occurring in the absence of mass unemployment, would be greatly magnified in our present economy.

Establishment, expansion, and continuation of manpower programs is going to depend on favorable evaluation of benefits in relation to costs.

Factors that must be considered include program uptake by individuals, the rate of dropouts attributable to program features or to its failure to motivate its clients, and the rate of withdrawals despite positive motivation. Eventual earnings (calculated by considering placement rate, new wage levels, and the duration of the income gain) must be compared with previous earnings. Experience under a program must be compared with the experience of other groups that had to seek jobs without training, and the comparison must also take into account demographic and educational characteristics of trainees, the state of the economy, and, finally, the effect of incentives to employers as distinct from training per se. Finally, if the training opportunity is administratively linked to an income-transfer program, the benefit-loss ratio facing an individual recipient electing to work has to be allowed for.

Even a careful evaluation may not offer a safe means of extrapolation to large-scale training proposals. For example, selection of trainees and instructors encounters more problems as scale increases. If unemployment is too high, direct job creation without training may seem a superior alternative.

Studies of five different training programs [63] show that results vary with sex, education, race, and age; there is a need to support training with other programs such as affirmative action and child care if earnings levels are to be improved.[64] Nevertheless, without additional training, many individuals now suffering from discrimination would not be able to take advantage of measures that do open up opportunities for qualified workers.

Improved information and referral services may make a difference for some persons. Information/referral may be significant in conjunction with affirmative-action programs in assuring that qualified individuals appear for each vacancy, and in connection with job development.

Another aspect of mobility is the transportation of individuals to jobs, quite important in view of poor public transportation in many areas. Competition with local suburban residents, however, may limit the effectiveness of transportation subsidies for residents of central cities as a solution that many metropolitan communities could adopt.

The development of child-care services on a local level, in a suitable geographical relation to job sites, represents a capital investment in improved job choices for women. Meeting current costs at such facilities, wholly or partially, or allowing realistic tax deductions amounts to an indirect wage increase. Of these choices, tax deductions are less effective because the initial expense must be met, i.e., women must have initial capital so as to seek and take work.

PUBLIC-SERVICE EMPLOYMENT

For many years, the economy has failed to provide an adequate supply of jobs. More jobs are needed. This does not mean separate job programs for the poor, which would feed into the low-wage sectors of the economy and help to maintain inequality. Typically, too, separate programs for the poor tend to deteriorate, whereas a broadly based job program would have a wider political base and more chance of success. In any event, unemployment occurs among all kinds of workers.

What factors would make for a workable public-service employment program, and what are some of the constraints?

A good program must be large, or it cannot make a dent in

the problem. Moreover, a broadly based public-employment program is less likely to be relief oriented. (Relief-oriented programs
tend to become stigmatized and to offer wages below the market
level.) To be most effective, public-service employment should be
a permanent program, not simply triggered by unemployment, as in
the 1974 legislation. A long-term commitment is a necessity if any
stabilizing effect on employment is to be achieved.

A public-service employment program must not be limited
to the disadvantaged, for changes in the economy affect workers
who have had stable employment for years. Still, a program must
serve proportionately more of the disadvantaged. It must penetrate
into the depressed labor markets of urban ghettos. A specified proportion of jobs must be reserved for the disadvantaged, and hiring
standards must not screen out the poor. Moreover, discouraged
workers who have dropped out of the labor force, reluctant retirees,
and handicapped persons who are not looking for work but would
gladly take jobs should be reached although they are not considered
"unemployed."

A public-service program should offer meaningful work that
would help meet a vast number of unmet public needs. If jobs do
not meet some acceptable standard of productivity, taxpayer antag-
onism may be aroused. However, if jobs are "just like" ordinary
jobs, competition with private-sector jobs causes other difficulties,
including failure to increase aggregate employment. If jobs are to
be tailored to fit available skills, more investment in administration
is needed than if quantity and immediacy are the goals. According
to Levin's findings for Los Angeles, the wage spread is less in the
public (local) sector than in the private sector. If sustained over a
period of time, this differential would indicate a higher return to education in the private sector.[65] A flat or somewhat equalitarian
wage structure is a worry to some economists who believe that it
may discourage investment in education, with unfavorable long-run

effects on the labor supply. However, social policies could be applied to increase and rationally distribute such investment. Moreover, to the extent that unemployment of skilled categories exists, the reward for education offered by the private sector is placed in question.

Ideally, a large public-service employment program should be implemented when unemployment is low; then it would be politically easier to direct a higher proportion of jobs to low-income people. But immediate needs may override this consideration.

What are the prospects and probable costs? Our major experience with direct, government-financed job creation came during the Great Depression. The Works Progress Administration (WPA) would not be a good model today, since it was income tested and paid lower wages than equivalent private jobs. But it did prove that government could quickly create socially useful work on a large scale. At its height in 1938 it provided 3.3 million jobs.[66] The lesser-known Civil Works Administration (CWA), created in November 1933, put more than 4 million Americans to work at useful tasks and reached into every county in the nation; but it was short lived. CWA was not income tested and paid prevailing wages. The Emergency Employment Act of 1971, subsequently phased out and replaced by the Comprehensive Employment and Training Act (CETA), represented the first major public-employment program since the New Deal. Nevertheless, with 185,000 jobs at its peak in 1972—while unemployment exceeded 5 million—the program could have had only a minuscule impact.[67] The program was federally financed but was operated by state and local governments. Most of them were pleased with the results; real work was done. And the program was implemented rather quickly.

Although the program served a wide variety of people, Taggart and Levitan note that "veterans, minorities, and working age males received a disproportionate share of the jobs; women and younger and older workers were given low priority.'' [68] Moreover, the program tended to help the "most feasible" candidates in all groups, including the 12 percent who were welfare recipients.[69] Women, though better educated than men, earned less and were mostly relegated to low-level service and clerical jobs. The different local programs varied in the extent to which they served the disadvantaged and women, suggesting "that it is possible, given commitment and proper incentives, to hire a much different mix.'' [70] But because program agents wanted to hire the most qualified workers, the program often did not reach far enough down to the hard-core unemployed. Civil-service rules did not bend easily and proved a barrier to the disadvantaged. Yet even the best-designed program could not have helped much because of the smallness of scale. Aside from the meagerness of size, the philosophy of the public-employment program was that the jobs it created were transitional. At the time, state and local government payrolls were growing, and some of these workers were eventually to be absorbed into nonsubsidized jobs in both public and private sectors.

Times change, and new methods are needed. But valuable lessons can be learned from WPA, CWA, and CETA. The new CETA, launched in 1974, was not considered an emergency measure. Unfortunately, Congress specified that half the CETA workers each year were to go on nonsubsidized payrolls, that is, state and local government jobs. Local officials were reluctant to add new employees whose wages they would eventually have to absorb. Nor could localities use CETA funds to pay permanent civil servants, who were being dismissed as the recession deepened in 1975.

Public-service employment should no longer be considered simply an expansion of regular state or local government. If a federal agency served as an additional route to public-service jobs, traditional civil-service rules would not screen out the poor, as in the public-employment program, and administrative problems that surfaced in CETA would be avoided. Such a mechanism would also be useful for reaching into rural areas. In any event, the notion that local governments, with their fiscal problems, would fund the jobs themselves is untenable; so the federal government must provide all funding.

How many public-service jobs could the American economy absorb? In 1965 and 1966 (years of relatively low unemployment), the Office of Economic Opportunity and the National Commission on Technology respectively estimated a need for 4.3 and 5.3 million additional socially useful public-service jobs.[71] Whatever a current estimate would be, obviously it is more than the hundreds of thousands of jobs provided for in recently enacted programs. As for cost, it seems reasonable to estimate that 1.5 million jobs would carry a net cost of $5 billion (after subtracting taxes produced and saving in income-maintenance payments).[72] The cost would depend, of course, on the wage level.

Part of the benefit from public-sector jobs will come through more private-sector jobs; another part, significantly, will come through reducing the low-wage labor supply and increasing low wages.

To be sure, public-service employment is not the same as full employment. It could be a step in that direction, but full employment requires more than the creation of public-service jobs. Federal legislation is needed to coordinate public- and private-sector activities to achieve both social and employment goals.

Public-service employment would be unnecessary in the long run if monetary and fiscal policies eliminated unemployment, or if, failing this, the highest-risk groups received special attention. Public-service jobs are needed, therefore, because plainly it is going to take time for the positive effects of macroeconomic policies to be felt in specific job markets and because public-service employment programs can be earmarked for high-unemployment groups. As we are discussing a program of major proportions, the possibility of inflationary effects must be considered. Such a program would have less inflationary effect if it were financed through taxation rather than borrowing, since taxation is more likely to involve reduced spending by the taxpayer, an offset to public expenditure. Although such a route would probably not be used exclusively, it is important in enacting the program to estimate consequences of taking alternative percentages of its total cost from the income-tax system. At any magnitude, public-service employment represents less of an addition to effective demand (and to inflation) than its gross payout would suggest, because the comparison is not with zero income but with current levels of assistance and unemployment benefits. Also, some debt repayment and even saving can occur (with counterinflationary effect) as enrollees receive income. In the long run, public-service employment may contribute to productive capacity, and so to a broad counterinflationary effect, though this cannot be counted on as a short-run safeguard against inflation.

UNIONS AND MINIMUM WAGE: THE WAGE BARGAIN

At a given level of skill, wages may be below decent levels because of poor bargaining power of workers (or low productivity, as for health reasons). Two major approaches to this problem have been used in the past—unionism and minimum-wage laws. In estimating their potential on the basis of past experience, a distinction must be made between the uneven focus of their past application to certain industries and occupations and the theoretical and practical limitations attending broader application. One theoretical limitation is that unionism and wage minimums may increase costs to the point where goods cannot be sold. Cutbacks, bankruptcies, and job reduction can result. A second limitation is that an employer may be motivated to substitute capital for labor, with similar effect on jobs. The employer could also relocate to an area where an unprotected labor force exists. Within the domestic economy, this desire can be checked by nationwide policies, including tax penalties for relocation (and for capital substitution); but in an open world economy the behavior of rival producers and multinational firms must be taken into account. In addition, both approaches can encounter political opposition because of the possible contribution of higher wages to inflation.

Despite these constraints, the very fact that the economy is complex and dynamic intervenes; unanticipated events and interactions can prevent the rigorous operation of these limiting factors. Strategies based on direct bargaining (unionism) or raising the minimum wage appear useful, at least within limits. Demands on employers are adjusted to economic conditions, and productivity has absorbed wage rises in many industries while profits have mounted. Employers and stockholders too have learned to live with unions. How to avoid a simple "pass-through" of wage increases into price increases, thus causing or sustaining an inflationary spiral, nevertheless remains one of the tough questions of overall policy.

Support of unionization as a partial solution to income inequality is based on the belief that increased bargaining power can raise low wages in a given occupation or industry. This belief has some foundation in fact. A recent Bureau of Labor Statistics study found that "with age, education, region, and occupation held constant the union effect [on earnings and wages] was estimated to be about 12 percent for all workers." The payoff was higher for blacks and women. It was 8 percent for white union men, compared to 27 percent for black men with similar characteristics, 19 percent for black women, and 22 percent for white women.[73]

Less than one-half of all workers in nonagricultural industries are unionized.[74] In 1971 a slightly larger proportion of black than white workers (21.8 percent compared to 20.2 percent) belonged to unions.[75] Proportionately fewer women than men are union members. Women were 18.1 percent of union members in 1952 and 21.7 percent in 1972.[76] In recent decades, as employment growth for women has been heavily concentrated in traditionally nonunion and low-wage white-collar and service jobs, their labor-force participation has far outpaced increases in union membership. However, these fields have some of the fastest-growing unions.

Unionism encounters political opposition, economic retaliation (as in plant relocation) and indirect checks on its effectiveness when inflation wipes out wage gains. It may also fall victim to internal inertia and bureaucracy and fail to take on the hard tasks. Nevertheless, it is one of the components of wage improvement. Unions too may be a good instrument for manpower programs on a large scale. And although they have little leverage on total employment, and no national fulcrum for raising those who do not have a regular attachment to the labor market to better status, unions do have substantial political influence. All this underscores the necessity of applying national policy and not just hoping for "market solutions."

THE MINIMUM WAGE

The minimum wage represents a special approach to correcting earnings inequalities. The Fair Labor Standards Act (FLSA), passed in 1938, gave minimum-wage protection to some who needed it least, those in relatively high-wage and more unionized sectors, although others, as in the textile and needle trades, were low paid though covered from the beginning.

Although coverage has lately been substantially extended, about 9.5 million workers—largely low wage and nonunion—are still not protected. In many of these uncovered sectors women are a large part of the work force. There are about 700,000 uncovered workers in agriculture, 3 million in retailing, 2.4 million in services other than domestic, and 0.5 million domestic workers.[77] Coverage of many domestic workers in May 1974 represented a first step toward granting them some protection. Seven out of ten were making less than the minimum for them ($1.90) at the time they were brought in.[78] Amendments raised the minimum to $2.10 an hour in 1975 and $2.30 in 1976. Special minimums, as low as $1.80 an hour, applied to more recently covered farm workers.

The minimum wage has been revised six times since 1938—in 1949, 1955, 1961, 1966, 1974, and 1976, and mandated increments may be scheduled between revisions. Although there is no automatic adjustment to the Consumer Price Index, recent increases exceeded rises in the CPI. In 1968, the minimum wage was 56 percent of the average wage of nonsupervisory workers in the private nonfarm sector.[79] By April 1974, the month before the effective date of the $2.00 minimum, the minimum wage had dropped to 40 percent of the average wage. The new minimum raised the ratio to 49 percent of the average wage; by October 1974 it had fallen once more to 46 percent. The relative position of the minimum-wage worker may decline unless the level of the minimum wage keeps pace with consumer prices. The $2.00 minimum effective May 1974 did not restore, let alone raise, the purchasing power of minimum-wage workers. To compensate for price changes after 1968, $2.19 would have been required.[80]

Figures for 1973 show that a husband and wife both working the year round at minimum wages would not have earned enough to live at the Bureau of Labor Statistics' lower level for a four-person urban family. The question arises, What size family should a minimum wage support, and at what level of living?

It is not unreasonable to believe that a wage earner with a modest-sized family of four should be able to earn enough to achieve a minimum standard of adequacy. The BLS lower-level budget provides a realistic budget standard that assesses minimum social as well as physical needs. But because of the problem of disrupting firms that would go under if they had to pay at this level, it will very likely be necessary to select a more modest immediate goal and to plan to attain it in stages over a period of time. A percentage above the poverty line could be used as a goal, and when it is reached, a higher wage target could be legislated. In order to prepare for orderly change, a national commission on low-wage industries should be established to investigate how improvements can be made in each industry. This was essentially the approach of the original FLSA. The mechanism should not be misused to depress wages below what would have been the statutory minimum. Some industries may need no assistance. Large, technologically advanced agribusiness firms may need regulation more than assistance. But maximum government effort should be extended to help small firms or those industries that may genuinely need financial help.

Exclusions from coverage under FLSA should also be eliminated. Exclusions maintain dualities. They are usually based on size of firm or industry. A fast timetable should be set to complete the elimination of exclusions so that all workers are protected. Otherwise a large locus of low wages remains embedded in the economy. Here too an industry or firm may need government help to adjust, and this should be given where it is feasible.

While redistributing income requires that low wages be raised, opponents of minimum-wage increases have always claimed that raising the minimum displaces workers and creates unemployment. Despite numerous detailed studies by the Labor Department on the impact of the minimum wage, this remains one of the most controversial areas of economics,[81] complicated by vested interests, ideology, and differing interpretations. It is not easy to measure the impact on employment of changes in the minimum wage in an economy in which other things are also changing. The impact may not be the same in a recession as in a period of expansion. The dire consequences predicted by opponents each time coverage has been extended or the minimum raised have generally failed to materialize. Agriculture was in a long-term employment decline *before* the minimum wage was partly extended to that sector. As a Labor Department report pointed out, "no evidence was found that higher wages tend to accelerate the introduction of labor-saving technology [on covered farms] in the short run." [82] But the report also added: "Should displacement eventually occur, the need for programs to assimilate farmworkers into other occupations would be intensified." [83] That is the heart of the entire matter. *If* there is any labor displacement, jobs must be available for those who are displaced.

There has never been a substantial increase in the minimum wage, and never one that brought it anywhere near a decent level that would enable a family of a minimum-wage worker to live in dignity. Even proponents of large increments, such as economists Thomas Vietorisz, Robert Mier, and Bennet Harrison, say that government help would be necessary to cushion the impact on the affected industries. They feel that raising the minimum substantially implies a series of measures such as upgrading of low-productivity firms, labor and management retraining, financing of added working-capital requirements of weak businesses, cushioning the foreign-trade impacts, and so forth. So raising the minimum wage substantially is best viewed as part of a total manpower and employment policy and should be coupled with finding ways to transform low-wage industries into higher-wage ones.[84]

Under the circumstances, it is difficult to view the minimum wage as an independent strategy, since evidently a set of efforts is needed to transform marginal industries into "solid citizens" and to protect individual workers against loss of jobs. It is true that, in other cases, enabling workers to broaden their job opportunities may be more feasible. Yet it is also difficult to conceive of solving the low-wage problem for workers who cannot easily transfer out of marginal industries without embarking on the efforts described, in accordance with a commitment and a plan. However, the minimum wage is a real means of lifting wages in some cases, especially when new workers are covered.

THE MACROECONOMY

A strategy to correct our current income distribution has to take into account the relationships between the possible success of all policies focusing on earnings and work and the overall or macroeconomy. The condition of the macroeconomy, through its effect on the labor market, helps to determine the size and composition of the poor population and the relative economic status of the poor. Macroeconomic conditions also influence the effectiveness of many antipoverty policies besides those based on employment.

One of the effects of economic expansion is a decline in the percentage of families below the poverty line when median family income goes up. In recent years, for families, a 1 percent rise in median income resulted in a 0.97 percent fall in the incidence of poverty before receipt of transfer payments. For individuals without families, a similar rise in income resulted in a 0.63 percent fall in poverty incidence. It follows that successive rises in income will have progressively smaller *absolute* effects of diminishing poverty. The subgroups that are typically left behind as growth occurs because they can't connect effectively with the labor market are evidently least likely to benefit from still more growth through wages. Comprehensive redistribution policies, and not growth alone, are needed to reduce poverty.

Another effect of expansion is that reduced unemployment per se reduces the numbers of the poor. In recent years we have experienced the converse: for a 10 percent rise in unemployment, there was a 0.27 percent increase in the number of poor families (before transfers). This statistical effect is produced by the receipt of income by those previously counted as unemployed, expansion of part-time to full-time work, and reentry into the labor market of those who had dropped out.[85]

A long-run effect of the condition of the macroeconomy is felt by the young and by older workers. When jobs are scarce the young fail to get on-the-job training that might help future employability and wage prospects, while many older workers are severed from their jobs and find it harder to form new attachments than it would have been to keep the old ones.[86] The converse occurs in expansion periods.

The positive impact of growth on economic position is greatest for families with male heads under 65, both white and black. For families headed by women, however, the percentage living in poverty actually rose for whites, and showed a meager drop for nonwhites.[87] *Hence, the notion of a "trickle down" effect whereby full employment and high growth take care of poverty is clearly not equally applicable to all groups. Therefore, redistribution policy must take care of both the diminishing impact and the differential effects of growth. At the same time, stabilization of the economy is directly helpful for many of the poor.* Furthermore, it prevents the disruption of many programs intended to benefit the poor that occurs when state, local, and even federal budgets feel the impact of a recession and reduced revenues. And it prevents the frustration of manpower programs that depend on a brisk demand for labor.

Stabilizing the Macroeconomy

The chronic but frustrated longing for a full-employment policy was referred to earlier. One example of the form a revitalized full-employment guarantee at the federal level might take is the Hawkins-Reuss bill, introduced on January 14, 1975.[88] The bill states the right of all adults "able and willing to work" to the opportunity for "useful paid employment at fair rates of compensation." No more than 3 percent unemployed is the immediate goal, and this job goal is not to be sacrificed to price stability or a favorable balance of payments. In this legislative approach, age 16 defines an adult (for whom a job will be required), and persons with health impairments are deemed willing and able to work.

The bill sets up a Job Guarantee Office that would provide employment through contracts with public, nonprofit, or limited-profit organizations. It could also give special assistance to those needing day care, training, etc. A Standby Job Corps would be available for public-service work, with pay not only conforming to minimum-wage standards, but also related to qualifications. However, as wages policy is also supposed to encourage clients to advance to other employment (that is, wages should not be too high) obviously some conflict is implied.

Any full-employment bill would work only if supported by effective coordination of all national policies to avoid both recession and inflation. Lekachman [89] attributes present immoderate rates of inflation to the pressure of world population on food supplies and to the historic reversal of terms of trade between resource-exporter nations and importers. Nevertheless, he is optimistic about the possibility of the United States's combining price stability with full employment if it accepts the need for significant "rearrangements of power, privilege, income and wealth." His program combines: (1) an unqualified federal guarantee of full employment; (2) income maintenance for those unable or even unwilling to work; (3) wage and price controls to prevent "cost-push" inflation; (4) redistributive taxation used in part to give relief to workers trying to make their incomes keep up with rising prices; and (5) a long-range shift to social investment if private investment should be depressed by altered profit expectations. These measures, price control in particular, would be supported by credit restraints and in turn would support them, for manufacturers would lose interest in inflationary borrowing to acquire inventories if prices were held in check.

Not all economists are as optimistic as Lekachman, in view of the worldwide problems that are involved, the difficulties of applying Keynesian solutions if the military budget cannot be controlled, and other complexities. Equalization itself would make it harder to control inflation, since new income received by the poor tends to be spent quickly.

Some of the differences among economists relate to whether the classical market has any resilience and tends to result in meaningful competitive adjustments without excessive human cost, or must be replaced by social controls. But economists also differ as to how much unemployment would result from given efforts to control inflation in order to control unemployment, and how to read the empirical evidence. Because of conflicting interpretations and ideologies, as well as strong political obstacles, it does not seem likely that the stabilization problem will be readily solved.

Nor do we know how soon a determined effort will be undertaken, using all the stabilization tools we have. But if a stabilization policy is to help the poor, it must aim to reduce unemployment rates far below recent and present levels. Residual unemployment would be dealt with by a public-sector jobs program and by training workers who need to adapt to changes in the type of labor demanded.

If a stabilization policy were achieved, the need for income maintenance would be reduced; to what extent this would occur would depend on the target level of employment. Without recessions and depressions, unemployment insurance would cushion persons for short periods of time between jobs and would not have to serve to the same extent as a major means of family support. Older or disabled persons desiring work would be more able to find it. More stable jobs at decent wages would help create the conditions that enable stable families to form and to remain together, and so there should be less need for AFDC. And welfare mothers able to work and desiring work outside the home would be more able to find jobs. Hence a keen concern with stabilization is relevant to income-redistribution efforts.

OTHER SOCIAL POLICIES

Government policies that help shape the level and distribution of unemployment and earnings include a commitment to a given level of employment and specific policies as to taxing, spending, public debt, and the money supply, but also include antidiscrimination policies and the whole gamut of labor legislation.

Most New Deal legislation had exclusions and exemptions that separated the labor force into two parts. The trend has been to extend coverage, but part of the job remains undone. Farm workers, for instance, are still excluded from labor legislation.

Less obvious policies also exert considerable influence. Agricultural policies have led to massive displacement of workers from southern agriculture. Housing and transit policies have influenced the location of industry and made it more difficult for blacks and the inner-city poor to gain access to jobs in the suburbs. Educational policies have often worked against the poor. And there are many ways in which corporate tax policies exert an influence. For example, American multinational corporations operating abroad have received tax benefits not available for domestic operations, encouraging the flight of jobs overseas. Another example is accelerated depreciation allowances, which have encouraged rapid investment in new equipment, in some places displacing labor faster than new jobs were created. Migration policy—and enforcement of it—also affects the low-wage labor supply and the international spread of poverty.

Business and union policies should not be ignored. Wage policy, discriminatory hiring practices, plant location, choice of technology—nearly every business decision has its impact. But with profit the driving force, it is naïve to expect business to change its ways unless forced to do so by government or unions. Today business firms no longer have unlimited power to hire children or to damage the environment. Similarly, a firm should not be permitted simply to leave an area if high unemployment will result. The introduction of equipment also needs more social controls to avert mass displacement of workers. Advance warnings and restrictions on layoffs are common in European nations and should be required here. Otherwise the burden is borne partly by the income-maintenance system and partly by the victims themselves.

Unions play a crucial role. They have vastly improved the pay scale, working conditions, and fringe benefits that accrue to unskilled and other workers. But historic patterns of discrimination on the part of some unions have injured minority-group members. Legislation now forbids such discrimination, but one cannot create by legislation a commitment on the part of organized labor to run a massive campaign to organize low-wage workers. Yet such a policy would be a major boost for low-wage workers and would help reduce earnings inequalities.

As this book goes to press, economic recovery is under way—but chronically high unemployment has been a major factor in preventing achievement of the goals set forth in this chapter and in eroding the modest gains of the decade. With substantial unemployment, the income-maintenance system is being made to support millions of additional productive persons who are cruelly prevented from utilizing their labor to enrich the country by producing goods and services. A permanent full-employment policy, supported by public employment and manpower services, is the bedrock of an improved income-maintenance system designed to support adequately those who cannot support themselves or who experience temporary loss of income. Toleration of higher and higher levels of unemployment over the past two decades and more recently the use of planned recessions to tame inflation have brought us to a tragic state. It is time to reverse the course.

Conclusion

In this chapter, we have presented material showing how employment and macroeconomic policy are integrally related to income-distribution objectives. First, the job market provides the major part of the income of most Americans. Manipulation of other forms of income (e.g., transfer payments) may affect distribution, but nothing will substitute for a sound employment and wage policy.

Second, the structure and organization of the labor market gives "special" treatment to disadvantaged groups. Later, these same groups show up at the bottom of the income distribution. That means, on one hand, that if we wish to eliminate or reduce such castes as a feature of American life, we must attack the problem in employment policies as well as in income-maintenance policies. It means, on the other hand, that we should not be surprised to see such groups turn up in disproportionate numbers seeking income maintenance.

Third, as entitlement and the benefit levels of most transfer programs (except public assistance and related programs) depend on work experience, disadvantage at work is likely to become translated sooner or later into disadvantage in transfer payments—

retirement insurance, for example. Hence, more equality in income transfers rests in part on more equality at work.

Fourth, work and the success of training programs depend in the end on the availability of real work. Work and training requirements that are built into welfare or social-insurance programs are meaningless—and are perceived by applicants to be meaningless—in situations of general or particular high unemployment.

Fifth, as social policies, work and income transfers are in some measure mutually substitutable, but one may be far more suitable for a given individual at a given time. Jobs wiped out require the creation or expansion of income transfers, unless people are to be allowed to remain in serious need. Other considerations may determine that the nation should budget such expenditures as transfers rather than the provision of work, or vice versa; but the expenditures themselves cannot be avoided.

Sixth, employment and income transfers are also complementary social policies. Again, this should not be taken to mean the use of income transfers as a wage supplement for individuals. Little that is done by way of providing employment or decent wages will support the retired, the disabled, the ill, children, or the women who because of maternity or other reasons should not work. Taking the preceding conclusion and this one together, sound policy would require full employment *and* well-developed transfer programs.

3

Taxation

DAVID GAYER

Taxes are a prime instrument in the redistribution of income and have been used in that capacity by many civilizations. Laws for taxing and redistributing income were mandated in ancient Israel. The middle ages saw both the Church and the nation states impose taxes, with the partial aim of income redistribution. The unfairness of the tax system is sometimes given as an underlying cause for the American Revolution.

In our own time, controversy over the proper burden of taxation figures prominently in public and private debate. Discussion revolves around the fairness of the tax system and its economic consequences. Questions of tax equity are more difficult to answer because of the turbid quality of the subject matter. It is often unclear who actually bears the tax burden. Taxes legally levied on one individual or firm may be paid by someone else. For example, a tax on real property in New York City may be paid by owners of residential, industrial, and commercial property. Or, it may also be paid by tenants and consumers of products through higher rents and prices. Taxes may depress wages, thereby falling on wage earners. Under certain circumstances, property taxes in a large city may be paid by individuals living far from its borders. Likewise, the economy of a city is affected by the tax structure. Its employment, growth, and income ultimately may depend on the types of taxes levied. Taxes also influence the nation's economic structure: its growth rate, its employment profile, and its level of output.

This chapter examines the issues in taxation with emphasis on their role in the distribution of income. Because distribution touches on a number of other issues, other fiscal functions of government are also discussed. The first section deals with the rapid increase of taxes as a proportion of gross national product (GNP). The next reviews the government's responsibilities for allocating resources for competing uses—how government influences what is produced and consumed. This section also looks at the basis for equity in taxation. The third section deals with the assignment of functions of allocation and distribution to various levels of government in a federal system. The fourth reviews the findings on incidence of taxation in several major tax studies. The fifth discusses costs of taxation in terms of efficiency. Much of what is said here depends on the assumption that the individual himself is best capable of determining his own welfare. The conclusions depend upon the acceptance of this proposition. The last section reviews the characteristics of six major taxes in the United States, and also looks at their probable economic effects.

Trends in Taxation

Controversy over redistribution has been accentuated in the United States in the twentieth century because of the rapid growth of the public sector of the economy. Both expenditures and tax collections at all levels of government have increased dramatically. In 1902 total revenue collections by all levels of government were 6.2 percent of the GNP; by 1940 they were 14.5 percent. The decades after World War II saw even faster increases in taxes compared to the GNP. By 1970 taxes stood at 30 percent of the GNP (see table 3.1). The relative growth occurred while the GNP itself rose from $21.6 billion in 1902 to $974.1 billion in 1970.

Most of the relative increases were in federal taxes. In 1902 federal tax collections were 37.4 percent of the total collected by all governments. By 1960 federal taxes represented 68.5 percent of the total, dropping slightly to 65.8 percent in the next decade. On the other hand, local governments' share of taxation dropped to only 14.1 percent in 1970, a decline from over 50 percent in 1902 and 57.6 percent in 1913. The state share increased between 1902 and 1940, but has fallen since. It did rise between 1960 and 1970, standing at 20.1 percent in the latter year.

There have been commensurate shifts in the composition of taxes. Direct taxes have increased compared to indirect taxes.[1] Personal income taxes, which did not exist in 1902, represented 35.4 percent of all tax dollars in 1970. Likewise, payroll taxes rose from zero to 18.5 percent. Comparative declines were in property taxes, death and gift taxes, and customs duties. The relative size of sales taxes decreased only slightly between 1902 and 1970.

States have largely relinquished to localities property as a base for taxation. In 1902 states collected 52.6 percent of their revenues through the property tax. It was only 1.9 percent in 1970. Most of the shift occurred during the period between World War I and World War II. States relied more heavily on sales taxes and income and payroll taxes. In 1970 the three taxes combined were 84.6 percent of all collections, as compared to 17.9 percent in 1902 (see table 3.1).

Table 3.1 Development of United States Tax Structure

	1902	1913	1922	1927	1940	1950 [a]	1960	1970
I. Tax Revenue as Percent of GNP								
1. Federal	2.3	1.7	4.6	3.6	5.7	13.6	18.2	19.8
2. State	0.7	0.8	1.4	1.8	4.4	3.4	4.5	6.0
3. Local	3.2	3.3	4.2	4.7	4.5	2.9	3.8	4.2
4. Total	6.2	5.8	10.2	10.1	14.5	19.9	26.5	30.0

II. Percentage Composition of Tax Revenue

Federal

	1902	1913	1922	1927	1940	1950 [a]	1960	1970
5. Individual income tax	—	—	} 56.8	25.6	16.9	40.7	45.4	48.1
6. Corporation income tax	—	5.3		36.6	19.8	27.1	24.0	17.5
7. Sales and excises	47.6	45.6	24.4	14.6	31.6	19.2	12.8	8.4
8. Customs duties	47.4	46.8	9.3	17.0	5.8	1.1	1.2	1.3
9. Death and gift	1.0		4.1	2.6	6.3	1.8	1.8	1.9
10. Payroll			1.2	2.1	14.2	9.0	14.2	22.3
11. Other	4.1	2.3	4.2	1.4	5.5	1.1	0.7	0.5
12. Total	100.0	100.0	100.0	100.0	100.0	100.0	100.0	100.0

State

	1902	1913	1922	1927	1940	1950 [a]	1960	1970
13. Individual income tax	—	—	4.1	4.0	4.7	7.4	9.9	16.0
14. Corporation income tax	—	—	5.5	5.3	3.5	6.0	5.3	6.5
15. Sales and excises	17.9	19.9	27.2	42.8	51.0	55.6	54.0	52.2
16. Property tax	52.6	46.5	33.0	21.2	5.9	3.1	2.7	1.9
17. Payroll			10.1	7.9	24.5	18.8	19.4	16.4
18. Death and gift	29.5	33.6	20.1	18.9	10.3	9.1	1.9	1.7
19. Other							6.9	5.2
20. Total	100.0	100.0	100.0	100.0	100.0	100.0	100.0	100.0

Local

	1902	1913	1922	1927	1940	1950 [a]	1960	1970
21. Individual income tax	—	—	—	—	} 0.4	0.8	} 1.3	} 4.1
22. Corporation income tax	—	—	—	—		0.1		
23. Sales and excises	—	0.2	0.6	0.6	2.8	5.9	7.7	8.1
24. Property		91.0	96.4	96.8	91.3	86.2	85.0	82.1

Table 3.1 (Continued)

	1902	1913	1922	1927	1940	1950 [a]	1960·	1970
25. Payroll		0.2	0.5	0.6	1.5	2.3	2.9	3.2
26. Other	11.4	8.6	2.5	2.1	3.9	4.7	3.0	2.5
27. Total	100.0	100.0	100.0	100.0	100.0	100.0	100.0	100.0

All Levels

	1902	1913	1922	1927	1940	1950	1960	1970
28. Individual income tax	—	—	⎫		9.8	8.1	29.3	33.0	35.4
29. Corporation income tax	—	1.5	⎬ 27.0		13.9	8.7	19.6	17.3	12.8
30. Sales and excises [b]	19.8	16.1	15.1	13.2	28.5	23.6	19.1	17.2
31. Customs duties	17.7	13.6	4.2	6.0	2.3	0.7	0.8	0.9
32. Property	51.4	58.6	44.0	48.8	30.3	13.0	12.7	11.9
33. Payroll		0.1	2.1	2.4	13.3	9.7	13.4	18.5
34. Death and gift	11.1	10.1	7.5	5.8	8.9	4.2	1.5	1.6
35. Other							2.1	1.7
36. Total [c]	100.0	100.0	100.0	100.0	100.0	100.0	100.0	100.0

III. Levels as Percent of Total

	1902	1913	1922	1927	1940	1950	1960	1970
37. Federal	37.4	29.1	45.2	35.5	38.8	68.3	68.5	65.8
38. State	11.4	13.2	13.9	18.0	30.0	17.3	17.1	20.1
39. Local	51.3	57.6	40.9	46.5	31.2	14.4	14.5	14.1
40. Total	100.0	100.0	100.0	100.0	100.0	100.0	100.0	100.0

Source: Reprinted from Richard Musgrave and Peggy Musgrave, *Public Finance in Theory and Practice* (New York: McGraw-Hill Book Company, 1973), pp. 190–91, by permission of the publisher.

1902–50: U.S. Bureau of the Census, *Historical Statistics for the United States; Colonial Times to 1957,* pp. 724, 727, 729.

1960 and 1970: U.S. Bureau of the Census, *Governmental Finances, 1959–60* and *1969–70.*

[a] Calendar years through 1950, fiscal years 1960 and 1970.

[b] Local motor vehicle and operator's licenses included in "other" to 1950 and in sales taxes thereafter.

[c] Detail may not add to total due to rounding.

Reasons for Taxation

The three major economic functions of government are distribution of income, allocation of resources, and stabilization of the economy. Tax policy is a prime instrument for accomplishing all three goals. Stabilization is concerned with maintaining taxes and expenditures at levels which keep the economy at full employment while minimizing inflation.[2] The allocative function serves to adjust the mix of goods and services to be produced and consumed in the economy by moving resources from the production of private goods, such as automobiles and vacations, to public services, such as police protection and national defense. Finally, the distributive function reassigns resources from one economic class to another. The necessity for this function of government implies that the private market's mechanism for distribution, through payments for factors of production, labor, capital, and land, leads to unsatisfactory results. Government redistribution programs involve the use of taxation, transfer payments, and government services to shift real resources among individuals in society. To obtain the whole picture of redistribution, we must analyze the three instruments concurrently.[3]

The most suitable role of taxation is best seen when revenues are compared with the government's uses of the money. Much of the tax revenue collected by government is not intended for redistribution, but rather for providing public services, since providing them through government is most practical. These include police protection and defense. Government undertook other services because of convenience or historical accident. Trash collection, a government service in some communities, can be supplied just as efficiently by a private company. Essentially, taxes used to support the allocative function can be viewed as payment for services received, much as consumers pay for goods they get in the private market. But public goods are usually provided by government for free, and there is no direct link between what is received and what is paid in taxes. Therefore, most taxpayers will try to have someone else pay for the public services they receive. A preferable system would be one in which the benefits taxpayers receive are known and are taxed accordingly. As with private goods, the rich expend more dollars but in turn obtain more goods and services. Their expenses for such things as restaurants and skiing trips may be a higher proportion of their incomes; likewise their demand for police and fire protection is probably larger in relation to their income. If this is the case, a progressive tax which taxes higher-income people proportionately more than lower-income people is not redistributive.

The major drawback with a tax system in which taxes are levied according to benefits is that it presupposes a proper state of distribution, so that it cannot solve the problem of income redistribution. An alternative principle, "ability to pay," has therefore been proposed. This principle completely divorces expenditures from tax collections. Its applicability lies in its ability to designate tax funds for transfer purposes. It cannot be used where expenditures and revenues are inexorably linked.

The ability-to-pay principle can be seen as satisfying the criterion that there be equal sacrifice by all taxpayers, a concept that has many interpretations. If income is used as a measure of capacity to pay taxes, then logically those with equal incomes should pay equal amounts of taxes. An extension of this principle implies that those with higher incomes should pay more taxes. The problem arises in ascertaining how much more the rich should pay compared to the poor. Whatever differences there are in applying this principle for higher-income taxpayers, few will argue that the very poor have been treated well with regard to the taxes they pay and the benefits they receive.

Fiscal Federalism

One disadvantage of ignoring benefits in a taxation policy is that tax differences between localities which are not compensated for with benefits may injure local economies. With a federal system of government, it is necessary that different functions be undertaken by different levels of government and that a suitable taxing mechanism exist for each level of government. As we have noted, the federal share of taxes has risen steadily in the twentieth century. The central government has directly provided more services, especially in defense and social security, and it has increased its grants to states and localities. At the same time, the federal government has tax bases that automatically produce large increases in revenues as income rises: the individual income tax and the corporation income tax. The former is progressive and the latter is based on profits, so that both expand more than proportionally as income rises. In fact, for a time before the heavy involvement of the United States in the Vietnam War, there were claims that the federal government needed to reduce its taxes so that tax collections themselves would not reduce aggregate demand and produce unemployment. At that time too, states and localities needed to raise taxes in order to increase their services. With this "fiscal imbalance," the whole question of the proper assignment of the allocative and distributive functions was carefully scrutinized.

One system of assigning the allocative function calls for multilevel government provision of services. Under this scheme the size of the service area is adjusted so that benefits accrue only to those living within its borders. This requires that defense be assumed by the federal government, while street lighting be provided by small localities. Flood control is best provided by a regional government. Thus a different size of service area may be required for each service. Failure to adhere to this principle may lead to underconsumption, since benefits would accrue to those outside the area who did not pay for them. For the system to operate well, benefits being provided by local governments must be paid for with local taxes.

In such a system distribution should be a federal responsibility, because areas over which labor and capital are mobile require a unified tax system for distribution.[4] Differential tax and benefit rates will induce the poor to cluster near the rich and the rich to escape to lower-taxed areas or to build barriers against entry by the poor by means of zoning codes. Factors of production too will tend to move toward lower-taxed areas, creating costs to the economy because of the altered location of firms and individuals.

A unified national plan for redistribution is also required if beneficiaries of transfer programs who are in similar economic circumstances are to get equal benefits. However, differences in the size of transfer payments may be needed if there are differences in prices of consumer goods in different localities. To equalize benefits among individuals living in different places, a high-rent area would require a larger dollar transfer than a low-rent area. But these differentials should be instituted nationally rather than on a statewide basis. Permitting states to set their own levels of payments and to pay for them with their own taxes creates disparities, because the poorer states cannot afford to support programs which redistribute income at the same level as richer states. If responsibility for redistribution is imposed on state and local governments, localities and states may be rendered incapable of performing even the functions which they do best, such as police and fire protection.

Taxes used for redistributing income need to be uniform nationally in order to avoid economic losses from inefficient location of firms and workers and to advance equity. State and local taxes for services benefiting people and businesses in a locality will not induce relocation that is economically deleterious. Only differences in the net tax-benefit amounts between locations cause such distortions. Not many taxes are intended for expenditures that lead to such direct benefits. (One example of such taxes is special assessments on property for sewer pipes that enhance the value of property.) However, it is possible to devise a set of state and local taxes which approximate benefits received and thereby minimize the net tax-benefits differentials among areas. Failure to do this may impoverish localities in which labor and capital are highly mobile. The fiscal crises of central cities are in part an outgrowth of localities' having to bear some of the burden of redistribution. New York City, for example, which pays for approximately one-quarter of its welfare bill, has lost over half a million jobs in the private market in recent years. Although the causal link between the two factors is not direct, there can be little doubt that the heavy load to support public assistance borne by the city has adversely effected its economy.

Empirical Studies of Tax Burden

After years of study by competent economists, the issues of who bears the burden of taxation still remain in dispute. This is not surprising; answers to these questions rest on detailed knowledge of the complex relationships of economic forces. Theoretical models and empirical investigations have produced inconclusive results. Testing techniques have borne out conflicting conclusions on the value of essential parameters, and sometimes they have yielded no results at all.

The essence of the problem is that taxes levied on one individual are often shifted to another. This situation arises from the modifications in behavior due to changing taxes, which in turn alter the price of final products and factor payments. For example, an excise tax levied on producers of automobiles may be partly shifted forward to consumers or backward to workers, shifted to capital or labor in other industries, or shifted to buyers of other products. The relationships are complex, and not all are deserving of equal attention.

A number of studies have been undertaken to determine who actually pays taxes. Because of empirical uncertainties and logical difficulties, the results of studies differ according to the assumptions made by the investigator. First, a measure of capacity to pay taxes must be defined. The one usually used is income, but it is also possible to include assests in such a measure. The taxpaying unit must also be established; households and persons are two possibilities. The time dimension has a bearing on the results—yearly income may produce a different pattern of tax burden than does lifetime income. Finally, investigators must make assumptions as to how taxes are shifted from one person to another. For example, a tax on the sale of cigarettes may be borne entirely by smokers. In order to allocate the tax burden by income classes one must know how much is spent for cigarettes by each income class.

A pioneer in such studies of tax incidence is Richard Musgrave. His most recent effort, for 1968, was done with Peggy Musgrave. In the Musgraves' study, total taxes on all levels of government were found to be almost proportional (i.e., the rates stayed constant with a rise in income), over a wide spectrum of the income distribution. For annual family incomes between $5,700 and $35,500, the rate of taxation varied from 32.4 percent to 33.9 percent. A the top and bottom ends of the distribution, taxes were progressive.

The totals are composed of a number of different taxes by federal, state, and local governments. The federal tax structure alone was progressive. This was neutralized by the regressiveness

Table 3.2 Estimated Distribution of Tax Burdens by Income Brackets, 1968 (Taxes as Percent of Total Family Income)

	Income Brackets [a]			
Taxes	Under $4,000	$4,000– $5,700	$5,700– $7,900	$7,900– $10,400
Federal Taxes				
1. Individual income tax	2.0	2.8	5.9	7.1
2. Estate and gift tax	—	—	—	—
3. Corporation income tax	5.1	6.1	5.0	4.0
4. Excises and customs	2.5	2.8	3.1	3.0
5. Payroll tax	5.5	6.3	7.0	6.9
6. Total [b]	15.2	17.9	20.8	21.6
7. Total excluding line 5	9.7	11.6	13.9	14.7
State and Local Taxes				
8. Individual income tax	—	0.1	0.3	0.6
9. Inheritance tax	—	—	—	—
10. Corporation income tax	0.4	0.5	0.4	0.4
11. General sales tax	3.4	2.8	2.5	2.3
12. Excises [c]	2.7	3.0	3.3	3.0
13. Property tax	6.7	5.7	4.7	4.3
14. Payroll tax	0.2	0.5	0.8	1.0
15. Total	13.4	12.5	11.9	11.6
16. Total excluding line 14	13.2	12.1	11.1	10.6
All Levels				
17. Total	28.5	30.5	32.8	33.1
18. Total excluding lines 5 and 14	22.9	23.7	25.0	25.3

of state and local taxes. The federal rates for all taxes were progressive throughout most of the distribution. The exception is for the brackets $12,500 to $17,500, and $17,500 to $22,600. A slight dip in rates here is accounted for by the social-security tax, which imposes a ceiling on the earned income that is taxable (see table 3.2). When the social-security tax (which was highly regressive for incomes over $12,000 in 1968) was left out of consideration, the federal distribution of taxes was progressive throughout. The most pro-

Table 3.2 (*continued*)

		Income Brackets [a] (*cont.*)				
$10,400– $12,500	*$12,500– $17,500*	*$17,500– $22,600*	*$22,600– $35,500*	*$35,500– $92,000*	*$92,000– and over*	*All Brackets*
7.9	10.1	10.6	12.7	14.8	18.5	9.9
—	—	—	0.6	2.0	2.7	0.4
4.3	4.6	4.8	5.1	5.3	6.6	5.0
2.9	2.7	2.1	1.1	0.9	0.6	2.3
6.7	6.1	5.2	4.2	1.5	0.6	5.2
21.6	23.4	22.6	23.8	24.5	29.1	22.7
14.9	17.3	17.4	19.6	23.0	28.5	17.5
0.7	1.1	1.4	2.3	1.6	1.3	1.0
—	—	—	0.2	0.6	0.8	0.1
0.3	0.4	0.4	0.4	0.4	0.5	0.4
2.2	2.0	1.7	1.0	0.5	0.3	1.8
2.9	2.5	1.9	1.0	0.8	0.6	2.1
4.0	3.7	3.3	3.0	2.9	3.3	3.9
1.0	1.0	1.1	1.2	0.2	0.1	0.8
11.1	10.6	9.7	9.1	7.1	6.9	10.3
10.1	9.6	8.6	7.9	6.9	6.8	9.5
32.8	33.9	32.4	32.9	31.6	35.9	33.0
25.0	26.9	26.0	27.5	29.9	35.3	27.0

Source: Reprinted from Richard Musgrave and Peggy Musgrave, *Public Finance in Theory and Practice,* (New York: McGraw-Hill Book Company, 1973), p. 368, by permission of the publisher.

[a] Uneven bracket limits are used for computational reasons.

[b] Totals may not add due to rounding.

[c] Line 12 includes motor vehicle licenses, excises, and miscellaneous revenue.

gressive element of the federal tax structure was the individual income tax. It accounted for nearly half the revenue for incomes over $12,500. The corporation tax was progressive in the middle and upper income ranges, but was regressive at low incomes. As was already stated, the social-security tax is highly regressive, since it imposes a ceiling on taxable income and taxes only earned income. Those with incomes below $8,000 per year actually paid more in social-security taxes than they did in income taxes.

State and local government taxes were on the whole regressive. This is because under the assumptions used in the Musgraves' study the sales, excise, and property taxes are all highly regressive.[5] The first two taxes were assumed to be paid by consumers of the taxed products. The property tax was divided. The property tax on residences was assumed to be borne by homeowners and renters. The property tax on business was paid half by consumers and half by people with capital income.

The Musgraves also estimated tax burden with an alternative set of assumptions. When the entire corporation income tax was assigned to shareholders it became somewhat more regressive at low incomes but highly progressive at incomes over $92,000 per year. When it was assumed that the entire tax was paid by consumers, the tax became extremely regressive (see table 3.3).

That state and local taxes are much more regressive than federal taxes should not be surprising, since their primary tax bases do not lend themselves to progressiveness as much as the income tax does.[6] This is because the income tax, which is a major federal tax, can account for income from all sources in determining rates of taxation. The property and sales taxes that are the largest revenue producers for state and local treasuries cannot. The incidence of those taxes (i.e., who pays what proportion of them) is determined mainly by consumption patterns of taxed products, while the rates are set according to the value of sales and property. Nor is it neces-

Table 3.3 Effective Tax Rates under Various Assumptions of Tax Burden (Tax as Percent of Total Family Income)

	Selected Income Brackets			
	$4,000–$5,700	$12,500–$17,500	$35,000–$92,000	$92,000 and over
Corporation Tax				
1. One-half capital income, one-half consumption	6.6	5.0	5.7	7.2
2. Dividend income	4.7	2.6	8.8	28.2
3. Capital income	6.1	3.7	10.0	13.7
4. Consumption	7.1	6.3	1.4	0.6
5. One-half capital income, one-fourth consumption, one-fourth wages	6.0	5.0	5.8	7.3
Property Tax [a]				
6. OR on owner; R on tenant; B—one-half capital income, one-half consumption	5.7	3.7	2.9	3.3
7. All on capital income	4.4	2.7	7.2	9.9
8. OR on owner, R and B on capital income	4.4	3.3	5.4	7.1
9. OR on owner, R on tenant, B on capital income	5.3	3.3	4.5	5.8
10. OR on owner, R on tenant, B on consumption	6.1	4.1	1.2	0.8
Payroll Tax				
11. Employer tax on consumption, employee tax on wages	6.8	7.1	1.7	0.6
12. All on wages	5.6	7.4	1.7	0.4
Total, All Levels of Government [b]				
13. Line 17, Table 3.2	30.5	33.9	31.6	35.9
14. Substituting lines 2 for 1, 7 for 6, 12 for 11	26.1	30.8	39.0	63.2
15. Substituting lines 4 for 1, 10 for 6	31.4	35.6	25.6	26.9

Source: Body of table reprinted from Richard Musgrave and Peggy Musgrave, *Public Finance in Theory and Practice* (New York: McGraw-Hill Book Company, 1973), p. 370, by permission of the publisher.

[a] OR stands for owner-occupied residences; R stands for rental property; B stands for other business property.   [b] Includes the payroll tax.

sarily undesirable that federal taxes be more progressive if the proper functions of state and local government are allocation of resources. Given the uncertainty of the distribution of benefits, there may be no strong case for progressive state and local taxes. But neither is there a case for the regressive pattern that now exists.

In a similar study, Pechman and Okner found that the tax rates for federal, state, and local taxes combined were mildly progressive throughout the distribution. This, of course, depended upon the assumptions employed about the incidence of taxation. The eight sets of assumptions used by the two authors produced considerable differences in burden at the extreme ends of the distribution. The tax burden in the middle portion of the distribution was affected little by varying the assumptions (see table 3.4).

An alternative way of looking at burden is to examine groups of individuals rather than income classes. Persons or households can be ranked by their income from the lowest to the highest individual income. The tax rate is then computed for people at various points on the distribution. This allows for comparisons of equal-sized groups of taxpapers. It avoids the difficulty of classes of income that contain few members. For example, high-income classes may pay higher rates of taxation than low-income classes. However, this may have little impact on income distribution because there may be few people whose incomes fall within the high-income brackets.

The findings by Pechman and Okner reveal that tax rates are regressive for 10 percent of the lowest-income people under the various assumptions. Tax rates are almost proportional for people with higher incomes. They become progressive only at the very top of the distribution. This means that taxes do not significantly redistribute income under any of the assumptions used in their study (see table 3.5). However, the regressiveness found at the bottom of the scale is probably exaggerated. This is because people have low in-

Table 3.4 Effective Rates of Federal, State, and Local Taxes under
Various Assumptions of Tax Burdens, by Family Income Class, 1966
(Income classes in thousands of dollars; tax rates in percent)

Adjusted family income	Incidence variants [a]							
	1a	1b	1c	2a	2b	3a	3b	3c
0–3	19.5	19.4	18.7	21.4	23.2	23.6	28.1	20.9
3–5	21.7	21.5	20.4	21.3	22.1	22.9	25.3	21.3
5–10	23.5	23.4	22.6	23.2	23.2	25.1	25.9	23.5
10–15	23.6	23.4	22.8	23.5	23.2	25.3	25.5	23.5
15–20	24.0	23.8	23.2	23.5	23.3	25.0	25.3	23.7
20–25	24.7	24.6	24.0	23.8	23.7	24.9	25.1	24.1
25–30	25.4	25.3	25.1	24.2	24.1	24.4	24.3	24.8
30–50	26.8	26.8	26.4	24.9	25.0	23.9	24.4	25.8
50–100	31.2	31.2	31.5	29.4	29.8	26.8	26.4	30.2
100–500	38.5	39.1	41.8	40.5	40.5	34.0	30.3	39.6
500–1,000	41.5	42.7	48.0	47.5	47.2	38.2	30.3	44.6
1,000 and over	41.2	42.9	49.3	49.3	48.8	38.5	29.0	45.7
All classes [b]	25.5	25.4	25.2	25.3	25.3	25.7	25.9	25.4

Source: Body of table reprinted from Joseph A. Pechman and Benjamin A.
Okner, *Who Bears the Tax Burden?* (Washington, D.C.: The Brookings Institution,
1974) p. 49, by permission. Computed from 1966 MERGE file.

[a] Each of these variants represents a different set of assumptions concerning
who bears the burden of taxes; e.g., 1a assumes that the payroll tax is borne by
employees, the corporation income tax and the property tax on improvements by *all*
property owners, and the property tax on land by landowners. See *Who Bears the
Tax Burden?*, table 3.1, for a detailed explanation.

[b] Includes negative incomes not shown separately.

comes for only part of their lives. Students and retired workers
have higher lifetime incomes. Their consumption patterns regarding
certain items such as housing and cars may be more closely related
to their lifetime incomes rather than to their current yearly incomes.
Nevertheless, it is surprising that the tax instrument is in fact not
redistributive for a wide range of income and is probably regressive
at the low end of the distribution.

Table 3.5 Average Effective Rates of Federal, State, and Local Taxes for Selected Population Percentiles, Various Incidence Variants, 1966 (Percent)

Population percentile	Incidence variants [a]							
	1a	*1b*	*1c*	*2a*	*2b*	*3a*	*3b*	*3c*
3d	24.3	24.1	24.4	31.5	33.8	31.9	35.6	29.2
5th	19.1	18.9	18.2	21.7	24.1	24.2	28.9	20.8
10th	18.3	18.3	17.4	18.9	20.5	21.0	25.4	18.9
20th	22.2	22.1	20.6	21.3	22.1	23.3	25.5	21.8
25th	23.1	22.9	21.6	22.1	22.6	24.3	26.4	22.9
30th	23.3	23.2	22.1	23.0	23.1	24.7	26.1	23.4
40th	23.4	23.1	22.7	23.1	23.2	24.7	25.7	23.3
50th	23.5	23.5	22.9	23.7	23.5	25.6	26.0	23.8
60th	23.5	23.3	22.7	23.5	23.2	25.3	25.6	23.5
70th	23.7	23.5	22.9	23.5	23.2	25.2	25.4	23.6
75th	23.7	23.5	23.0	23.5	23.2	25.2	25.4	23.6
80th	23.8	23.5	22.9	23.4	23.2	25.3	25.6	23.5
90th	24.6	24.4	24.0	23.9	23.7	24.9	25.0	24.1
91st	24.6	24.4	24.0	23.9	23.7	24.9	25.0	24.1
92nd	24.6	24.4	24.0	23.9	23.7	24.9	25.1	24.1
93d	24.9	24.9	23.9	23.7	23.6	24.8	25.3	24.2
94th	25.0	24.9	24.0	23.6	23.6	24.6	24.7	24.2
95th	25.0	24.9	24.5	23.7	23.5	24.3	24.1	24.4
96th	25.7	25.7	25.7	24.7	24.6	24.5	24.6	25.1
97th	25.6	25.6	25.2	24.2	24.2	23.8	24.0	24.7
98th	26.8	26.8	26.7	25.3	25.5	24.3	24.4	26.1
99th	29.2	29.1	28.3	25.9	26.2	24.1	25.2	27.5
Top	36.0	36.6	39.2	38.1	38.2	31.8	28.6	37.1

Source: Body of table reprinted from: Joseph A. Pechman and Benjamin A. Okner *Who Bears the Tax Burden?* (Washington, D.C.: The Brookings Institution, 1974), p. 51, by permission. Computed from the 1966 MERGE data file.

[a] See table 3.4.

Another shortcoming of using current income as a measure of capacity to pay taxes is that it ignores variations in need among tax-paying units. Larger families need more income in order to be as well off as smaller families.[7] Thus two families paying the same tax rate who have the same incomes but have different numbers of members cannot be said to be bearing the same tax burden. For this reason recent studies have used welfare ratios as a measure of capacity to bear taxes rather than income classes. The welfare ratio is the ratio of income to the poverty line; families with the same welfare ratio are grouped together. Families whose income is twice their poverty line form one group, while families whose incomes are half their poverty line form another group. In one such study, Benjamin Bridges compared the tax rates by the two classifications, income and welfare ratio. As in the Pechman and Okner study, he ranked people according to their income and their welfare ratio. The welfare-ratio approach produced less regressive tax burdens for the bottom 5 percent of the population and consistently lower tax rates for the bottom 70 percent of the population. For the top 30 percent of the population tax rates were found to be higher with the welfare-ratio measure than with the income classification. However, taxes were only slightly more progressive for the entire population with the welfare ratio as compared to the income measure of capacity.[8]

As can be seen, much of what we perceive of the distribution of the tax burden depends on the measure of capacity to pay taxes that is used, the definition of income, and the assumptions on the incidence of taxation. However, there seems to be a general agreement that in the middle-income range the differences are not large no matter what assumptions are used. There is much less agreement on the effects of taxation at the extreme ends of the distribution, since the results are most sensitive to changes in assumptions. These uncertainties as to the effects of taxation are distressing because one might particularly like to alter distribution at the extreme ends of the income scale. Nevertheless, under just about any assumption, there is very little redistribution through taxation at the low-income end of the distribution, and taxes there may actually be regressive.

No investigation of taxes alone gives a complete picture of the extent of redistribution in the system. Government expenditures and transfers too play an important role. Musgrave and Musgrave did such an analysis. They divided government expenditure into three categories and attempted to determine the share of benefit from each accruing to different income groups. The first category looked at government expenditures for such things as hospitals and education, where benefits could be attributed to specific individuals within income groups. For example, benefits from education were based on number of children in each income group. The second category contained transfer payments such as public assistance and social security, which could also be directly attributed to groups of beneficiaries. The third type of expenditures, those which could not be attributed directly to specific beneficiaries (such as defense), was distributed on the basis of three alternative assumptions: taxes paid, family income, and population in each income group. With any of the assumptions used by the authors, expenditures by government redistribute income to the poor. The Musgraves added taxes and benefits for each income group to show net benefits. The break-even point for all taxes and expenditures occurred at about $10,000 income level. Those below $10,000 generally benefited from the tax and expenditure structure in the United States, while those with income above that amount lost. The break-even point for federal taxes and expenditures alone was lower, around $8,000, while for state and local taxes and expenditures it was over $11,000 per year. This is because the federal structure is much more favorable to the poor than are state and local taxes, both because federal taxes are more progressive and because federal expenditures favored the poor to a greater degree. The largest amounts of benefits accrued to those whose income was below $4,000 annually. This is because most transfer payments in the United States are given to people in these groups. Those with incomes up to $5,700 a year also benefited substantially from the tax-expenditure structure. The net benefits were quickly reduced for incomes above $6,000 a year (see table 3.6).

Caution needs to be employed in analyzing these results because of the large differences in benefits received by individuals in the same income group. Doubt is more serious with respect to benefits than to taxes, because benefits are received according to special characteristics of the poor. Thus social-security benefits are received by the old and disabled, and public assistance is given mainly to families with absent fathers. These groups generally pay few taxes compared to low-income workers who may pay both social-security and income taxes. Thus the beneficiaries are not the same individuals as the taxpayers, even though they may be in the same income group. The net tax-benefits concept would have more meaning if subgroups of like populations were compared. Nevertheless, it is clear that the expenditure patterns of government have redistributed more income to lower-income groups than has the tax system.[9]

Efficiency Costs

Just as modifications in behavior affect who pays taxes, they also alter production so as to affect the efficiency of the economy. The economic definition of efficiency relies on consumer sovereignty. Efficiency is a state in which consumers, producers, and factors of

Table 3.6 Distribution of Net Benefits and Burdens (Net as Percent of Total Family Income)

					Income Brackets					
	Under $4,000	$4,000–$5,700	$5,700–$7,900	$7,900–$10,400	$10,400–$12,500	$12,500–$17,500	$17,500–$22,000	$22,000–$35,500	$35,500–$92,000	$92,000 and over
Federal										
1. Specific allocation	76.7	17.7	4.1	−1.9	−4.2	−5.6	−5.6	−5.1	−5.1	− 5.1
2. General, variant A [a]	4.3	2.7	1.0	0.7	0.6	−0.4	−0.1	−0.6	−1.0	− 3.6
3. Total	81.0	20.5	5.1	−1.3	−3.6	−6.0	−5.6	−5.7	−6.1	− 8.7
State and Local										
4. Specific allocation	15.7	8.2	5.9	2.7	0.2	−1.4	−3.2	−3.7	−3.4	− 4.4
5. General, variant A	− 1.1	− 0.8	− 0.6	−0.5	−0.3	−0.1	0.2	0.4	1.1	1.2
6. Total	14.6	7.4	5.4	2.2	−0.1	−1.5	−3.0	−3.2	−2.3	− 3.2
All Levels										
7. Specific allocation	94.0	27.0	10.6	1.2	−3.7	−6.9	−8.9	−9.1	−9.4	−11.0
8. General, variant A	1.6	0.9	− 0.1	−0.3	—[b]	−0.5	0.3	0.3	1.1	− 0.9
9. Total	95.6	27.9	10.5	0.9	−3.7	−7.4	−8.6	−8.9	−8.4	−11.9

Source: Reprinted from Richard Musgrave and Peggy Musgrave, *Public Finance in Theory and Practice* (New York: McGraw-Hill Book Company, 1973), p. 375, by permission of the publisher.

[a] Lines 2, 5, and 8: General expenditures are allocated in proportion to family income levels and tax distributions as in table 3.2.

[b] Less than 0.05.

production are in optimal position. Changing neither the mix of goods consumed, nor work effort, nor savings schedules will improve consumer welfare. The position of producers will not be improved by changing the mix of goods produced, factor inputs used, or business location. Any distortion in consumption, work, savings, or investment imposes a burden on someone. These distortions may lead to a lower level of GNP, a smaller growth rate, or greater unemployment.

THE CONSUMPTION-LEISURE CHOICE

A tax imposed on workers' incomes or wages may rearrange choices regarding work and leisure. This may impose an efficiency cost upon the economy. The fundamental principle underlying the behavior of workers is that they are free to choose between income through work and leisure. An important determinant in the decision is the wage rate. Taxes affect the net amount of wages a worker will earn. This in turn influences how much workers will work.

Empirical evidence in a study by Greenberg and Koster indicated a moderate change in the number of hours worked on the part of male heads of families as a result of changes in wages.[10] In a study of a similar nature, Michael J. Boskin found little evidence of changes in work hours by male heads because of changes in wage rate.[11] Some of these results may be due to poor data and some to the omission of relevant behavioral variables. Today there seems to be no strong evidence of major changes in labor supply because of changes in taxes.

THE CONSUMPTION-SAVINGS CHOICES

Just as the family can vary its decisions on how much income it earns through its choices of work and leisure, it can also decide what proportion of its income it will save. Savings can be regarded as a reduction of current consumption in order to increase future consumption. The amount saved is a function of the rate of return. But the direction of the influence of interest rates is not known. If higher interest rates lead to greater amounts of savings, taxes that reduce the rate of return will diminish savings. However, it is usually assumed that household savings do not rise with higher interest rates. In fact, the opposite may be the case. If households set goals of specific amounts of assets that they wish to accumulate, higher interest rates require less savings in order to meet such goals. Therefore, a reduction in the returns on savings because of increased taxes may actually lead to an increase in the amount of savings.

A more important factor in the amount of savings is family income. The proportion of income saved rises with family income. The greater the progressiveness of the tax, the bigger the reduction in savings is likely to be. The amount will therefore depend on the final disposition of the tax burden. For example, if a corporation income tax is borne by consumers, the reduction in total savings is likely to be less than if the tax were paid by owners of capital. This is because the rich who own proportionately more capital save a larger proportion of their money than do the rest of the population. An analysis of the total effect on savings of a corporation tax must take into consideration effects on households as well as on businesses. An increase in the corporation income tax may lower savings by reducing cash flow to corporations. Some of this reduction in corporation savings may induce owners of corporations to save more, thereby increasing savings by households.

The differentials between types of incomes will also tend to alter the choice of investment portfolios. Income from state and local bonds for which no individual income tax need be paid is favored by high-income individuals. Similarly, capital gains may be a superior choice to dividend income because of postponements in paying taxes in the individual income tax. This may turn to complete avoidance of tax payment if there are no effective death taxes. We will return to this matter.

EFFECTS ON INVESTMENT

Does a change in taxes lead to a change in investment, and does this in turn lead to a change in growth of GNP? The answer seems to be yes, although the magnitude of change is unknown, as are the most effective policy variables to encourage investment. Which factors determine investment rates is still a controversial question. In the traditional economic approach, investment is considered to be dependent upon the relation of the interest paid for borrowing funds to the rate of return on investment. Recently, economists have emphasized the availability of funds to the firm, especially from internal sources. Thus, Jorgenson states that investment credits and accelerated depreciation, both of which affect internal liquidity, encourage investment.[12] Also, different kinds of investment may react to varying extents to the different policy variables; thus, for example, a given policy might encourage replacement capital more than investment for plant expansion. If new capital formation is to be encouraged, investment credit and accelerated depreciation may be more effective than a reduction in the corporation profits tax.

In the context of encouraging investment, the effects of taxation on risk taking are important. Although taxation may result in some investment's being reallocated between projects of unequal risk, there seems to be no reason why total risk taking should be reduced because of taxation, assuming that write-offs for all investment losses are permitted in the individual income tax.

The impact of added savings and investments on growth is also controversial. There seems to be a wide margin in the empirical estimates. Solow claimed that a 1 percent increase in growth rate can be produced by a 2.5 percent rise in investment.[13] Harberger states that a 10 percent rise in investment is needed to increase growth by 1 percent.[14]

A more important stimulus than investment to economic growth may be technological improvements and investment in human capital. Tax credits and direct grants may facilitate the former. The latter may be accomplished by more equitable distribution. Since the remaining potential effect of improving the quality of labor is biggest among low-income people, better distribution and larger GNP are compatible in this case.

OTHER EFFECTS OF TAXATION

Taxation may lead to inefficiencies in allocation among industries, locations, and factors of production. For example, an unwarranted depletion allowance may lead to distortions favoring extractive industries. It may interfere with short- and long-term capital investment decisions. It may also create complete losses to the economy by shortening capital life.[15]

Taxes' influences on work-leisure decisions, saving, investment, and consumption patterns can be depicted as an extra cost to the economy. Taxes paid to government shift resources away from private uses to public uses. This approach assumes that the real burden is equal to the amount of taxes collected. Most tax experts recognize that tax burden exceeds the amount of revenues collected by government treasuries. This added burden stems from the distortions in economic choices imposed by the tax system on taxpayers. A tax on the sale of shoes reduces taxpayer welfare by the amount of the tax paid. It further reduces welfare by inducing consumers to decrease the purchase of shoes relative to other commodities. The foundation for this welfare approach to viewing the tax burden is that individuals determine their own optimum welfare. Such an approach does not recognize that the collective interests of society may diverge from those of the individual. It also ignores the way in which individual welfare calculations are influenced by outside, even insidious forces. For example, advertising is often accused of creating satisfaction from products where none exists. A product may be consumed which is actually harmful to individuals' long-term interest but nevertheless creates welfare in an economic sense. Cigarette smoking is such an example. The efficiency cost in such a system is equal to the total loss of welfare minus the loss of welfare without distortion. It can be measured by applying a completely neutral tax, one that does not influence patterns of economic behavior such as consumption, work, and savings.

EMPIRICAL ESTIMATES OF EXCESS BURDEN

Empirical estimates of these extra tax burdens have indicated only modest losses to the economy, however. The major losses through excess burden seem to result from the corporation income tax and from excise taxes. Musgrave and Musgrave have estimated the losses from the corporation income tax and excise tax as $1 billion and $3 to $4 billion respectively. Harberger places the excess burden of the corporation tax between $1.5 and $2.5 billion.[16] The Musgraves state that excess burden for all taxes is about $10 to $15 billion. The additional $5 billion administrative and compliance costs leads to a surprisingly small total of $20 billion. This is less than 6 percent of all tax collections.[17]

Tax Characteristics

The incidence of a tax depends upon the type of base used and the manner in which the tax is imposed. The choice of base may be income, expenditure, or wealth. Within these categories the breadth of the base may vary greatly. Income from all sources, earned income alone, or some combination which omits certain incomes but includes others may be taxed. Taxes may be general or selective, as in the case of a tax on all consumer purchases or a tax on cigarettes. It may also vary by industry—for example, an excise tax on automobile production.

As was stated above, the imposition of taxes may produce modifications in behavior of consumers, producers, and owners of factors of production, all influencing the tax burden. A tax on the sale of gasoline may alter its consumption and its price. A tax on income may alter work effort. A tax on factors of production may change the input mix as well as the location of individuals and firms.

THE INDIVIDUAL INCOME TAX

The individual income tax is the vehicle most suited to include equity features in taxation. It is also the tax that has produced the greatest controversy over the fairness of these features. It allows for a structure which is compatible with individual circumstances but which may give extraordinary benefits that few people can justify. Whatever the argument for special consideration for certain groups, the ability-to-pay principle dominates these debates.

A number of decisions have to be made in order to tax people's incomes. The definition of taxable income must be based on a concept of capacity to pay taxes. The proper taxpaying unit must be established—for example, the family, the household, or the individual. Finally, preferential treatment for some individuals may be desirable in order to achieve equity between people with the same incomes and people with different incomes. To accomplish this, some (e.g., those with large families) must be allowed to pay less than others. Lastly, tax relief can be given for preferred economic activities.

THE PAYING UNIT

The federal individual income tax allows some choice by taxpayers of the taxpaying unit. Married couples can file joint returns or pay taxes separately. Under certain circumstances it pays to combine parents and children into one taxpaying unit. At other times they may be separated. Differential treatment of families and unrelated individuals is evident in the tax law. In 1969 separate tax-rate schedules were constructed for these two groups. This is probably a compromise between mandating the household as the taxpaying unit and viewing individuals as taxpayers. Under the first approach, all income by all members in the family would be taxed on a single tax-rate schedule. Reduction in taxes for larger families should more realistically reflect the amount required to support an extra member in the family. The law now permits an exemption for an additional member in the family, but in an amount far below that required to support an extra member. However, it gives preferential rates to married couples. Although there are sound arguments for a unified tax schedule for the entire household, married couples with two wage earners would be worse off than under the present law. Treating individuals singly as taxpaying units would mean imposing an unequal tax on families with the same income but a different number of earners.

INCOME CONCEPT

A more controversial aspect of the tax is the definition of income used. If taxpayers with the same incomes are to be treated alike by the tax law, a global concept of income is required and the tax must be levied in the period it accrues to the taxpayer. Such a definition of income should be net of the costs incurred in earning the income.[18] The definition in existing law is far from global. While income from various sources—wages, interest, rent, dividends, profits, and income from unincorporated businesses—is included in the definition, interest derived from state and local bonds is excluded, as is part of capital gains. Also excluded are government transfer payments such as social security and unemployment insurance. Nor is account taken of in-kind income such as imputed rents. Adjustments are made by excluding expenses incurred in earning income. This include outlays for relocation and employee business expenses. However, no reduction is made for investment in human capital (i.e., educational outlays).

There are certain unavoidable personal expenditures which vary even among taxpayers with similar incomes. The inclusion of itemized deductions in the federal income tax recognizes the need to account for these expenses. Extraordinary medical expenditures and state and local taxes are recognized as legitimate personal deductions. Other deductions, such as contributions to charitable institutions, are avoidable but are considered desirable and hence allowed. There is also the standard deduction option. Under present law, this option is preferable for those whose itemized deductions are below the allowed standard deduction.

Finally, exemptions are allowed for variations in family size, each member producing a reduction in taxable income of $750. Additional exemptions are given for the blind and the aged, perhaps in recognition of greater need.

Taxable income is derived by application of these deductions and exemptions to adjusted gross income (AGI), which is itself not a global concept of income. It becomes apparent that, depending on the amount of exclusions from AGI and the size of the deductions and exemptions, the effective tax rate is very different from the marginal rates in the tax tables. For example, at $100,000 income per year the marginal rate is 62 percent, but the effective rate (tax as a proportion of AGI) is only 34.5 percent. With a broader income definition of taxable capacity than the present AGI definition, this difference grows. It is the effective rate that is the better measure of tax incidence. Changes in the laws with regard to the definition of taxable income can play an important role in the incidence of taxation.

THE MERITS OF EXCLUSIONS, DEDUCTIONS, EXEMPTIONS, AND SPECIAL TREATMENTS

The arguments for treating some income in a special way vary with each case. Reduced rates for earned income are sometimes justified on grounds of merit, such income being earned by "sweat of the brow." Arguments may also be based on fears of reducing work effort. Because earned income is a larger proportion of all income for those near the bottom of the income distribution, the reduced rate is sometimes seen as a method of aiding the poor. But the law limits the marginal tax rate on earned income to 50 percent; that is, only high-income earners benefit.

The most controversial case of special treatment is capital gains. Realized long-term gains are taxed at a maximum of 36.5 percent. This provides incentives to receive income in this way for those taxpayers whose marginal tax rates on income from dividends and profits are above 36.5 percent. Unrealized gains are not taxed at the time of accretion to the taxpayer. With ineffective death taxes, taxes on unrealized gains may be postponed for long periods of time or avoided altogether. There are problems in taxing unrealized gains at the time of accretion: the difficulty of valuing some assets, the change in the general price level, and the problem of having to pay taxes when there is no cash flow. In addition, the oft-stated argument in support of the favoritism is the fear that the income tax is a deterrent to risky business ventures. As was mentioned earlier, with a complete offset for loss against all types of income, there seem to be little grounds for such fears. The other obstacles can probably be overcome as well.

Omissions of imputed rents in AGI produce unequal treatment of renters and homeowners. Treatment of income from pension plans and from Old Age, Survivors, and Disability Insurance (OASDI) also need revision. Under present law the income on which the employee pays the social-security tax is also taxed by the individual income tax. Employer contributions are not taxed at all. Neither are benefits taxed. It may be better to tax all transfer payments, including OASDI, at the time received. A nagging problem remains whether OASDI still contains some features of insurance and therefore should not be taxed at the time benefits are received.

Interest on state and local bonds is tax free. This is a way of aiding states and localities by reducing their interest rates for borrowing. However, it is inefficient, since not all the loss to the federal government is passed on to the states and localities. It also limits the number of buyers of state and local bonds to those who profit by this arrangement. It may be more advisable to give such subsidies to states and localities directly.

Itemized deductions are an attempt to account for hardships due to variations in expenditures. However, the value of the deductions differs according to the marginal tax-rate paid, so that high-income taxpayers benefit more than low-income taxpayers from a dollar of deductions of state and local taxes. A tax credit instead of a deduction would help even out the benefits among taxpayers. Interest rates paid by households are deductible. This is probably not justified in case of residences, but is in the case of businesses. However, encouraging home ownership may be desirable in itself as well as a way to maintain the housing stock in better physical condition.

The use of the standard deduction has also been questioned. Rate changes may accomplish the desired distributional impact more directly. The justification for the minimum standard deduction is that all taxpayers have certain expenditures on which a tax should not be levied. Costs of administration and compliance by taxpayers are reduced if deductions do not have to be itemized. In addition, there is a feeling by some taxpayers that the allowable itemized deductions are not justified. State and local taxes, for example, also represent benefits received by taxpayers.

The worth of a $750 tax exemption is $375 for individuals with a 50 percent marginal tax rate, while it is worth only $150 for those in the 20 percent bracket. This can be altered by converting the exemption to a credit or by altering the tax brackets.

Of the arguments used to justify tax preferences, only some have been presented here. Indeed, preferences need justification, since they lead to unequal treatment of people with the same incomes. They substantially redistribute income. Their effect is felt most at the extremes of the income distribution. The poor benefit mainly through the standard deduction and exemption, the rich through the treatment of capital gains and interest on state and local bonds. The middle-income group gains from deductions because of home ownership. These preferences should be viewed as subsidies to be included in the federal budget. Making these trade-offs visible might lead Congress to greater reluctance or wisdom in dispensing these favors.

Important issues for consideration remain in this area of taxation. The move to a broader definition of income and lower marginal tax rates needs to be debated. There is a need to smooth out the discontinuity in marginal tax rates from zero to 14 percent.

This may be bridged by a subsidy that decreases as income rises. The problem of the taxing period needs to be discussed. There is already some income-averaging arrangement in the personal income tax for those whose income has risen substantially. This may have to be expanded to include those whose incomes have fallen.

THE INCIDENCE OF THE PERSONAL INCOME TAX

A change in the federal tax on earned income has made certain adjustments in behavior beneficial but not others. No advantage is gained from moving to a new industry or region. However, taxpayers may improve their welfare by altering work effort. Empirical evidence suggests that even here few adjustments are made. This may be due to the rigidities in the labor markets which block workers' options for altering hours of work. It may also be caused by the importance of nonmonetary variables in decisions on work behavior. Imperfections in the extent of competition in the market may lead to some shifting of the personal income tax through salary raises that compensate for increased tax. Union power may allow for such shifts, if unions were not maximizing income of their members before the tax was imposed. Likewise, self-employed individuals such as doctors and lawyers may have greater latitude in shifting the tax to the consumers of their services.

THE CORPORATION INCOME TAX

The corporation income tax (in 1975) imposes a 20 percent tax on profits under $25,000, ranging up to 48 percent tax on profits above $50,000. Four-fifths of all corporations pay only the lower rate, but profits are distributed in such a way that 90 percent of taxes are derived from the highest rate.[19] Although this tax has progressive marginal tax rates, its progressiveness is not due to this feature. Large corporations with large profits may be owned by many poor stockholders, while small corporations may be owned by rich individuals. The incidence of the corporation income tax is due to asset ownership and the degree of tax shifting.

The main theoretical controversy surrounding the corporation tax is whether to consider it as a supplement to the individual income tax or as wholly new tax on a different tax base. The position taken depends partly on whether one believes taxes are paid only by individuals. Those advocating a separate corporation income tax contend that institutions derive benefits from the existence of government, which they should support. The size of corporations, especially if they have monopoly power, needs to be curtailed. The best way to do this is through taxation. Besides, the argument continues, undistributed corporate profits need to be taxed directly; otherwise a tax-avoidance mechanism would be created.

Proponents of the corporation tax as a supplementary tax claim that the corporation tax creates double taxation: one income stream is taxed at two points. Instead, they propose a unified system which merges income from all sources. Under such a scheme, undistributed corporate profits would be assigned to individuals owning the stocks. Total income would be taxed at individual income-tax rates.

The corporation income tax is usually viewed as a progressive element in the federal tax structure. This is because at least part of the tax is believed to fall on profits, which are a much larger portion of income of the rich. However, progressiveness is reduced if account is taken of its effects on the individual income tax. The effect of a corporation income-tax payment is to reduce the individual income-tax liability. The higher the marginal rate, the bigger the savings to the taxpayer. This reduces the progressiveness of the corporation income tax.

In fact, combining the individual and corporate income taxes would make for a more progressive tax structure. This is because a tax shelter develops from undistributed corporate profits. The higher the marginal tax rate and the bigger the proportion of undistributed corporate profits, the larger the shelter. Integrating the system removes the shelter, thereby increasing progressiveness. The impact of integration on progressiveness depends on the proportion of corporation profits that are undistributed. Several methods of integration have been proposed. One is to treat corporations as partnerships. Profits would be imputed to stockholders' incomes based on their share of stocks. Both distributed and undistributed profits would be taxed under the individual income tax.[20]

THE INCIDENCE OF THE CORPORATE PROFITS TAX

The distribution of the burden of the corporation tax is in doubt, although it has been studied extensively.[21] The significance of important variables is still unknown. For example, it is clear that the corporation tax is not neutral, since it is levied only on corporations. However, even among corporations the tax is not neutral. Because it is levied on profits, the amount of tax paid by various firms and industries differs. The impact upon the reallocation of capital and labor among industries and locations depends upon the mobility of capital and labor. It also depends on the market structure of the firms that pay the tax. Pure monopolies that try to maximize profits pay the entire tax. Firms that attempt to maximize sales or work on markups may shift part of the tax. The time frame is also important. In the short run the entire tax falls on capital. In the long run it is shifted to lower-taxed industries until net return on investment is equalized. The effects of the present structure of the corporation tax are like a sales tax with differing rates on different products depending on the profit position of each firm and how well it can shift the tax. Thus the corporation income tax imposes substantial efficiency costs on the economy.

THE PAYROLL TAX

The federal payroll tax to finance social security has risen greatly in recent years. Inflation has made the cost of financing retirement and disability under the program more costly. Adding the Medicaid program to the system has also increased outlays. Since social security is financed by a payroll tax, the need for larger revenues has forced increases in tax rates on a larger earned-income base. The effect has been to burden low-income workers with large regressive taxes. The tax stands at 11.7 percent of wages and salaries up to $15,300 per year, divided equally between employers and employees.[22]

There are two ways to view the social-security tax; as a benefit tax, and as an independent tax completely divorced from social-security benefits received. The first approach treats the tax as insurance for retirement and disability. The tax was made compulsory because society did not want dependent people who had failed to insure themselves. Viewed in this way, the regressiveness of the social-security tax itself is not bothersome. Taken together with benefits, the system actually redistributes income to the poor.

A more convincing view, set forth at length in the next chapter, is that there is only a tenuous link between what is paid and what is received. There are transfers between income groups and generations. The effects of the social-security tax must therefore be looked at independently of benefits. As such, the tax is regressive and discriminatory against earned income. It should therefore be replaced with an independent income tax which is broadly based and progressive.

THE INCIDENCE OF THE PAYROLL TAX

There is general agreement that the part of the payroll tax legally levied on employees remains on workers. This is because there is little change in work effort as a result of the tax, just as in the case of the individual income tax.[23] Therefore, there is no incentive to substitute capital and land for labor in production.

There is some controversy as to who bears the employers' share of the tax. Drawing on an empirical study of industries and countries, Brittain claims that workers bear the entire burden of the employers' share.[24] However, the Musgraves and Bridges assume that it falls at least in part on consumers.[25] Theoretically there should be no difference in incidence between the employer and the employee portion of the tax. But with imperfections in the market, some shifting is possible. If employers are unable to lower wages to compensate for higher employer payroll taxes, they may try to increase prices to consumers instead in the short run. In the long run, subsequent wage increases may be smaller as a result of the previous rise in the social-security tax.

The tax revisions of 1975 extended relief to low-income wage earners. Those with earnings below $4,000 received a cashable credit of 10 percent of their earnings upon filing their income-tax returns. This government action contained the implicit judgment that the employee's part of the payroll tax and almost the whole of the employer's part were borne by the wage earner. However, if the employer's portion of the tax is in actuality shifted to consumers, workers' credits should have been limited to what the employees legally pay, i.e., 5.85 percent of earnings.

Progressiveness of the tax may also be increased by raising the ceilings of taxable income and allowing exemptions, as in the case of the individual income tax. A more radical approach to relieving the tax burden of the poor is to integrate it with the individual income tax.

THE SALES TAX

The sales tax remains the largest revenue producer for states. Localities too have collected increasing revenues from this source in recent years. Because of differences in rates and coverage among locations, its impact is unevenly distributed. The possibilities of bases include value added (wages, interest, rents, and profits of a firm), gross national product, and net national product (GNP minus depreciation). Sales taxes can be legally imposed on the buyer or on the seller. Localities usually tax most sales to consumers, but sometimes they tax only particular products, such as cigarettes. Broadly based taxes are imposed on the value of sales. Single-item taxes may sometimes be levied on volume—for example, gallons of gasoline or liquor.

The choice of a particular base determines the economic costs of the tax as well as its incidence and its equity. A tax on the value of all business turnovers pyramids the tax at each stage of production. This leads to inefficiency, because it is advantageous to produce inputs within the firm rather than buying them from other firms. A tax which includes all transactions, even if it has no pyramiding effect, discriminates against savings. It is unfair and economically unsound because it taxes gross income without taking account of the cost of producing the income (depreciation).

Consumption taxes now imposed on sales by states and localities are in proportion to the value of sales. However, it is feasible to replace a progressive income tax with a progressive consumption tax.[26] Proponents for such a switch have argued that fairness requires taxing how much is taken out of production (consumption) rather than how much is put in (income). Consumption taxes have the added advantages of encouraging savings.

The sales tax is inequitable in that it taxes people with the same income different amounts. This is because even families with equal incomes consume different amounts of taxed goods. The inequity is diminished if the base is broader. The tax is regressive when the base is all consumer goods. For this reason certain consumer items, important in low-income family budgets, are often not taxed (food, rent, drugs).[27] Another reason for excusing such goods from taxation is that the government does not want to discourage their consumption. The sales tax may also be considered a user charge. The tax on gasoline is a charge for using highways.

SALES-TAX INCIDENCE

The incidence of a sales tax on one commodity is determined by supply and demand of taxed goods. If a consumer cannot do with less consumption of the taxed commodity, a new tax will be paid for entirely by the consumer.[28] Although such a pure example is difficult to find, cigarettes and other habit-forming consumer goods come close. Consumers also bear the entire tax burden in an industry whose cost per unit of production does not vary with the amount of output. On the contrary, if supply is fixed, as in the case of a farmer who has harvested his crop, the entire tax is borne by the producer.

A sales tax on all consumer goods at one rate in all localities will fall on consumers. Those saving all their money will pay no tax, while consumers cannot escape the tax by altering consumption patterns. Differences in rates and coverage between localities, especially within metropolitan areas, may induce some shifting. For example, Henry Levine found that New York City lost about 6 percent in sales for every 1 percent of tax rate above the surrounding area.[29] This may have serious implications for local economies. Taxes on items which consumers are unwilling to give up at any price produce least economic-efficiency costs, but these taxes are usually on goods consumed in large proportion by low-income groups and are thus regressive. In such a situation a policy choice must be made between what is fair and what is efficient.

THE PROPERTY TAX

Just as taxes on income and expenditures can be based on either ability-to-pay or benefit principles, so can the property tax. Three types of benefits may be perceived which justify the property tax. The value of property may increase because of public expenditures which are supported by the property tax. More outlays for public schools attract families seeking better education, thereby raising the value of property in the area. A second benefit to property owners may be derived from the services provided by government. Sidewalks, trash collections, and street lighting are but a few of the government services from which property owners benefit. The third benefit is more general. The existence of government protects property rights; therefore property owners should pay for government's outlays. However, benefits received are linked to the general property tax in a tenuous way only. This is because many other variables determine rates and benefits. For example, large school-tax rates are often found in poor areas with many children. This may have the effect of lowering property values rather than raising them. Existence of government benefits all individuals, not only property owners. Likewise, services should be paid for by those who receive them, not only by property owners. A government outlay which enhances property values, such as the construction of sewers, is better financed through a special assessment rather than a general property tax.

The ability-to-pay principle applied to tax property suggests that ownership of property is not merely represented by the income derived from it. This is already taxed by the individual income tax. Another tax on property is needed because wealth gives something more to its owner than merely an additional income flow. It gives him the possibility of converting his assets to cash, something a wage earner cannot do for the value of his future labor. It offers power to the rich in some cases well out of proportion to the income produced by the assets. Government may, therefore, wish to control the distribution of wealth.

If the property tax is justified on the ability-to-pay principle, it is because it is part of a tax on all wealth. However, it is difficult to tax liquid assets, especially for localities. Such assets usually disappear across jurisdictional lines in order to avoid taxation. A tax on wealth to limit the power of the rich is perhaps less effective than circumscribing the areas in which money can be used. Limiting the use of money in politics may be more desirable. Nevertheless, there remains the justification for taxing wealth in order to influence its distribution. But the tax on real property is a poor vehicle for accomplishing this purpose. The main reason why the real-property tax remains such an important part of the tax structure of localities has nothing to do with either principle. It has remained because it has produced surprisingly large amounts of revenues for long periods of time.

Property taxes differ between localities even in the same metropolitan area. This leads to an excise-tax effect on property with differing effects of burden depending on location, industry, and firm. Property-tax rates are very high compared to sales taxes on commodities. Property tax is estimated to be about 25 percent of rental values in the United States. However, it is lower than the tax on stockowners in corporations. Corporations must pay both a property tax and the corporation income tax. In addition, property owners can claim the property tax as a deduction in their individual income tax, an option not open to stockholders. Corporation owners may, therefore, pay twice the rate of property owners.[30]

PROPERTY-TAX INCIDENCE

The real-property tax on unimproved land has no distorting effects, as demonstrated by Henry George at the turn of the century. He claimed that because land was nature's gift to man its entire value should be taxed so that all of society could benefit from it.[31] The property tax in its present form, however, taxes both the value of sites and their improvements. Therefore, the property tax now in existence has deleterious effects on the economy. Because it is difficult for capital to move on short notice, the tax is borne in the short run by those owning the property. Even in the long run, owners of land bear the entire burden of the tax. But, given time, people and capital adjust their welfare position by moving out of highly taxed areas. The extent of the movement depends on the size of the property-tax differentials among areas as well as on a firm's capacity to shift the tax. There will, therefore, be differences in the incidence of the tax among firms and industries. Firms serving the local industry, such as barbershops and restaurants, can shift the tax to consumers through higher prices. Monopolies in the national market may also be able to shift part of the tax to consumers. However, for the most part the tax will fall on local residents and businesses, some of which are located outside the area. Businesses that compete for national markets will be forced to absorb the local property tax. Those businesses that are mobile will be stimulated to move outside the taxing jurisdiction, possibly causing economic hardships in the area.[32] This may leave the highly taxed locality with less capital, lower wages, and a smaller tax base.

The property tax on residences is generally considered to be regressive because it is assumed to be shifted to tenants. Recent studies have cast doubt on this assumption. Buchanan concluded that the shifting of the tax to renters is much less than generally believed.[33] Richman has argued that the landlord bears the property tax.[34] Much of the debate depends on the proportion of values of properties attributable to site value. If it is larger, more of the burden is borne by the owners than by the tenants. On the basis of a more complex economic model, Aaron suggests that the property tax is actually borne by all owners of capital.[35]

Since the property tax produced over 82 percent of tax revenues of localities, the lack of certainty as to who actually bears the burden is unfortunate. For this reason and because of the possible impact upon a local economy the tax must be used cautiously, especially where there are large rate differentials among communities even within metropolitan areas.

DEATH TAXES

Death taxes (estate, inheritance, and gift taxes), which annually produce only about $5 billion in revenues, are a source of irritation in their implication on the distribution of wealth. The primary reason for these taxes is presumably control of the distribution of wealth, but their impact has clearly been minimal. Death taxes are also used as a mechanism to tax those who have successfully escaped payment of some of the individual income tax. The present federal tax applies to estates of over $60,000, with higher rates for larger estates. Gifts and trusts are convenient mechanisms for tax avoidance. The latter device allows generation skipping in applying the tax. Another feature which makes the estate tax ineffective is the unlimited charitable contributions which are sometimes controlled by the contributors for their own purpose after they have been donated.

The system should be altered so that the inheritance tax is substituted for the estate tax. Taxes would then be based on the total amount inherited (including gifts) rather than the size of the estate. Progressive tax rates can then be applied depending on the size of the inheritance, with appropriate exemptions. Undoubtedly there are many legal and technical problems to overcome, but the modest goal of taxing wealth once in a lifetime does not seem unattainable.

Summary and Conclusions

The rapid increase in taxes, especially federal taxes, has provided the government with an important vehicle for redistribution. Large amounts of money can be shifted from the rich to the poor; thus it is vexing that little income has actually been redistributed through taxes in the United States. This is partly because a large portion of taxes are used for reallocation of resources from the private to the public sector, but mainly it is due to social unwillingness for the task.

Issues of equity in taxation are complex. Separating the allocative and distributive functions of government, and therefore the uses of taxes, helps to clarify some of these issues. Since it is best to assign the various functions to different levels of government, it becomes necessary to fashion a tax structure for each level of government in a manner that is consistent with its functional responsibilities. Taxes used for allocation should be different from those used for redistribution.

Under a federal system the allocative function should be divided among various levels of government. In order to minimize economic loss from taxation, services should be assigned according to size of the area serviced. Defense is properly a federal responsibility, while local governments should undertake fire protection. There is a strong argument for assigning the function of redistribution of income primarily to the federal government, in that this reduces loss in economic efficiency due to location patterns of firms and allows for equal treatment of people in the same circumstances no matter where they live.

An examination of redistribution is complicated by the fact that the redistributive effects of taxation and their impact on economic efficiency are not clear. The exact incidence of the property tax and the corporation income tax is still unknown. The incidence of the individual income tax and the payroll tax is more easily understood. Empirical data suggest that the tax structure is proportional for middle-income families while it is progressive at the extremes. But this conclusion rests on the uncertain assumptions of tax shifting and the method for measuring burden. When burden is compared among income classes the tax structure appears progressive at low-income levels. However, when people are ranked according to their income, the tax system seems to be regressive at the low end of the distribution. A larger proportion of income is paid in taxes by people at the very bottom of the distribution than by those somewhat above them. Federal taxes are progressive on the whole, while state and local taxes are regressive. An analysis of tax incidence is also complicated by the plethora of taxes whose impacts are interrelated. For example, the existence of the federal individual income tax alters the incidence of the corporation income tax.

Inefficiency due to taxation appears to create only moderate costs to the economy. Work-leisure decisions are hardly affected by taxes on earned income. The biggest economic costs on the national level are from the corporation income tax. The Musgraves estimated total costs to be in the neighborhood of $20 billion or 6 percent of all collections. The efficiency costs of taxation for localities appear to be more serious, although there have been few extensive studies on the subject. Taxes that are placed on commodities and services considered essential by consumers lead to fewer economic distortions than taxes on commodities and services whose consumption is sharply reduced as prices rise. Thus a tax on cigarettes would produce fewer economic losses than a tax on perfumes. However, essential commodities are frequently consumed largely by lower-income people. A tax on these commodities would, therefore, be more regressive than a tax on luxuries.

Estimates of costs in efficiency are based on the concept of consumer sovereignty: the consumer is best able to determine his own welfare. Taxes that alter consumption patterns reduce the well-being of consumers. However, government policies aimed at encouraging consumption of services such as housing and education through subsidies may vitiate this concept, since they ignore consumer preferences for these items.

The main avenue for restructuring the tax system which also minimizes the costs to the economy is the federal budget. Its prime tax instrument, the individual income tax, is particularly suited for the task since the magnitude of tax rates has little impact on work patterns. Reform of the federal individual income tax should begin by widening the definition of adjusted gross income. This would enhance equity by treating people with the same income more equally regardless of the source of their income. It would be a major step in making the tax more progressive. Treatment of two types of income, capital gains and income from interest on state and local bonds, needs to be altered. Interest from state and local bonds should be considered as normal income. Direct subsidies to states and localities can be given by the federal government to compensate them for the higher interest rates they will have to pay for borrowing. Realized capital gains should be treated as normal income with a complete write-off for losses against any income, not only capital gains. Since this type of income is likely to be clustered, income averaging for years of declining income should be allowed as well as for years with rising income. In order to help avoid investor "lock in," stringent death taxes which preclude tax avoidance need to be imposed.

A personal deduction for state and local government income and sales taxes is justified because the actual burden is on income recipients and consumers. It reduces the possibility that tax rates on income will reach confiscatory levels because of the effect of taxing income at different levels of government. It is also an incentive for state and local governments to utilize the income tax. Allowing property taxes as deductions in the federal individual income tax is unjustified because the tax may be borne by homeowners as investors. Since taxes paid by other types of investors—for example, stockholders in corporations—cannot be deducted, deductions by investors in housing is unwarranted. Even if the tax is actually paid by homeowners as consumers of housing, the deduction is not justified because the property taxes paid by renters are not allowed as a personal deduction. This feature of the tax law is perverse in that homeowners, who are generally higher-income individuals, benefit at the expense of the poorer renters, thereby reducing the progressiveness of the individual income tax.

In place of the present exemption, which is worth more to high-income taxpayers, a credit against taxes would be given based on family size. Those whose tax liability is lower than their credit would receive the balance in cash. The existing credit extends only to wage earners. This credit acts to reduce the regressiveness of the social-security tax and therefore should be retained.

These alterations in the tax law would go a long way toward increasing the progressiveness of the individual income tax. Direct changes in the rate schedules could then be used to further increase its progressiveness. Similarly, the tax on the sale of gasoline should not be allowed as a deduction. This tax is really a highway user charge whose tax levies are offset by benefits received.

In spite of the technical difficulties, it would probably be better to eliminate the corporation income tax so that all income from corporation profits could be taxed by the individual income tax at normal rates. This would eliminate a tax shelter which now exists for high-income recipients, thus making the net effect of the tax more progressive. Losses in revenues from the new arrangement could be made up by adjusting individual income-tax rates.

Most economists agree that if there is to be a depreciation allowance for extractive industries, it should be at a much lower level than at present, with the alterations in the Tax Reduction Act of 1975.[36] The allowance should be lowered and perhaps eliminated in cases where sufficient mineral extraction to meet national needs would exist without it, and in cases where the rate of extraction is unaffected by the allowance.

Death taxes, which include estate, inheritance, and gift taxes, need drastic revision. Under the present law, two ways to avoid payment of inheritance and estate taxes are the use of gifts and trusts. Use of trusts magnifies tax abuses because the trust is a vehicle for avoiding income-tax payments. It is difficult to overcome the legalities of the trust fund, which have been set up to avoid tax payments. However, the principle of taxing wealth once each generation does not seem beyond reach.

Taxing problems of state and especially local governments are much more severe, since economies of localities are more likely to be adversely affected by taxation. It is important that tax-benefits differentials among localities, especially those within the same metropolitan area, be minimized. Thus, the redistributive function should be shifted to the federal government. State and local taxes can then be reformed to make them less regressive. This requires that states rely more heavily on the individual income tax. It has been demonstrated that states can administer such taxes efficiently. Localities which could not administer such a tax by themselves could share in the receipts, thereby reducing their reliance on the property tax. A preferred system may be one individual income tax administered by the federal government, with surcharges at different rates for states and localities. Sales taxes could be made much less regressive by giving a credit for sales taxes against the state income tax. Individuals whose tax liabilities are lower than the credit would receive the refund in cash.

The property tax needs reform, especially in administration. More frequent general assessments, for example, would reduce the difference in rates paid for old and new dwellings. Basing the tax on the full value of property instead of on assessed value would also reduce differences in tax rates paid for different types of property. There should be higher property-tax rates on unimproved land to reduce the incentive to speculate in land.

Other changes in the tax structure could also improve its equity. However, enactment of these proposals would substantially increase the progressiveness of the tax system in the United States and could finally make it a vehicle for social reform.

4

Social Insurance
and Redistribution

MARTHA N. OZAWA

It was not until the Great Depression of 1929 that the federal government got involved in public income-transfer programs. Since then, the social-insurance programs enacted under the Social Security Act of 1935 and its subsequent amendments, as well as other existing social-insurance programs, such as state workmen's compensation programs, have been thought to be the first defense against income loss due to social and industrial hazards. However, four decades after the enactment of the Social Security Act, in spite of increasing expenditures for social insurance,[1] especially for Federal Old Age, Survivors, and Disability Insurance, these programs have not diminished the need for residual programs of public assistance.

On the contrary, during the past decade, public-aid programs have expanded faster than social-insurance programs. During this period, we have seen the introduction of Medicaid for the medically indigent, a growth in payments under Aid to Families with Dependent Children (AFDC), the expansion of work and training programs, and the initiation of Supplemental Security Income (SSI). Since these programs provide only for those who can prove themselves to be in financial need, they are generally called "income-tested" or "income-conditioned" programs. They are also called "residual," since they supplement non-income-tested programs, e.g., social-insurance programs.[2]

If public-aid programs are to be truly residual, the roles of wages and social insurance need to be maximized. A logical way to develop a system of income maintenance is first, to provide jobs with decent wages; second, to strengthen social insurance; and third, to establish equitable and humane cash and in-kind public-aid programs for those who were nevertheless missed. Public policy in income maintenance seems to have moved in the opposite direction in recent years.

Strengthening social insurance rather than public aid is more acceptable to the public and is also more effective for logistic reasons. If jobs and social insurance can provide for those who are normally attached to the labor force, income-conditioned cash-transfer programs can be separated from the heated question of work incentives. Second, the provision of an adequate minimum benefit under social insurance can keep the number of concurrent recipients of social insurance and public aid to a minimum —keeping the value of social-insurance programs in the public eye. Third, since social security (a form of social insurance) spends much more than public-aid programs such as AFDC and SSI, it has a greater potential for redistributing income.

One objective of social-insurance programs—generally accepted without question—is to *replace a portion of income loss* due to social and industrial hazards. Another objective is to *provide adequate income* to eligible families in order to prevent poverty; this objective is generally accepted in principle, but the degree to which social-insurance programs can or should accomplish it is questioned.

The problem of providing adequate income through social insurance is enmeshed with the issue of work incentives on one hand and with the issue of meeting family needs on the other. Concern for work incentives leads lawmakers to develop benefit formulas related to previous earning. However, earnings-related benefits often do not meet family needs, that is, they are insensitive to family size. This dilemma must be confronted if social insurance is to prevent beneficiary families from becoming poor.

A related question is public willingness to spend more to provide a higher minimum. If social-security benefits were increased proportionately, so that no insured worker would remain poor, the expenditures would have to be increased enormously. The nation does not seem ready for such an increase. Therefore, if social insurance is to channel more income to low-wage beneficiary families, the distributional pattern of benefits must be changed in their favor.

Finally, any reform attempting to provide an adequate minimum to beneficiary families is constrained by the need to retain social-insurance principles. The transformation of social-insurance programs into another system of welfare programs in an effort to eliminate public assistance seems a meaningless exercise.

All the constraints identified above compel a look at social-insurance programs from a new perspective. With such a perspective, we examine the legitimacy, potentiality, and limitations of social-insurance programs in redistributing income.

This chapter is divided into four parts. The first part presents the scope of social-insurance programs within the context of the American economy and within the system of social-welfare programs. It reviews the overall distributive impact of social-insurance programs on various income classes and considers the antipoverty potential of social-insurance programs. The second part shows how and why certain groups of people are provided for inadequately or not at all under selected insurance programs. The third part argues the legitimacy of redistributing income through social insurance and empirically reviews the direction of income redistribution under existing social-security programs. The fourth part presents a reform package of social-insurance programs and advocates a children's allowance program as an integral part of it.

The social-insurance programs mainly dealt with in this chapter are: federal Old Age, Survivors, and Disability Insurance (OASDI), popularly called "social security"; state unemployment insurance; state workmen's compensation; and state temporary disability insurance.

Scope and Distributive Impact
of Social-Insurance Programs

A distinctive characteristic of the post–World War II era in the United States was public willingness to spend increasingly for publicly financed social-welfare programs. Social-welfare expenditures under public programs increased from 8.9 percent of the GNP in 1949 to 17.6 percent in 1972. Social-welfare expenditures increased twice as fast during these years as the growth of the economy. One element in increasing social-welfare expenditures was the tremendous growth of social insurance. Between 1949 and 1972 expenditures for social insurance increased from 1.9 percent to 7.0 percent of the GNP.[3]

Within social insurance, the rate of growth in social-security programs was most noticeable. Expenditures for OASDI increased from $784 million in 1949 to $39 billion in 1972. The number of beneficiaries increased from 3 to 28 million. This phenomenal growth reflects not only the liberalization of eligibility requirements and benefit levels but also the gradual maturation of the programs. During the same period, expenditures for state unemployment-insurance programs increased from $2.1 billion to $5.9 billion, and for state workmen's compensation programs from $943 million to $4.3 billion. In the recession year 1975, expenditures for unemployment insurance were close to $18 billion.

Nevertheless, the United States is far behind other industrialized countries in its commitment to social insurance. The major shortcoming in the system is its lack of universal health insurance and national temporary disability insurance. Even for existing social-insurance programs, the United States spends a smaller proportion of the GNP than other industrialized countries. This country also lacks programs for children's allowances and maternity benefits, which exist in most industrialized countries.

On the other hand, the United States has a relatively large commitment to such public-aid programs as AFDC, SSI, general assistance, Medicaid, and public housing.[4] Public aid has been accelerating during the past decade.

DISTRIBUTIVE IMPACT OF SELECTED SOCIAL-INSURANCE PROGRAMS

Since social insurance is a vehicle through which society deliberately transfers income from one segment of the population to another, distributive patterns of social-insurance benefits are inevitably spread unevenly across the population. For example, OASDI tends to redistribute income from the young to the aged. Unemployment insurance redistributes income from the securely to the insecurely employed. Children's allowance programs transfer income from childless families to families with children.

These transfers are regarded as horizontal redistribution. So-called vertical redistribution—from the rich to the poor—is believed to take place through social insurance, although the extent and direction of redistribution are not clear. Which income class receives what portion of social-insurance benefits depends on a number of factors: whether workers in the income class are covered by the program; the probability that a worker in that class faces recognized industrial risks; and the level of benefit. Combining these factors, one can imagine, for example, that families headed by workers in the lowest income class, though unemployment prone, may receive a relatively small share in unemployment insurance benefits, since many are not covered by the program, and many, if covered, receive a small benefit. Some unemployed workers from the lowest income class may not be insured for benefits for one reason or another. On the other hand, the share in unemployment-insurance benefits by the highest income class may be relatively small, since workers in this class, though covered by the program, are not likely to be unemployed. Another factor that depresses the share in benefits of the highest income class is that a ceiling on benefits may prevent them from receiving a full 50 percent of wages.

Figures 1 and 2 illustrate shares in benefits received by different income classes.[5] Figure 1 applies to unrelated individuals and families headed by a person under 65, and figure 2 to those headed by a person 65 or over. The separation of the figures for two age groups is important because the distribution of social insurance is generally "age biased." Public assistance is included in the figures for comparative purposes.

These figures were developed by plotting on a semi-log paper the ratio of the proportion of benefits under a social-insurance program going to a given income class to the proportion of total families falling into that income class. Suppose 10 percent of the

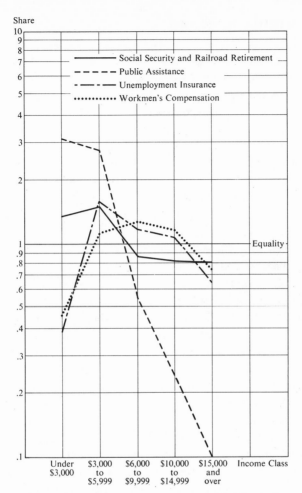

Figure 1. Selected Social-Insurance Programs and Public Assistance: Shares by Families and Individuals of Aggregate Benefit Payments, Relative to Equality, by Income Class, 1970 (Head under 65).

Source: Derived from Dorothy S. Projector and Judith Bretz, "Measurement of Transfer Income in the Current Population Survey," in James D. Smith, ed., *The Personal Distribution of Income and Wealth*, Studies in Income and Wealth, vol. 39 (New York: National Bureau of Economic Research, 1975), tables 1, 5, 6, and 7, pp. 380, 390–92, and 394–401.

families fell under a certain income class and received 20 percent of the total benefits under a social-insurance program; their share of benefits in the program would be twice as much as "the equal share." If benefits were distributed absolutely equally across income classes, one would expect the plotted ratios to form a horizontal line with a ratio of one. If an income class received more than the equal share, its ratio would be greater than one; the reverse is also true. One can see the size of the share in benefits by an income class, in relation to equality. Relative "progressivity" involved in a program can be also seen, thus presenting an interprogram comparison.

Figure 1 illustrates patterns of distribution of social-insurance benefits and public-assistance payments received in 1970 by unrelated individuals and families headed by a person under 65 in various income classes. The greatest degree of progressivity in benefits is seen in public assistance, as it should be. Among social-insurance programs, social security and railroad-retirement benefits present the clearest case of progressive distribution. The lowest two income classes received more than their equal shares. Families receiving disability-insurance benefits are headed, in the majority of cases, by a person between 55 and 64; and those receiving survivors-insurance benefits by a person 55 and over. Retirement beneficiaries between 62 and 65 are also included in figure 1. All these families typically have relatively little income from sources other than social security. Thus they end up with relatively little total income. Note, however, that the range of ratios (describing the variation of shares) is confined to the range between 1.3 and 1.5.

Distribution of benefits from unemployment insurance and workmen's compensation follows similar patterns. Income classes between $3,000 and $14,999 received more than their equal shares; however, the lowest and highest income classes did not. A plausible interpretation has already been offered. Lower-income workers tend less to be covered. If covered, they receive a meager amount for a shorter period of time. Upper-income workers, on the other hand, are less likely to become unemployed or injured on the job.

Figure 2 illustrates patterns of distribution for unrelated individuals and families headed by a person 65 and over. Distribution of benefits and assistance payments follows patterns similar to those of families headed by the nonaged, with the exception of social security and railroad-retirement benefits. A plausible explanation for this difference is as follows: Unlike death and disability, the risk of old age hits everybody regardless of his income background, thus making all persons aged 65 and over potential beneficiaries. Once a person has retired, only earnings affect his social-security benefits—not other forms of income or status. Moreover, the benefit itself is based on prior earnings. Therefore, even moderate- or middle-income families show a ratio over 1. Beyond $10,000, shares of benefit payments gradually decline as incomes become higher. Here the effects of the earnings test and the ceiling on benefits seem to set in. Families headed by the aged that fall in income classes with $10,000 or more were in the minority, however: they were only 12.5 percent of the total families, and they received just about an equal share, 12.7 percent of the total benefits.

Low-income classes receive a greater share of benefits when the distribution of benefits is more progressive, but this is not a full indication of the importance of a given program. The magnitude of distribution depends not only on progressivity but also on total program outlay. Simply put, a 100 percent share of a peanut is still a peanut, but a 50 percent share of an elephant is half an elephant. Effects of these two factors—the extent of the share and the size of the pie—are seen in table 4.1, which shows aggregate benefit payments as a percentage of total money income received by each income class.

One sees, for example, that a relatively large share (42 per-

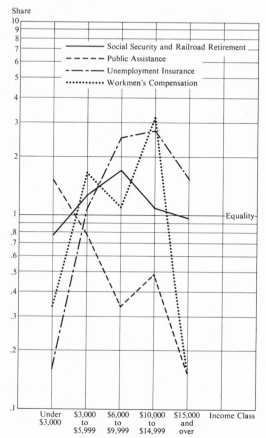

Figure 2. Selected Social-Insurance Programs and Public Assistance: Shares by Families and Individuals of Aggregate Benefit Payments, Relative to Equality, by Income Class, 1970 (Head 65 and over).

Source: Derived from Dorothy S. Projector and Judith Bretz, "Measurement of Transfer Income in the Current Population Survey," in James D. Smith, ed., *The Personal Distribution of Income and Wealth,* Studies in Income and Wealth, vol. 39 (New York: National Bureau of Economic Research, 1975), tables 1, 5, 6, and 7, pp. 380, 390–92, and 394–401.

cent) of total public-assistance payments went to the lowest income class (less than $3,000). However, only 14 percent of the class's total money income came from public assistance. In contrast, as much as 41.3 percent of its total money income came from social security and railroad-retirement benefits, although a relatively small share (30 percent) went to this income class. Yet, on a simple measure of which set of programs was more completely devoted to poor people, public assistance would rank higher.

The data for families headed by a person 65 and over in table 4.1 provide a clearer illustration. The lowest income class (less than $3,000) had a relatively small share (35 percent) in social security and railroad retirement; yet benefits from these programs constituted as much as 65.6 percent of its total money income. Its share of public assistance was overwhelmingly large (70 percent), but public-assistance payments constituted only 9.7 percent of the total money income. In short, although public assistance is strictly geared for low-income classes, it is not as important as social security in terms of the magnitude of distribution involved, even for the lowest income class. This implies that changing the shape of distribution in social-security benefits even slightly in favor of eligible low-income families could redistribute more financial resources to them than reforming public assistance.

This does not mean that there is no need for public assistance. For those not eligible, obviously social security does not provide income. One can see this in the data for families headed by a person under 65. These families are less likely to be on social security or railroad retirement than older families; social-security income is not as important to them. The younger families in the lowest income class received only 13.8 percent of their income from social security. In contrast, 18.8 percent came from public assistance.

Less progressive distribution and relatively smaller total out-

Table 4.1 Selected Social-Insurance Programs and Public Assistance: Aggregate Benefit Payments as Percent of Income by Income Class [a] and Age of Head, 1970

	Under $3,000	$3,000 to $5,999	$6,000 to $9,999	$10,000 to $14,999	$15,000 and Over	All Income Classes
			All Families [b]			
Social Security (OASDI) and Railroad Retirement	41.3	15.6	3.8	1.6	.8	4.1
Unemployment Insurance [d]	.5	1.0	.4	.3	.1	.3
Workmen's Compensation	.2	.2	.1	.1	— [c]	.1
Public Assistance	14.0	4.0	.6	.2	— [c]	.9
			Head under 65			
Social Security (OASDI) and Railroad Retirement	13.8	4.4	1.4	.9	.5	1.2
Unemployment Insurance	1.0	1.3	.5	.3	.1	.3
Workmen's Compensation	.3	.2	.1	.1	— [c]	.1
Public Assistance	18.8	5.5	.6	.1	— [c]	.8

lays involved in other programs—unemployment insurance and workmen's compensation—make only a minimal impact on the economic life of low-income classes. Less than 1 percent of the total money income of the lowest income class came from unemployment insurance. But obviously, such income was important to the families that received it.

To understand net redistributive impact, one has to know not only about benefits but also how much beneficiaries have contributed. This cost-benefit relationship is an important phenomenon and will be touched on later in this chapter.

The proportions of families headed by the aged and the

Table 4.1 (*Continued*)

	Under $3,000	$3,000 to $5,999	$6,000 to $9,999	$10,000 to $14,999	$15,000 and Over	All Income Classes
			Head 65 and over			
Social Security (OASDI) and Railroad Retirement	65.6	44.3	22.4	12.2	5.9	28.1
Unemployment Insurance	.1	.3	.4	.2	.1	.2
Workmen's Compensation	.1	.2	.1	.1	— ᶜ	.1
Public Assistance	9.7	1.9	.4	.4	.1	2.0

Source: Derived from Dorothy S. Projector and Judith Bretz, "Measurement of Transfer Income in the Current Population Survey" in James D. Smith, ed., *The Personal Distribution of Income and Wealth,* Studies in Income and Wealth, vol. 39 (New York: National Bureau of Economic Research, 1975), tables 1, 5, 6, and 7, pp. 380, 390–92, and 394–401.

ᵃ Term "income" used here means total money income.

ᵇ Families include individuals and families.

ᶜ Less than 0.05 percent.

ᵈ About $2 billion of the total $14 billion benefit payments under unemployment insurance, workmen's compensation, government employee pensions, and veterans' payments, reported through the March 1971 Current Population Survey, was reported by persons who received income from two or more of these programs or who did not identify the source of their "other public transfer" income. Therefore, the portion of this $2 billion attributable to unemployment insurance and workmen's compensation is excluded from the calculation of the percent of income provided by these two programs.

nonaged falling into a given income class were "standardized" in figures 1 and 2 in order to facilitate an intergenerational comparison. One has to be aware that the same income class does not mean the same relative economic position (or the same level of economic well-being) for families headed by the aged and families headed by the nonaged. For example, only 11.2 percent of families headed by the nonaged had income less than $3,000, while 45.5 percent of families headed by aged had less than $3,000. Families with aged heads are relatively more deprived, even though such families tend to be smaller. Finally, in table 4.1 and figures 1 and 2, total money income has not been related to size of family.

SOCIAL INSURANCE AS AN ANTIPOVERTY INSTRUMENT

As already indicated, social-insurance programs distribute more financial resources to low-income families than public assistance does, even though social insurance is not income tested. One study [6] shows that all social-insurance benefits, taken together, brought 32 percent of families, who were poor before such benefits were provided, above the poverty threshold. Beyond this, welfare benefits pulled an additional 11 percent out of poverty.

Since social-insurance programs favor one segment of the population over another, their distributive impact in preventing poverty is felt differently by families of different demographic backgrounds. Table 4.2 shows distributive effects of social insurance and welfare in preventing poverty among different types of families.

Social insurance does most to prevent poverty among families headed by the aged; 52 percent of pretransfer poor families headed by the aged were made nonpoor by social-insurance benefits. This indicates the overwhelming magnitude of retirement insurance within the social-insurance system. Social-insurance programs, on the other hand, do least to prevent poverty among families with children headed by a nondisabled, nonaged man. Only 6 percent of such families are made nonpoor by these programs. Welfare benefits tend to make up for inadequacies of social-insurance programs. For example, only 11 percent of pretransfer poor families with children headed by a nondisabled, nonaged woman became nonpoor because of social-insurance benefits; welfare lifted out of poverty an additional 28 percent.

Table 4.2 Extent of Poverty Prevention by Social Insurance and Welfare Programs, 1971 (Percent) [a]

	Pretransfer Poor Made Nonpoor by Social-Insurance Benefits	Pretransfer Poor Made Nonpoor by Social Insurance and Welfare Benefits	Net Incremental Effect of Welfare Benefits in Poverty Prevention
All families	32	43	11
Families with aged head	52	57	5
Families with nonaged, disabled head	20	36	16
Families with nonaged, nondisabled head without children	18	23	5
Families with nonaged, nondisabled male head with children	6	21	15
Families with nonaged, nondisabled female head with children	11	39	28

Source: Derived from Michael C. Barth, George J. Carcagno, and John L. Palmer, *Toward an Effective Income Support System: Problems, Prospects, and Choices* (Madison, Wis.: University of Wisconsin, Institute for Research on Poverty, 1974), tables 5 and 6, pp. 26 and 28.

[a] Families include childless couples and unrelated individuals. Social-insurance programs include social security (OASDI); unemployment insurance; workmen's compensation; temporary disability insurance; railroad unemployment, retirement, and disability insurance; and public retirement programs. Welfare benefits include public-assistance and general-assistance payments and food stamps.

Disadvantaged Persons in
Social-Insurance Programs

Despite its impact, social insurance as currently administered is not a panacea; it does not eliminate poverty among its beneficiaries, let alone the ineligible. In 1971, for example, about half (48 percent) of pretransfer poor families headed by the aged stayed poor after receiving their social-insurance benefits (see table 4.2). One of every five aged persons in that year was poor after all forms of public income transfers.[7] A more startling picture is seen among the severely disabled persons. According to the most recent nationwide Survey of the Disabled, in 1966, 35 percent of the beneficiary units with severely disabled workers on social security in 1965 were poor. Of course, the incidence of poverty among the household units with severely disabled not on social security was higher.[8]

This part of the chapter selects groups of people who tend to receive inadequate benefits under social insurance and shows how this happens. The groups were not identified on the basis of an exhaustive review, nor are they mutually exclusive.

LOW-WAGE EARNERS, WOMEN, BLACKS,
AND CHILDREN UNDER SOCIAL SECURITY

Low-Wage Earners. As social-security programs mature, lifelong earnings increasingly determine the level of benefits that workers receive on retirement. Thus, if a worker has always worked in a low-paid job, he receives a small benefit, notwithstanding the benefit formula, which somewhat favors those with low earnings.

What level of wages does a worker have to earn in his lifetime to receive a social-security benefit high enough to put him over the poverty threshold if he does not have any other income? A worker retiring at age 65 in January 1973 would need to have earned just about 1.5 times the minimum wage continuously since 1956. Earnings at this wage level would have entitled the worker to 112 percent of poverty-line income. Minimum wages during those years would have provided the retiring worker a benefit equivalent to only 90 percent of poverty-line income. Ironically, if he had a dependent spouse eligible for benefits, he—the minimum-wage earner—would be bailed out of poverty. The couple would receive 106 percent of the poverty-line income. If he had dependents in addition to his spouse, it would become more difficult for him to receive a benefit high enough to put his family over the poverty threshold.

The problem is compounded because low-wage earners tend not to have tenure on the job. Their employment is often intermittent and part time. As the level of benefit depends on length of employment as well as earnings level, the retirement benefit suffers for both reasons.

Early retirement is a third problem. If a worker decided to retire at 62, his benefit would be reduced by 20 percent. The incidence of early retirement is especially high among those with records of low earnings,[9] and persons who retire early tend to have stopped working long before retirement.[10] So one understands why social-security benefits for those retiring at age 62 in 1968 were averaged at 65 percent of benefits for those retiring at 65 even before the 20 percent actuarial reduction.[11] After that mandatory reduction, they averaged only 52 percent.

Female Workers. Women's work experiences, involving less regular and less extended employment, low-paid occupations and industries, and discrimination in pay for the same work, all contribute to their poor showing in social-security benefits. At the end of

1972, female retired workers received, on the average, $140.20 a month in benefits, which was 21 percent lower than benefits for male counterparts.

A major reason for the difference is that women often do not have as sustained employment as men. A study shows that less than 50 percent of the women retiring in 1965 had 14 years or more of employment, compared with 71 percent of men.[12] To make the matter worse, women more often retire early. For example in 1972, 73 percent of retired female workers chose early retirement, compared with 61 percent of retired male workers.

Second, women retirees tended to earn low wages while working. During the period 1959–67, women's median earnings ranged from 42 to 44 percent of men's. Among "four-quarter wage earners," women's median earnings ranged from 54 to 56 percent of men's.[13] Even if women had worked for the same number of years, only 16 percent of female workers retiring in 1971 would have been in the high-benefit bracket ($190 or more) in comparison to 33 percent of men.[14]

As social security was developed to keep "families" from suffering income loss, the benefit formula was developed to provide relatively well for wives and widows but not so adequately for single women. A dependent wife under disability insurance and under old-age insurance receives 50 percent of the primary insurance amount of the insured, a relatively generous benefit compared with European countries. It is also generous in the light of the official definition of poverty, which allots 29 percent of the income needed to support the head of the family for an additional dependent. Under survivors insurance, a surviving wife is entitled to 100 percent of the primary insurance amount when there are no other survivors.

As a result, benefits based on a woman's own earnings are often smaller than the benefits they could receive as the wife or widow of a retired or deceased male worker. In 1972, 19 percent of female retired workers had chosen to receive benefits as a wife or widow instead of on their own earnings records.

Black Workers. Black workers tend to be deprived of social-security benefits in relation to white workers, just as female workers are in relation to male workers, although the causes and consequences of deprivation are somewhat different.

Retired black workers in 1972 averaged about 80 percent of the benefits received by white beneficiaries—$130.76 a month against $165.10. For disabled black workers, the relative disparity in benefits was slightly less; the average monthly benefit for blacks was 85 percent of that received by whites.[15] Since the black breadwinner earns less than the white one, and since black beneficiary families tend to be larger, the average benefit per black child is smaller than that of a white child.

Factors contributing to a relatively low level of social-security benefits for black workers are low wages, discrimination in pay, and less stable employment than among white workers. However, for black workers, in contrast to women, low wages seem more important than less stable employment in explaining the low level of benefits. Median annual earnings of black wage and salary workers are still less than two-thirds of those of white workers, a fact that has been noted in earlier chapters.[16] During June 1970, 60 percent of the black men who had 25 years tenure in their longest job and were awarded social-security benefits had less than $150 a month in benefits; only 30 percent of their white counterparts had earned so little.[17] The point is that, although the black unemployment rate is twice that of whites, most blacks work all their lives at lower wages than whites. So in the end they receive smaller social-security benefits.

Black workers are more often forced to retire early for reasons of ill health, with permanently reduced benefits; and more often than white workers, they supplement their meager social-security benefits by working after retirement, despite ill health.[18] Disabled black workers also tend to supplement social-security benefits with earnings more often than white counterparts.[19] An important difference is that blacks are underrepresented among retired workers since they die younger than whites, and blacks are overrepresented among disabled workers since they are more exposed to hazardous jobs than whites.

Child Beneficiaries. The amount of social-security benefit that a child receives depends on two factors: the primary insurance amount (PIA), calculated from the average monthly earnings of the breadwinner, and the size of the beneficiary family. Dependent children of a retired worker or a disabled worker on social security are entitled to 50 percent of the PIA, and those of a deceased worker to 75 percent. However, since social security sets a maximum benefit that a family as a whole can receive, each child in a large family receives less than the statutory proportion of the PIA. (A family that includes the insured worker and two or more dependents faces the rule of maximum family benefit.) In such a case, each dependent's benefit is proportionately reduced to bring the total benefits of all eligible family members within the maximum.

Table 4.3 shows the impact of the rule of maximum family benefit under social security. When the rule is applied, obviously children receive much smaller benefits, on the average. The average monthly benefit per child in large families facing the rule was $49 in 1972 under old-age insurance, $46 under disability insurance, and $91 under survivors insurance; these figures compare with $87 under old-age insurance, $91 under disability insurance, and $135 under survivors insurance paid to children in other families. The erosion in proportions of PIA is also clear.

Table 4.3 Estimates of Average Monthly Social-Security Benefit per Child,[a] Expressed as a Percentage of PIA, by the Effect of the Maximum Family Benefit Rule and Type of Insurance, 1972

Type of Insurance	All Benefits		Benefits not Affected by the Maximum Family Benefit Rule		Benefits Affected by the Maximum Family Benefit Rule	
	Amount	Percent of PIA	Amount	Percent of PIA	Amount	Percent of PIA
Old-Age Insurance	$ 60	(37)	$ 87	(50)	$49	(28)
Disability Insurance	49	(28)	91	(50)	46	(24)
Survivors Insurance	110	(63)	135	(75)	91	(48)

Source: Social Security Bulletin: Annual Statistical Supplement, 1972, tables 67 and 97, pp. 83–93 and 113–14.

[a] Data apply to 305,000 disabled children aged 18 and over and 634,000 students aged 18–21 as well as to 3,576,000 child beneficiaries aged 1–17.

Slightly more than half—52 percent—of beneficiary families with children had benefits reduced because of the family maximum, but 70 percent of all children were affected. Children of disabled workers suffered most; 94 percent of such children were not receiving the full statutory proportion of benefits.

Black children on social security pay penalties through maximum family benefits and the low level of their parents' earnings. They receive smaller benefits not only in absolute terms but also in relation to an already low PIA. The average monthly benefit of black children in 1972 was $43.82 under old-age insurance, $36.96 under disability insurance, and $82.14 under survivors insurance. Benefits for black children were in each case 67 to 70 percent of the average benefits for white children.[20]

Over the years, black children have come to constitute a large proportion of black social-security beneficiaries. Also, black children have increased as a proportion of all children on social security. However, blacks in general are not overrepresented among social-security beneficiaries. All told, black beneficiaries in 1972 constituted only 9.7 percent of all beneficiaries, less than their percentage in the general population. Their share in social-security benefits is even less, in that year 7.3 percent of the aggregate amount of benefits.[21]

UNEMPLOYMENT-INSURANCE PROGRAMS: IMPACT OF INADEQUATE DEVELOPMENT

Although state unemployment-insurance programs were launched as an integral part of the Social Security Act, their subsequent development has been inadequate compared with the development of social-security programs (OASDI). Inadequate development of unemployment insurance has stemmed from these facts: program development has depended heavily on state legislative initiative; the majority of state legislatures have been conservative; employer interests have dominated the state legislative scene. The House Ways and Means Committee and the Senate Finance Committee have given little stimulus to breaking down state-employer dominance of unemployment insurance.

Various indices illustrate inadequate development in unemployment insurance. The first is the inadequate funding of the programs. The maximum taxable base in all but six states was only $4,200 in 1975 compared with $14,100 under OASDI, although both programs had the identical maximum taxable base of $3,000 in 1939. In 1950 only 29 percent of all wage and salary workers had earnings in excess of the maximum taxable base of unemployment insurance, compared to 54 percent in 1972.[22] Indeed, unemployment-insurance contributions have steadily declined as percentages of *total* payroll in covered employment—currently generating less than 1 percent of total payroll in covered employment.[23]

The second indication of the outdated character of unemployment insurance is meager benefit levels. In 1972 all but 14 states and the District of Columbia provided maximum weekly benefits below poverty-line income for a family of four.[24] The program provides, on the average, only one-third of prior weekly wages in the form of benefit. For example, 73 percent of male workers and 29 percent of female workers in Ohio received in 1972 less than one half of their wages in unemployment-insurance benefits.[25] Only workers with low wages can expect to receive the customary 50 percent of wages. But since their wages are already too low, unemployment-insurance benefits cannot possibly provide adequate income. On high wage levels, unemployed workers receive less than 50 percent of wages because of benefit maximums; again, such benefits would be inadequate to provide a decent living. Under these circumstances, families experiencing unemployment are often forced to join the ranks of the poor unless there is other income or unemployment is short lived. A study shows that the incidence of poverty among families whose male heads experienced unemployment during 1966 was over twice as high as among similar families with no unemployment experience.[26]

The third indication of inadequacy in umemployment insurance is incomplete coverage. In 1972, approximately 14 percent of all wage and salary employment was not covered by the insurance. Among those not covered, 9.1 million or 68 percent of the jobs were in state and local government, 1.2 million or 13 percent in agriculture, and 1.7 million or 19 percent in domestic services.[27] Noncoverage of farm laborers and domestic workers is especially serious as, even when they are working, the level of earnings for these workers is low. Noncoverage of state and local government employees can also present serious problems. Although their employment may be relatively secure, their numbers are large, and even a comparatively low unemployment rate would be noticed.

Although the majority of unemployed workers receive inadequate protection, certain groups of workers receive especially meager protection. These groups are identified in the following paragraphs.

Even among workers who are covered in principle, a sizable group do not receive benefits. Some have not worked long enough to qualify; some quit jobs for personal reasons; some were fired for misconduct. New entrants (mostly the young) and reentrants (mostly housewives) have yet to establish employment records so as to qualify. As many as one-third of all unemployed workers in 1967 were new entrants and reentrants.[28] If one takes nonqualified and uncovered workers into account, in 1973, for example, only 42 percent of the unemployed were insured for benefits. Proportions of the unemployed who were insured were especially low among women, the young, and nonwhites; 36 percent of unemployed women were insured for benefits, 15 percent of the unemployed under age 25, and 23 percent of unemployed nonwhites.[29] Thus, only a small minority of the unemployed in these groups actually receive unemployment-insurance benefits.

In short, the majority of unemployed workers receive no benefits from unemployment insurance. Many who do receive inadequate benefits. Benefits are inadequate in the sense that they are not equivalent to 50 percent of lost wages and are not enough to pay for items absolutely nondeferrable for daily living. When "inadequate" is so defined, it is interesting that a sense of relative deprivation is felt most acutely by families headed by a fairly well-paid earner with dependents and no other earner in the family. Such workers generally receive the maximum benefit, but it is less than 50 percent of their lost wages, and they have dependents to support. Insurance benefits for such families were reported as 26 percent short of the need for buying nondeferrable items. In these terms, families with two earners or with no dependents did not fare quite so badly. Families with dependents supported by a sole earner experienced various kinds of hardship more often than other types of families when drawing unemployment-insurance benefits—for example, exhausting savings, borrowing money, and resorting to relief.[30]

Needs of dependents are often recognized in the literature related to unemployment insurance but rarely met under the law. In 1975, only 10 states and the District of Columbia provided dependent allowances. Benefit levels are generally low; the most generous state, Connecticut, paid a maximum of $52 a week for all dependents.

THE DISABLED: FALLING THROUGH THE CRACKS

Social-insurance programs in the United States designed to protect against disability have developed piecemeal. They currently provide uneven and often inadequate benefits, and protection is incomplete, especially against temporary sickness and disability. The overwhelming majority of the disabled in the United States (17 million in 1965, the latest figures available) are not helped by any social-insurance program. The 1966 Survey of the Disabled reports that 69 percent of families with disabled adult persons aged 18–64 were not receiving any form of social-insurance benefit in 1965. Even among families with adults disabled severely enough to be eligible for social-security benefits on medical grounds, 54 percent did not receive any social-insurance benefit.[31] The survey also reports that, when either the married head or spouse was disabled, families with minor children had a poverty incidence of 41.2 percent, compared with 15.6 percent among similar families with a nondisabled head and spouse.[32]

Three major social-insurance programs currently protect against disability: (1) state workmen's compensation for work-related injuries and diseases; (2) state temporary disability insurance for short-term sickness and disability; and (3) federal disability insurance for long-term disability. How can it be, with three programs, that some disabled persons are provided for inadequately or not at all?

State Workmen's Compensation Program.[33] Despite various improvements made especially since 1972, as the result of a recommendation by the National Commission on State Workmen's Compensation Laws, these programs still leave much to be desired. They cover only 84 percent of civilian employees, generally excluding farm, domestic, and casual workers, workers in religious and charitable organizations, and workers in small establishments.

Many eligible workers do not receive the statutory percentage, 60 to 67 percent, of weekly wages in the form of benefits. This erosion of benefit, which is similar to that occurring under unemployment insurance, is caused by benefit ceilings set under the law. In 1973, even after momentous improvement in the programs, an average earner received 65 percent in wage replacement in only 18 jurisdictions, although the statutory percentage was at least that high in 43 jurisdictions. Nationwide, the average weekly benefit was $89, or 57 percent of the average weekly wage for covered workers.

A more significant shortcoming under workmen's compensation is seen in its benefit provisions for permanent total disability, permanent partial disability, and death. Permanent total disability is one which is expected to last for life and which totally incapacitates a worker. Permanent partial disability is one which creates a permanent residual condition, such as a loss of fingers, but which does not make a person totally incapable of working. For these types of disabilities and for death of a worker, states often set a maximum on lifetime benefits or on the duration of benefits. These limitations cause a serious erosion in the rate of replacement of wages. Another factor compounding the problem is that the benefit amount, calculated at the time of entitlement, is not increased to account for inflation, let alone wage hikes that mark a maturing career or union seniority. Thus, one study reports that in 30 states a 35-year-old worker who became permanently and totally disabled in 1972 could expect less than 40 percent of the lost wages to be replaced by workmen's compensation during the 30 years thereafter. The replacement rate for permanent partial disability was found to be even lower: only 13 to 29 percent in 29 jurisdictions where comparison was possible.[34]

State Temporary Disability Insurance. Rhode Island, California, New Jersey, New York, Hawaii, and Puerto Rico currently have temporary disability insurance programs. In these states, nearly 90 percent of wage and salary workers have protection against wage loss due to short-term sickness and disability. In other states, only half of such workers have coverage under voluntary group sickness and injury benefit plans. Where coverage is voluntary, well-organized workers tend to be protected and less organized, second-class workers ill protected.

Temporary disability insurance generally provides waiting periods of 2 to 7 days and maximum weekly benefits; it also requires minimum previous earnings for entitlement. Except in Rhode Island, pregnancy is not recognized as a compensable disability. As a result, the rate at which benefits replace wages is generally much smaller than the statutory rate of 50 to 67 percent. Benefits paid to private wage and salary workers in 1972 replaced 26 percent of lost wages in the six jurisdictions that had temporary disability insurance. In states that did not, private group plans in private industry replaced 22 percent of lost wages.[35]

Far fewer workers, certainly, are covered in states without

temporary disability insurance. Private plans in such states provided higher benefit rates to those actually covered than state plans where state insurance was provided. It is more important, however, that in states without this insurance about half of wage and salary employees did not have short-term disability coverage of any sort.

The degree of protection against wage loss due to short-term sickness and disability is related to family income. One study reports that workers from a family with an income of more than $10,000 were reimbursed, on the average, 65 percent of the wage loss, compared with only 26 percent for workers from a family with income less than $5,000. In terms of the percentage of days of work loss reimbursed, a similar observation was made. The disparity in protection given to the privileged and the disadvantaged was also observed in relation to occupation, age, and race.[36]

Disability Insurance under Social Security. Severe disability often leads to unemployability, and makes a person needy. The 1966 Survey of the Disabled found that in 1965 6.1 million noninstitutionalized adults aged 18–64 had been severely disabled for 7 months or longer; 38 percent of families involving these people were poor.[37]

The economic plight of severely disabled adults stems from their inability to earn income and the rigidity of the federal disability-insurance program. Survey findings show that 80 percent of the severely disabled were not in the labor force in 1965; only 16 percent were employed, most of them part time. Median annual earnings among men was $709, and $381 among women.

The survey's definition of "severely disabled" was almost identical to that used under disability insurance, but remarkably few benefit from the program. In 1965, only 13.9 percent of the severely disabled adults received disability-insurance benefits. An additional 12.8 percent received old-age insurance benefits—6.0 percent as retired worker and the rest as dependent.[38] The disabled in the survey who were on old-age insurance were presumed to be between 62 and 64, and receiving actuarially reduced benefits.

Many disabled adults are not receiving disability-insurance benefits because they have not worked long enough in covered employment, or they are not disabled enough to qualify for benefits, or both. Under the law, the disabled worker must be both "fully insured" and "disability insured." "Fully insured" means that the worker has been in covered employment at least one-fourth of the quarters elapsing after 1950 or after the year in which the worker became 21, if that is later. "Disability insured" means that the worker has worked at least 20 quarters during the 10 years immediately before the onset of disability. These two requirements for the insured status are stiff compared with other social-insurance programs, such as workmen's compensation, and, for that matter, private disability-insurance plans. Presumably, these requirements account for the large number of "severely disabled" who do not qualify for benefits.

Adequacy and Income Redistribution through Social Insurance

Can social insurance do better in providing adequate benefits? Is income redistribution a legitimate goal of social insurance? What is social insurance anyway?

WHAT IS SOCIAL INSURANCE?

John R. Commons, a pioneering student of social insurance, defined insurance as "an arrangement for distribution among many of the losses sustained by a few.'' [39] Social insurance is similar to private insurance in various respects. Both social insurance and private insurance are attempts to pool risks; both explicitly state all conditions related to coverage, benefits, and financing; both perform impartial calculations of benefits according to a set formula; and both specify contribution (or premium) rates. At the same time, social insurance differs from private insurance in important respects. First, private insurance is strictly based on the principle of individual equity, while social insurance implements the principle of social adequacy as well. Individual equity is generally understood to mean that the contributor receives benefit protection directly related to the contributions made. Social adequacy is generally understood to mean that benefits are so calculated as to provide the insured with an acceptable standard of living. Second, participation is compulsory under social insurance, while it is voluntary under private insurance. Third, social insurance provides a statutory relationship between the government as the ''insurer'' and citizens as the ''insured,'' while private insurance involves a strictly contractual relationship between two parties. The statutory provision can be changed by the legislature but the contractual provision cannot. Fourth, private insurance must be fully funded so as to protect the rights of the insured, but social insurance does not need to be fully funded because its financial soundness depends on the government's taxing power and because it is compulsory and statutory. [40] In fact, if it were funded fully, social insurance might have adverse effects on the economy.

From the major characteristics of social insurance, it seems apparent that implementing social adequacy—providing adequate minimum benefits—is one of its most important missions. Such implementation, of necessity, entails income redistribution. Isaac M. Rubinow long ago identified the redistribution of income from the rich to the poor as the major objective of social insurance. He wrote:

> The class which needs social insurance cannot afford it, and the class that can afford it does not need it. To solve this socio-political antinomy, legislative coercion becomes necessary. In the best sense of the word is social insurance true class legislation. It is nothing but an effort to readjust the distribution of the national product more equitably—not in accordance with the ideal demands of equity, but at least with those standards which due consideration for national vitality makes immediately imperative.[41]

INCOME REDISTRIBUTION THROUGH SOCIAL SECURITY: WHICH WAY?

In recent years, it has been argued that social security is stretching social adequacy—or the welfare objective—too far in favor of low-wage beneficiaries. Alarmed by such an argument, and to protect individual equity in social security, the Joint Economic Committee of Congress issued a welfare proposal that would further expand the current cash-transfer programs for the poor and near-poor.[42] On a somewhat similar note, Pechman and his associates proposed that a "negative income tax" provide a minimum income to retirees and that social security become a pure earnings-replacement program.[43] Brittain, who advocates a progressive social-security tax on one hand, is willing to let the social-security benefit structure be more earnings-related on the other hand.[44]

These critics believe that beneficiaries with low earnings are favored too much under social security. In their view, this is detrimental to the preservation of individual equity. The Joint Economic Committee presented a typical argument: Social security has acquired characteristics of a welfare program on the grounds that (1) benefits replace a progressively larger proportion of average monthly wages as the wage level declines; (2) the minimum PIA has increased faster than the maximum PIA; and (3) low-wage earners have more dependents, especially children.[45] How strong is their argument?

Benefit Formula. It is true that under the benefit formula a larger percentage of low than of high wages are replaced by benefits. This might give the impression that income is being redistributed from the retiree with a record of high earnings to the retiree with a record of low earnings. The fact is, however, that the bulk of redistribution is not from one group of retired workers to another but from the working population to the retired population.

The author investigated the current value of "intergenerational transfers" (subsidies from the working population to the retired) for workers who retired during the past decade. Two hypothetical cases were examined: a worker who always contributed the maximum and a worker who always contributed half of the maximum from the beginning of social security in 1937. The value of intergenerational transfers is defined as the difference between lifetime benefits discounted to the current value and the lifetime annuitized amount of benefits compounded to the current value. In other words, intergenerational transfers are subsidies added by the working population to what the retired worker might receive if he had joined an annuity program that would guarantee an inflation-proof return and 3 percent interest in addition. In calculating lifetime benefits, it is assumed that the retiree would live 14.8 years after age 65, [46] the present average life expectancy. Both employer and employee contributions are credited to the employee. Table 4.4 presents findings from the study.[47]

One observes that the maximum contributor retiring in 1973 could expect to receive intergenerational transfers of $25,808 in his lifetime compared with $18,415 for the 50 percent contributor retir-

Table 4.4 Intergenerational Transfers under the Federal Old-Age Insurance by Year of Retirement and Level of Contribution

Year of Retirement	Discounted value of retirement benefits for 14.8 years (in dollars of retirement year)	Lifetime Annuitized Amounts of Benefits [a] (in dollars of retirement year)	Intergenerational Transfers (in dollars of retirement year)	Intergenerational Transfers (in 1973 dollars)
		The Maximum Contributor		
1962	$17,339	$ 3,883	$13,456	$18,636
1963	17,482	4,320	13,162	18,031
1964	17,626	4,814	12,812	17,337
1965	18,872	5,329	13,543	17,554
1966	19,016	5,867	13,149	17,227
1967	19,474	6,560	12,914	16,493
1968	22,355	7,290	15,065	18,713
1969	22,999	8,120	14,879	17,734
1970	27,198	9,046	18,152	20,533
1971	30,537	10,025	20,512	21,891
1972	30,967	11,105	19,862	20,330
1973	38,132	12,324	25,808	25,808
		The 50-Percent Contributor		
1962	$11,651	$1,941	$ 9,710	$13,448
1963	11,676	2,160	9,516	13,035
1964	11,747	2,407	9,340	12,639
1965	12,604	2,664	9,940	13,271
1966	12,846	2,933	9,913	13,026
1967	12,879	3,280	9,599	12,260
1968	14,784	3,645	11,141	13,841
1969	14,995	4,060	10,935	13,033
1970	17,726	4,523	13,203	14,935
1971	19,818	5,012	14,806	15,801
1972	20,096	5,552	14,544	14,886
1973	24,577	6,162	18,415	18,415

Source: Martha N. Ozawa, "Individual Equity versus Social Adequacy in Federal Old-Age Insurance," *The Social Service Review,* 48, no. 1 (March 1974), tables 1 and 2, pp. 31 and 33.

[a] Equivalent to the compounded real value of contributions paid from January 1, 1937 to the end of year immediately preceding retirement. A full backward shifting of employer contributions to employee is assumed.

ing in the same year. Both the maximum contributor and the 50 percent contributor received substantial subsidies beyond what private insurance would have paid for their contribution. Moreover, the high-wage retiree is subsidized much more than the low-wage retiree. (The gap between the two has widened over the years.) Apparently, the magnitude of intergenerational transfers overrides whatever effects the formula has in favoring low-wage retirees. So what is at issue is not return on contributions, but who should get more of the transfer income that is provided by working people.

If social-security benefits were made more strictly proportionate, as is implied in some proposals, the disparity in the amounts of intergenerational transfers provided to the high-wage and the low-wage retiree would become even greater.

Benefit Levels. It is also argued that the ratio of the maximum to the minimum PIA has decreased over the years since 1935.[48] Evidence cited seems too simplistic, however. One should see the rate of increase in minimum and maximum PIAs over the years; also these PIAs must be related to average earnings in respective years. One should also look at the shape of distribution of benefits among retired workers and see whether it has changed over the years in favor of low-wage retirees. Trends during the past decade, when benefits increased so dramatically, should be taken into account.

Minimum and maximum PIAs have increased at a similar rate. The minimum increased by 111 percent, and the maximum by 119 percent between 1963 and 1972.[49] Also, both minimum and maximum PIAs have been kept in line with the rising levels of earnings. The minimum yearly benefit (the minimum PIA multiplied by 12) went up from 12.0 percent of average yearly earnings in 1963 to 14.2 percent in 1972; the maximum yearly benefit (the maximum PIA multiplied by 12) from 36.3 to 43.6 percent during the same period.[50]

As for the change in the shape of distribution of benefits over the years, it is clear from table 4.5 that it has hardly changed in the decade. The bottom fifth of retired workers, ranked by benefit levels, has received approximately 10 percent of the total benefits of retired workers, while the top fifth has received between 29 and 31 percent of the total benefits.

All told, one comes back to the earlier question: Has the level of adequacy increased in favor of those with low social-security benefits? It appears that retired workers on the bottom are as much deprived now in relation to fellow retirees as they were a decade ago.

Dependent Benefits. The report of the Joint Economic Committee alludes to the provision for dependents of the insured as another indication that the social-adequacy principle is being stretched too far. It is true that low-income families tend to be larger than high-income families. However, the rule regarding maximum family benefits wipes out any distributional advantage that might be gained by low-income families.

Table 4.5 Federal Old-Age Insurance: Shares of Total Paid Out to Retirees in Current Payment Status, by Fifths of Retired Workers Ranked by Monthly Benefit Amount (Percent)

Fifths of Workers	1962	1964	1966	1968	1970	1972
Lowest	10.3	10.4	10.0	10.9	10.7	10.5
Second	14.9	16.4	14.9	14.7	14.9	15.0
Third	19.8	19.2	20.1	19.8	20.1	18.4
Fourth	25.3	25.4	25.3	24.9	24.9	24.7
Highest	29.6	28.6	29.8	29.8	29.4	31.4
All Workers	100.0	100.0	100.0	100.0	100.0	100.0

Source: Derived from *Social Security Bulletin: Annual Statistical Supplement: 1962,* tables 62 and 63, pp. 59–60; *1964,* table 66, p. 66; *1966,* table 75, p. 84; *1968,* table 79, p. 94; *1970,* table 78, p. 91; *1972,* table 79, p. 101.

It has been noted that social security sets a ceiling in family benefits for each wage level. Ironically, the ceiling—the maximum family benefit—is equivalent to only 150 percent of the PIA at the lowest earnings level but 183 percent of the PIA at the highest level. The effect is that, under disability insurance, for example, after the disabled receives his own benefit, only one dependent may be included within the maximum benefits for the lowest-paid worker, but 1.6 dependents for the highest-paid worker. Dependents beyond these numbers do not increase the amount of family benefit. Thus, large family size among low-income families does not bring them proportionately larger benefits.

When one connects dependent benefits with intergenerational transfers a startling conclusion may be reached. Since the retired worker has not paid for the overwhelming portion of lifetime benefits, let alone for a spouse or other dependents, dependent benefits are a windfall. The amount of the windfall is greater as the PIA or prior earnings increases.

In addition to these widely understood aspects of social security—benefit formula, benefit levels, and dependent benefits—there is the question of how ethnic variations in life expectancy influence the degree of income redistribution to low-wage retirees. Government data show a 7-year difference in life expectancy at birth between white and black men and a 6-year difference between white and black women.[51] The disparity in life expectancy between white people and American Indians is even greater. Thus, these minority groups, typically with low wages, are less likely to live long enough to collect social-security benefits. If they collect, they do so for a shorter period of time. As a relatively small proportion of the minorities go to college, they start work earlier and contribute to social security longer. Thus the redistributive impact of social security is diluted for minority people at both ends of their lives.

What can one conclude? Most students of social security

agree that it is different, in principle, from private insurance. One different objective is implementation of social adequacy. Since adequacy is implemented in behalf of poorer beneficiaries, individual equity along the lines of private insurance is undermined. But data presented here lead to additional conclusions: (1) Social security implements social adequacy *in addition to* individual equity. All retirees receive the full value of their investment, and a lot more. (2) Social adequacy has not been stretched very far in favor of low-wage beneficiary families. Such redistribution as is built into social security does not favor low-wage more than high-wage beneficiary families. High-wage beneficiaries receive larger subsidies from the working population than low-wage beneficiaries.

Looking into the Future

What can we say about the future of social insurance? What direction should social insurance take in order to provide minimum benefits adequate to prevent poverty? The other objective related to preventing poverty is income redistribution. These two objectives must go together if relative poverty is to be eliminated. They must also go together if a better minimum in social-insurance benefits is to be provided without an excessive increase in social-insurance expenditures. The provision of a better minimum in turn results in making income-conditioned programs smaller in scope than they are now.

As was stated in preceding parts, social-insurance programs in the United States developed piecemeal without any coherent, coordinated policy on what level of minimum benefits they ought to provide or on how many persons in the family such a minimum is to support. No wonder many families are poor in spite of social-in-

surance benefits. Data collected by the most recent survey of the
aged indicate that 22 percent of aged couples on social security
were poor in 1967. Unmarried persons on social security had poverty incidence of 45 percent.[52] Social security is not as effective an
antipoverty instrument as it ought to be, considering the massive
transfers from the working to the beneficiary population. Under
unemployment insurance, since the majority of states provide maximum benefits which are short of poverty-line income for a family
of four, it can be inferred that many unemployed families receiving
benefits will be poor. The same bleak picture can be drawn of families headed by disabled workers.

Establishing an adequate minimum benefit under social insurance inevitably raises the question of how many family members
such a minimum is supposed to support. The question boils down
to what to do with support for children. Unless minimum benefits
are tied to a definite number of persons they remain an abstract
idea; but the problem goes deeper. As long as minimum benefits
are tied to previous earnings, they cannot meet the needs of families of all sizes. Minimum wages cannot support a family of four at
the poverty threshold, to start with. So how can social-insurance
benefits, which are set below the previous earnings level, support a
family of four? On the other hand, if dependent allowances are
added to benefits for the insured, the amount of total benefits for a
family may exceed previous earnings, causing the question of work
incentives to arise. The maximum in family benefits under social
security, for example, is detrimental to large families; but doing
away with it may create an incentive problem. It may be said that
the aged and the disabled on social security are not, by definition,
in the labor force and therefore do not create a work-incentive
problem. But the decision to retire and the decision to recover from
disability may often be influenced by the level of benefits they can
expect if they retire or stay disabled. Research indicates that auto

workers in Detroit tend to retire earlier when the level of retirement income is perceived as "adequate" than when it is not.[53] The dilemma between adequacy and incentive may be resolved by detaching the question of support for children from the domain of social insurance.

Under social security, a drastic change in the benefit structure, in addition to incremental changes, is required in order to redistribute income and to assure an adequate minimum benefit. Conventional approaches such as an across-the-board percentage increase in benefits are both costly and ineffective to change the distribution of benefits in favor of low-wage beneficiaries. Changing the *shape* of distribution (along with enlarging the size of the pie, if that is possible) seems to be the key to upgrading the income level of low-wage beneficiaries and, indirectly, all low-income families.

There is another reason why a change in the benefit structure that alters the distributive pattern is called for. Old-age insurance, which constitutes the bulk of OASDI benefit expenditures, favors those who live longer. The high-wage earner has as good or maybe a better chance to benefit from old-age insurance as the low-wage earner. Therefore, simply enlarging the size of the pie—increasing benefits across the board—may redistribute income more to high-wage beneficiary families.

Unemployment insurance, workmen's compensation, and temporary disability insurance need only incremental improvements, such as upgrading benefit levels and liberalizing eligibility requirements, in order to assure adequate minimum benefits and to redistribute income at the same time. This is possible because low-wage earners generally are more prone to become unemployed, injured on the job, or disabled for non-work-related reasons, and therefore more often tend to benefit from improvements in these programs.

WHAT CAN SOCIAL SECURITY BE?

In the last part, it was argued that social security, as it is currently administered, provides the retired worker with much more than he "has paid for." In effect, social security is an inadvertent two-tier or double-decker system, in which the high-wage retiree receives larger subsidies than does the low-wage retiree.

In a more conventional use of the term, the "two-tier system" is well known in many European countries and some other parts of the world. A two-tier system generally combines a contributory flat pension program and/or a noncontributory universal pension program with a contributory earnings-related pension program. A major objective of the two-tier system is to provide a basic floor of income to all beyond a certain age, and simultaneously to provide retirement income based on previous earnings.

As a way to cope with income-maintenance problems of the aged, disabled, and survivors, a few European countries followed the British tradition of poor laws. That is, they originally developed relief programs to provide for the needy aged poor through an income or means test. Some means-tested programs were later converted into universal noncontributory pension programs to eliminate the stigma attached to relief programs. In Britain, when a comprehensive social-security system was developed during the 1940s, the flat amount of benefit became the basis for the contributory pension program. Since the 1950s there has been a marked movement in countries with such programs toward adding earnings-related benefits to pensions.

On the other hand, more European countries began with contributory earnings-related pension programs, patterned after the pioneering German Law of 1889, which enacted Bismarck's social-insurance program. To assure an effective minimum floor in income to all pensioners, however, some of them later supplemented contributory earnings-related pension programs with contributory flat pension programs and/or noncontributory universal pension programs.

In short, European social-security systems have been moving from two different directions toward two-tier systems, further supplemented by income-conditioned relief programs in some countries.[54]

American social security appears to have the foundation and legitimacy for developing itself into an explicit two-tier system. In the process, the twin objectives of adequate minimum benefits and redistribution of income to low-wage beneficiaries seem achievable. As discussed earlier, even the highest-wage earner has paid for not more than one-third of his lifetime benefits, and the lower-middle-wage earner has paid for not more than one-fourth of his lifetime benefits. In terms of absolute amount, the high-wage retiree has received more subsidies than the low-wage retiree. Yet it seems reasonable that every aged person receive the same amount of subsidies from those still working.

If all retired workers received equal subsidies, either through internal redistribution of social-security funds or through financing from general revenues, the lower strata of retired workers would gain in benefits. In short, what is proposed here is a two-tier system of social security in which the retired worker receives social-security benefits consisting of two parts: one strictly *related to past contributions* plus real compounded interest, [55] and the other representing a ''basic benefit'' subsidized by payroll taxes levied on those still working and/or by general revenues. The words ''related to past contributions'' are italicized because the current relationship between the amount of contributions and the level of average monthly earnings is tenuous.

The benefit calculations for disability and survivors insurance might also be done according to the proposed two-tier scheme:

one layer representing subsidies, and the other representing the investment value of past contributions.

The level of basic benefit can be set at or above the current SSI benefit for an individual. Calculation by the author indicates that current old-age insurance funds alone could provide in 1974 a basic benefit of $135 a month, in addition to benefits representing a fair return on contributions. This basic benefit level contrasted with the minimum of $94 in that year. (In this calculation, savings derived from the conversion of benefits for spouses into a flat amount and the elimination of children's benefits as discussed below, both under old-age insurance, were used to help equalize subsidies to retired workers.) [56] The SSI payment for an individual in 1974 was $146. Thus with a relatively small amount of further funding from general revenues, social security could provide the basic benefit at or above $146 in 1974 dollars.

Since retired workers receive subsidies which they have not paid for, it is logical to extend the provision of the basic benefit to all individuals 65 and over. The basic benefit could also be extended to the disabled and the blind not on social security. This way, the current SSI program could be absorbed into a more comprehensive social-security system embodying two levels of benefits.

Setting apart the proposal of a two-tier system, other changes would move toward redistribution and adequacy.

First, dependent benefits for a spouse could be converted from the current 50 percent of PIA to a flat amount. The proportional benefit formula always favors spouses of workers in high-wage brackets. Such a formula is fair if social security is a strict insurance program for which the insured pays the actuarial costs of benefits. But retired workers currently on social security have not paid sufficiently to cover their own lifetime benefits, let alone their spouses' benefits. The benefit level for the spouse could be set somewhere between the additional income presumably needed to support one dependent at the official poverty line ($60 a month in 1974) and the average benefit for spouses of retired workers ($95 a month in 1974). The savings derived from the change in the benefit formula for spouses could be used to strengthen the basic benefit level for the insured worker.

Second, dependent benefits for children could be placed outside social security. Social security is not geared to support all children in beneficiary families adequately. Children of low-wage earners are doubly punished by the maximum family benefit and the low wage level of their parents.[57] Therefore, the provision of income for children through a program which is independent of the social-security system and the wage structure would facilitate a greater degree of income redistribution to low-income families with children. (More will be said about this a little later.) Again, the savings derived from the elimination of dependent benefits for children from social security could be used to strengthen the level of basic benefit for the insured worker. Currently, benefit expenditures for children on social security are approximately 10 percent of the total benefit expenditures.[58]

Third, the percentage reduction in benefit for those who retire before age 65 might be liberalized. Currently, a 20 percent reduction in benefit is imposed if a worker retires at age 62. If this provision is made less punitive, income tends to flow to low-wage retirees, since they more often tend to retire early. Actuarial calculation notwithstanding, it is advisable to cut the rate of reduction by half, and institute instead strong incentive measures for postponing retirement beyond age 65.

Fourth, the maximum level of social-security benefit that a retired worker can expect should be made explicit. After all, reshaping the pattern of benefit distribution requires the policy maker to specify both minimum and maximum ends of benefit. The minimum as proposed in this paper would be equivalent to the basic benefit level. The maximum could be expressed as a ratio of the minimum. As of 1974, the maximum PIA ($305) was 3.2 times the minimum PIA ($94). Another way to control the maximum benefit within a proper boundary is to keep the maximum taxable earnings at a proper level. The ceiling in taxable earnings in this country has been relatively low compared with those of other European countries.[59] However, under the proposed two-tier system, which incorporates financing from general revenues, it is advisable to maintain the $15,300 maximum on taxable earnings (1976), subject to changes according to wage levels. As social security matures, as previous earnings become more and more closely related to contributions, and as contribution-related benefits become closely related to earnings-related benefits, it becomes important to infuse funds from general revenues to keep the level of the basic benefit in proper balance; that, in turn, becomes the key to maintaining a fair share in benefits for low strata of retired workers.

Fifth, eligibility requirements for disability-insurance benefits should be liberalized. The criterion for meeting "disability insured" status should be 8 quarters of work during the 5 years immediately before the onset of disability instead of 20 quarters during the 10 years. Such liberalization would make it easier for young new entrants into the labor force to qualify for disability-insurance benefits when they become disabled. Also, workers approaching retirement age who are unable to work because of chronic illness and disability would find it easier to qualify for disability-insurance benefits. That would make it unnecessary for them to apply for old-age insurance benefits at a reduced rate.

Sixth, since the income-maintenance problem of children is dealt with outside the social-security system, surviors-insurance benefits—100 percent of PIA—should be provided only to the eligible surviving spouse or the first child in the absence of such a spouse.

Seventh, benefit increases should be enacted with the redistributive objective in mind. Not much income redistribution takes place with the customary across-the-board percentage increases, nor does the shape of the benefit distribution change. From the redistributive point of view, however, flat-rate benefit increases are preferable to across-the-board percentage increases.

The proposals that have been made, though aimed at the two objectives noted earlier, would offer several additional advantages.

First, the proposed two-tier system of OASDI would provide flexibility for upgrading either the basic benefit or contribution-related benefits, or both, depending on the legislative intent at a given time. If, for example, Congress wished to raise the minimum floor of benefits, it would need to improve the basic benefit only. This way, fiscal resources would be utilized efficiently. On the financing side, the proposed system opens the door to the use of general revenues, especially for improving the basic benefit. If general revenues were so used, the system would gradually mitigate the regressivity of current payroll taxes.

Second, if the basic benefit level were set at or above the current SSI benefit level, SSI could be absorbed into the proposed comprehensive social-security system. This would assure that those who worked and contributed to social security would receive greater benefits than those who did not contribute.

Third, flat payments for eligible spouses, the level of which is set below the basic benefit, would eliminate the current awkward situation in which some women who have worked many years receive a smaller benefit than some wives who never worked.

REFORMS IN OTHER SOCIAL-INSURANCE PROGRAMS

The following reforms in selected social-insurance programs would move transfer-income policy toward a more redistributional and antipoverty emphasis.

Unemployment Insurance. To provide adequate minimum benefits and an equitable and reasonable rate of replacement of wage loss due to unemployment, federal adoption of minimum benefit and duration standards applicable for all states seems imperative. Federal action is also needed to assure adequate coverage and financing.

The replacement rate should be increased from the current 50 to 67 percent. The maximum weekly benefit should be related to such state's average weekly wage—for example, 100 percent of that wage. With such a maximum, the great majority of beneficiaries would receive at least 67 percent of their gross wages.

If the above proposals were adopted, unemployment insurance would adequately replace lost wages and meet the basic needs of the family of the unemployed worker. For example, a worker earning the federal minimum wage at the 1974 rate of $2.00 per hour would receive a benefit, the level of which is close to the poverty-line income for a family of two and above poverty-line income for an unrelated individual. As with social security, it would be desirable to place the support of children outside the domain of unemployment insurance.

The variable duration of benefits, practiced in all but 7 states and Puerto Rico, is detrimental to the worker in unstable jobs. Therefore, it should be changed to a uniform duration of at least 26 weeks during normal economic conditions. The work requirement before a person can qualify for benefit should be kept within the prevailing level—20 weeks of employment in the base year, with earnings of at least $40 a week. Coverage should be broadened to include farm workers, state and local government employees, domestic workers, and workers in nonprofit organizations.

Not the least important reform lies in financing unemployment insurance. Experience rating as a mechanism to levy variable tax rates may have outlived its original objectives. It seems to have

been doing more harm than good: (1) it acts as an obstacle to raising adequate fiscal resources; (2) it encourages the employer's
undue interference with applicants for unemployment-insurance
benefits; (3) it creates unnecessary interstate competition in lowering the tax rates; and (4) it has adverse effects on the stabilization
of the economy. Thus, notwithstanding the vested interests in experience rating, the federal government should consider moving toward abolishing experience rating. As an interim measure, it could
require that at least half of the taxes for unemployment insurance be
raised by a proportionate tax on payrolls. Another change needed to
make unemployment insurance a more adequate and equitable social-insurance program is to broaden the tax base drastically, possibly to the same level as under OASDI. This would lighten the relative tax burden on industries that rely heavily on low-wage earners.

Workmen's Compensation. Although state workmen's compensation programs have made noticeable progress in recent years, they
still leave much to be desired. There is at present no federal statutory responsibility for this program, but federal minimum standards
seem imperative in the following areas.

First, weekly cash benefits should be at least two-thirds of
the worker's average weekly wage. A replacement rate of 67 percent would assure a minimum-wage earner income close to the
poverty-line income for a family of two and above-poverty-line income for an unrelated individual. Setting the maximum weekly
benefit at 100 percent of the state's average weekly wage would assure a fair and equitable replacement of lost wages to the majority
of insured workers.

Second, a drastic improvement needs to be made in benefits
for permanent total disability, permanent partial disability, and
death. These benefits should have a cost-of-living adjustment to assure at least a constant purchasing power to the beneficiaries in-

volved. For permanent total disability, benefits should be paid for the duration of disability or for life. In case of death, benefits should be paid to a widow or widower for life or until remarriage. In the absence of a surviving spouse, surviving children should receive benefits until they reach age 18, or 22 if they are full-time students.

Third, the coverage of workers should be broadened to include farm workers, domestic workers, workers in religious and charitable organizations, and workers in small establishments.

Fourth, full coverage of work-related diseases should be enforced. All states have full coverage of work-related injuries and accidents, but some do not provide completely for work-related diseases. As industries become more complex, particularly those utilizing chemical compounds, full coverage of diseases is rapidly becoming a decisive factor in determining the level of protection against wage loss due to work hazards. Full medical and physical rehabilitation services should be provided without statutory limits on dollar amount or length of time.

Temporary Disability Insurance. The nation needs a nationwide program to protect against wage loss due to non-work-related short-term disability. The use of federal subsidies and grants-in-aid to induce states to develop temporary disability insurance seems futile. Even if all states developed such programs, interstate variations in benefits, duration, and eligibility requirements would persist.

The nationwide program should be developed with close coordination with OASDI. Under such a plan, a disabled worker would receive his temporary disability insurance benefits during the first 5 months of his disability. Before the maximum duration expired, a determination would be made as to whether his disability would last 12 months or more from its onset. If the medical evaluation was affirmative, and if he met the work requirement for disability insurance, he would continue to receive benefits, without interruption; his case would be automatically transferred from the temporary disability to the disability insurance program. In the meantime, a rehabilitation plan should be laid out in behalf of the disabled person.

The most delicate part of coordinating temporary disability insurance with the two-tier system of social security is in relation to its benefit level. There seem to be two options. The first is to calculate temporary disability insurance benefits on a similar basis to that of workmen's compensation, providing two-thirds of lost wages up to a maximum amount. The second is to calculate temporary disability insurance benefits in the same way as disability-insurance benefits, providing the basic benefit, plus a contribution-related benefit, plus a dependent benefit for a spouse, as proposed earlier. The first option would be more likely than the second to provide higher benefits to the majority of temporary disability insurance beneficiaries. If this happened, the beneficiary would face a sudden cut in benefits when he was transferred to disability insurance. This question and others related to the coordination of the two programs need to be analyzed further and resolved.

The work requirement for temporary disability insurance benefits should be similar to that for unemployment insurance—20 weeks of employment in the base year with earnings of at least $40 a week. The two standards in work requirement for temporary disability and disability insurance mean that if a worker is transferred from one to the other, he has to meet a tougher work requirement before he is eligible for disability-insurance benefits. If he did not, he would have to settle for the basic benefit under proposed two-tier system.

On the basis of current data, it is estimated that new federal temporary disability insurance that provides two-thirds of wage loss in the form of benefits would cost approximately $3.1 billion in 1974, or less than 0.5 percent of taxable payrolls.[60]

A NEED FOR CHILDREN'S ALLOWANCES

By now it is apparent that children's allowances are an important ingredient in a comprehensive system of income-maintenance programs. A universal children's allowance program would be potent in making family income sensitive to family size without creating a problem of work incentive. To recapitulate, the minimum-wage earner, working year round, cannot keep a family with three or more dependents from poverty. Social insurance cannot support many dependents either. If it did, benefits might exceed earnings received by the worker just before the onset of insured risks. Thus, under social security, the maximum family benefit in the lowest wage bracket is high enough to cover benefits only for the insured and one dependent, and no more. However, children's allowances, to be provided to all children regardless of income levels of families and employment status of the breadwinner, could eliminate the conflict of adequacy vs. work incentives. Why is this possible? Since universal children's allowances would be provided to all children, rich and poor, the family would not need to adjust income levels to qualify for allowances. Children's allowances would not influence the work effort of the breadwinner, either, since they would be provided whether he worked or not.

Children's allowances are compatible with the redistributive objective. Families with children tend to have relatively low income.[61] Therefore, children's allowances would facilitate income flow to such families. If they were financed by progressive taxes, the magnitude of vertical redistribution of income from the rich to the poor would be that much greater.

Children's allowances, on their own, are a strong antipoverty instrument. One study showed that children's allowances of $600 per child per year would in 1966 remove 77 percent of poor children and 64 percent of poor families from poverty.[62] Since social-insurance benefits, as proposed in this chapter, would provide almost above-poverty-line income for the insured worker and his spouse, an income-maintenance system consisting of social-insurance programs and children's allowances would virtually bring most of current poor families out of poverty, if they are headed by a person employed or on social-insurance benefit rolls. Those who remained poor would be mainly individuals, small single-parent families, and childless couples neither employed nor on social-insurance benefit rolls.

Children's allowances originated in France in the 1870s when several French administrative services and railways began paying *allocations familiales*.[63] The provision for children as family dependents, however, was made in substance even earlier. In 1795, the British "Speenhamland system," instead of raising wages, provided "relief, in cases where there are a number of children, a matter of right and an honor instead of a ground for opprobrium and contempt." [64] Although children's allowances had become quite general in Europe by World War II, after the war they spread further and benefit levels became substantial. Children's allowances came to mean a flat payment, or demogrant, to all children, provided by the government, based solely on age of children, without regard to family income or other eligibility conditions.

The objective of children's allowances has changed somewhat over the years. When they were implemented in France toward the end of nineteenth century, the overriding objective appeared to be holding down wages by granting allowances only to those workers with children. This practice continued into the period of World War I and thereafter. However, after World War II, as children's allowances came to be provided under government auspices and paid regardless of employment status and wage level of the breadwinner, the idea of children's right to economic security emerged, along with the objective of equalizing the burden of child rearing. One theme has persisted: Children's allowances make up for the discrepancy between wages and their derivatives (e.g., social-insurance benefits) that are not based on family size, on the one hand, and family needs that depend on family size, on the other.

As children's allowances have become an institution in many countries, criticisms of the program as a depressant of wages or as an inducement toward a higher birth rate appear to have subsided. Indeed, since unions in all industrialized countries are much stronger than when children's allowances came into being, the provision of children's allowances by the government seems to have little influence in union bargaining with management. Evidence attests that children's allowances have had little influence on birth rates in countries with such provision.[65]

What type of children's allowances is desirable in terms of the major objectives of income redistribution and the provision of adequate minimum income? First of all, the level of allowances should be high enough to provide income to support a dependent in the family. Under the 1974 poverty-line income, the incremental income needed to support a dependent is $750. Therefore, children's allowances of $60 a month or $720 a year per child are a reasonable provision. This allowance level contrasts with the 1974 average children's benefit of $69 under old-age insurance and $56 under disability insurance.[66] Two particularly important policy questions to be resolved are these: Is a children's allowance (or taxable demogrant for children) preferable to the cashable tax credit suggested in chapter 3? Should the amount of allowances vary according to the order of birth or be uniform for all children?

The children's allowance requires a huge initial outlay that eventually could be recouped from high-income families by taxation. The cashable tax credit can minimize the apparent government outlay, since the credit for high-income families would simply be absorbed in their tax liability. Thus the tax-credit approach has public appeal. However, this approach is less efficient than the taxable-demogrant approach from a redistributive point of view, unless the federal tax law is drastically changed. This is because tax credits allow an equal amount of tax savings (or implicit after-tax income) to all taxpayers regardless of income levels. But if the taxable-demogrant approach is taken, the bulk of initial children's allowances is recouped from high-income taxpayers. In specific terms, a $720 tax credit means $720 in cashable tax savings to all taxpayers regardless of income level. But the same amount of taxable demogrant means $720 to the poor who do not pay income taxes, but only $216 in after-tax income to those in the highest bracket. The spill-over benefit for the rich is smaller under the taxable-demogrant approach than under the cashable tax-credit approach. Thus, from the viewpoint of efficient redistribution of income, a program of taxable demogrants for children is much to be preferred.

Some advocate variable children's allowances according to the order of the child's birth, because economy of scale indicates that a large family does not require a proportionately large income and because such variable children's allowances at least do not encourage a family to have many children. However, again from the redistributive point of view, the flat amount of allowances to all children is recommended, because under the variable allowance scheme the share for low-income families will be smaller. Among poor families only 55 percent of the children are either the first or the second child but among all families 69 percent of the children fall into this category.[67] If the third and fourth children, for example, are given a smaller allowance, high-income families will benefit proportionately more than lower-income families.

What will be the cost of a children's allowance program that provides $720 a year per child under age 18, takes the taxable-demogrant approach, and abolishes the current $750 exemption for each child under federal individual income tax? A rough estimate of costs for 1974 would be $34 billion. Savings in public assistance would be about $5 billion. Thus, the net public outlay to implement children's allowances of $720 to all children would be approximately $29 billion.[68]

Conclusions

The two objectives—the provision of adequate minimum benefits and income redistribution through social insurance—are not necessarily the same. The former can be achieved either through increasing the overall expenditures for social insurance or through changing the distributive pattern of benefits. However, the latter can be achieved only through changing the distributive pattern of benefits. Compared with European systems, the American system of social insurance is smaller in scope and expenditures. This country could expand the overall commitment to social insurance in order to provide a better minimum benefit. However, the objective of income redistribution requires that one look at how the division of shares can be changed. This chapter has been written toward such an end.

On the issue of an adequate floor to income for all, this nation could continue what it started a long time ago by expanding income-conditioned programs. But such a path appears to be a dead end from both practical and ideological viewpoints. If income-conditioned programs proliferated, these multiple programs with work-incentive measures tacked onto them separately, serving the same clientele, not only would be administratively confusing but, more important, would raise problems about incentive to work. Ideologically, such programs will draw a clear line between "the giver" and "the receiver," which may be detrimental in the long run to the character of this nation.

Providing adequate income first through jobs and then through social insurance, both supplemented by a children's allowance program, can escape these gloomy consequences. We have proposed in this chapter dealing with support for children quite independently of wage and social-insurance patterns. Then we could organize minimum wages and wage-related social-insurance programs so that they could provide an adequate income for a worker and spouse. Wages and social-insurance benefits cannot effectively provide adequate income to all families. Together with children's allowances, they could. There would be no fear of losing work effort on the part of the breadwinner in such a scheme.

The proposed income-maintenance system consisting of improved social-insurance programs and a new children's allowance program would create an ideology of universal coverage and membership among the general public both as contributors and beneficiaries. Of course, even under the proposed scheme, there will be a need for a residual program. However, the residual will be truly supplemental to the proposed system. It will cease to be a dominant element in income maintenance, as it is today.

5

Fair Share
in Health Care

RACHEL FLOERSHEIM BOAZ

The health-services sector of the economy, which has been expanding during the past three decades, is likely to continue doing so. Demographic characteristics, hazardous habits and jobs, and the achievements of biomedical research all point in this direction. With a rising number of older Americans, with disease-causing lifestyles and employment, and with the success of medicine in prolonging the lives of the sick and the crippled, it is only too likely that an increasing share of the national product will have to be allocated to the medical industry. And since taxpayers provide substantial amounts of dollars to support the construction of expensive facilities, the training of health professionals, and the development of biomedical research, the question of who should benefit how much from this endeavor is inevitably asked. The determination of a fair share in health care has become a major social issue, and its resolution requires conscious and explicit public policy.

Although medical care is not the only factor that contributes to attaining and maintaining good health, medical services have a unique and sometimes crucial role in prolonging life, curing disease, and relieving pain. If a person's health status and the imperatives of the medical-clinical requirements were the only factors in determining the allocation of such services, the issue of a fair share in health care would not have to be raised. However, when the market system allocates scarce resources, ability to purchase medical services may give a considerable advantage to those who can afford to pay for the prescribed diagnoses and therapy. Thus economic constraints can alter the distribution of health-care services. The actual distribution of medical services may be determined by both health status and economic restrictions; it may be shaped by the relative importance of these two components.

Medical services, by their very nature, are not equally distributed because people differ in their initial health, their environment, and their position in the life cycle. Some phases of the life cycle are relatively free from health problems and others are not. Good health without medical care can be enjoyed over relatively long periods of time. Hence, an equitable distribution of health care does not mean an equal distribution of medical services. Rather, it means that services are guaranteed to every member of the society whenever medically accepted standards suggest that such services should be provided. Equity mandates that medical care be "income blind," that is, that the consumption of medical services be independent of income and payments for them unrelated to utilization. The financing mechanism, which is instrumental in removing the link between services and payments, would have to be based on income so that the cost of health care could be universally shared. Thus, no person would be deprived of medically accepted care because he lacked the means to pay for it, and no individual would obtain preferred treatment because he had the income to pay for the essential services or the social prestige to secure them without pay.

The United States, unlike other major industrialized countries, still adheres to the principle that the individual patient, unless he proves poverty or indigency, is ultimately responsible for paying his medical bills. And with the soaring costs of health-care services, many families have become acutely aware that a prolonged illness or other major health problem could deplete their economic resources and plunge them into debt notwithstanding their private health-insurance policies or their Medicare benefits. Mounting dissatisfaction of the voting public with this arrangement has prompted many legislators to sponsor and introduce in the Congress national health-insurance programs designed to protect Americans against large outlays by placing a ceiling on the patient's responsibility for medical expenses.

The latest wave of national health-insurance bills began in 1970. Since then, many of the same bills, though with some modifications, have been reintroduced by their sponsors time and again. Conflicts of ideology and economic interests have thus far impeded legislative progress, though at times it seemed that a law was imminent. Nevertheless, there appears to be a wide consensus that the time is ripe for some system which as a minimum would subsidize the health insurance of the poor and provide protection against catastrophic payments for the entire population. Whether the anticipated legislation would be comprehensive and equitable or narrow and inequitable depends on the compromise that would be reached among widely different positions with respect to financing, administration, and governance of the national insurance program. Since the resolution of the conflict is likely to have a profound impact on the entire health-care delivery system, the proposed legislation and its implications ought to be viewed in a framework of long-term rather than immediate consequences.

This chapter focuses on some of these issues as they are

likely to affect the relationship between the distribution of income and the distribution of medical services among different population segments. The first part describes the health-care services rendered to different income groups and assesses the effects of private insurance and public programs (Medicare and Medicaid) on allocating the burden of paying for medical services. The second part discusses the national health-insurance proposals before the Congress and examines how different provisions can affect the distribution of the program's benefits. With these provisions in mind, we present arguments for a system where payments for comprehensive benefits could be equitably shared. However, successful implementation would require a rational organization of the health-care delivery system to eliminate deficiencies that stem from the prevailing maldistribution of expensive facilities and skilled manpower.

The Distribution of Health-Care Services and Payments

The effect of income on the distribution of medical services depends on the type of medical help that is needed. In particular, a distinction has to be made between emergency and nonemergency care. In general, the lack of income is not expected to affect the demand of emergency care. To put it differently, the inability to pay is not likely to constitute a barrier where life is at stake or when pressing symptoms of an acute disease require urgent medical attention. Income levels are expected to have more of a restraining effect in cases of nonemergency care. However, demand for medical services in the care of chronic diseases will occur regardless of income.[1] This is so because, while a chronic disease is of long duration and often incurable, modern medicine may be effective in relieving pain, slowing the process of deterioration, and increasing the capabilities of patients to perform at least some normal functions. The demand for medical services in nonurgent cases of preventive care and for what are perceived as minor health problems is likely to be income sensitive; that is, as more urgent and pressing claims are made on the family budget, expenditures for such health care are either postponed or foregone.

The distinction between different types of care is conceptually appealing and analytically helpful, but it has not yet been translated into measurable counterparts. Available information permits us (1) to distinguish between individuals who have had and who have not had contact with a physician or a dentist, and (2) to measure the quantity of some medical services and the amounts of payments made directly by patients. For the general population, it appears that income does affect access to the health-care system via physician services and care for health problems that do not require many physician visits or much hospital care. However, available information indicates that income differences may be immaterial when individuals obtain a large quantity of medical services either in an ambulatory setting or as hospital patients.

INCOME AND MEDICAL SERVICES

National expenditures for medical care reached a level of $104 billion in fiscal 1974, or almost $500 for each man, woman, and child. Two types of personal health services absorbed three-fifths of this amount: hospital care (two-fifths) and physicians' services (one-fifth). Drugs, nursing-home care, and dentists' services accounted for a little more than another fifth. And expenditures which affected consumers only indirectly, such as public-health activities, construction of facilities, and biomedical research, amounted to less than one-tenth of all health-care expenditures.[2] Put differently, institutional care (in hospitals and nursing homes) comprised 46 percent, and other personal care (physicians, dentists, drugs, eyeglasses, and appliances) 36 percent of all medical expenditures; the remaining 18 percent was divided between investment categories (construction and research),[3] public-health services, and administrative expenses.

How are these services distributed? The very nature of medical care suggests that the distribution of such services reflects differences in health status in the population. Some persons can enjoy good health without any health-care services, while many others require few services spread over a considerable time span, and relatively few individuals require continuous services over a long period or many services within a relatively short period. The question that may be asked is whether this expected inequality in the distribution of health-care services has been made more unequal by the inequality in income distribution.

The National Health Interview Survey (HIS) may provide some illuminating information on this subject, although its data are not adjusted for differences in health levels of the population. If economic constraints act as a brake on the utilization of medical services, we would expect the number of service units (the number of hospital days or doctor visits) to increase as income levels rise.[4]

A comparison of hospitalized persons (in 1968) suggests that income affected only relatively short hospital stays of 7 days or less; for each age group, the proportion of such persons among all hospitalized persons decreased with income levels. But income did not appear to have the same effect on individuals who spent 15 or more days in the hospital; the proportion of persons spending many days as inpatients decreased as income levels increased. No such clear relationship could be found for persons who were inpatients for more than 7 and less than 15 days; the proportion of such persons across all income levels was constant for the relatively young, decreased for the middle-aged, and increased for the elderly.[5]

The distribution of physician and dentist visits by income levels (in 1969) indicates that income was a restraining factor on persons who had no contact with physicians or had only few (less than 5) such contacts per year; the proportion of persons who had no contact decreased when income increased, and the proportion of persons with less than 5 visits increased as income levels rose. But income did not seem to have had such a restrictive effect on persons reporting 5 or more contacts.[6] Visits to dentists, however, showed sensitivity to income at all service levels, although, even at relatively high income levels, a third of all individuals had no dental care.[7]

The relationship between income and the utilization of medical facilities points toward a consistent pattern: where a health problem is perceived as serious, the lack of income may not act as a barrier to obtaining health care. The initial contact with the physician or dentist is made by the prospective patient and depends on his decision; this may be influenced by his income level. Similarly, sporadic visits and return visits to the physician may be determined by the patient and may be affected by income levels, especially if the health problem is not considered pressing and urgent. Likewise, short-term hospitalization, if applied for elective therapy, may be affected by income. However, when a patient's health problem is serious or critical, the consumption of medical services is determined by the attending physician; and it is unlikely that a sick person would not follow the physician's prescribed treatment because of economic constraints. Thus, irrespective of their income, seriously ill patients may have many visits to their physicians and spend many days as inpatients in a hospital.

INCOME AND SOURCES OF PAYMENT FOR MEDICAL CARE

If the lack of income is not a barrier to obtaining care when a health problem is serious, how is such care paid for? This question is pertinent because some surgical procedures and other modes of therapy are expensive and may require a large fraction of the patient's income. In many cases, however, the patient to whom services are rendered does not pay the total bill for such care. Private health insurance and government programs together have paid nine-tenths of all hospital expenditures and three-fifths of physician services; but they paid only one-third of the expenditures for other personal health services.[8]

The public sector paid for almost two-fifths of all personal medical expenditures in fiscal 1974. Medicare and Medicaid were by far the largest programs, comprising 60 percent of government expenditures in this area.[9] Medicare is strictly a federal program and its enrollees are entitled to uniform benefits across the land; Medicaid is a federal-state program and its benefits differ among states. Medicare enrollment was originally limited to the elderly; but since July 1973, its coverage has been extended to the long-term disabled (who have been receiving cash benefits for a period of two years and longer) and to persons with kidney malfunction. Medicaid enrolls all recipients of public assistance; at the discretion of individual states, its benefits may be extended to the indigent whose income does not exceed the comparable public-assistance payments by more than one-third (the 133.3 percent rule).

Medicare. Health status is expected to deteriorate with age. In comparison with young persons, the elderly are more prone to health impairments, more seriously affected by them, and find it harder to recover from illness to regain and maintain a satisfactory health status. It is therefore expected that they would consume more medical services than their younger peers. Table 5.1 compares the personal health-care expenditures of the two groups and shows that, on the average, an old person's expenditures were almost four times as high as those of a younger person in fiscal 1974.

Table 5.1 Personal Health-Care Expenditure by Age and by Type of Payment: Fiscal Years 1972–74

Type of Payment	1972	1973	1974 [a]
		Under Age 65	
Per Capita Expenditure ($)	278	302	330
Per Capita Expenditure (Percent)	100.0	100.0	100.0
Direct Payments (Percent)	*38.4*	*37.8*	*35.5*
Indirect Payments (Percent)	*61.6*	*62.2*	*64.5*
Private	34.8	35.1	35.9
Insurance	33.0	33.3	34.2
Other	1.8	1.8	1.7
Government	26.8	27.1	28.6
Medicare	—	—	1.3
Medicaid	9.2	9.6	10.6
Other	17.6	17.5	16.7
		Age 65 and Over	
Per Capita Expenditure ($)	1,034	1,120	1,218
Per Capita Expenditure (Percent)	100.0	100.0	100.0
Direct Payments (Percent)	*35.5*	*34.7*	*34.1*
Indirect Payments (Percent)	*64.5*	*65.3*	*65.9*
Private	5.6	5.6	5.6
Insurance	5.2	5.2	5.2
Other	0.4	0.4	0.4
Government	58.9	59.7	60.3
Medicare	38.6	37.9	38.1
Medicaid	11.9	13.6	14.6
Other	8.4	8.2	7.6

Source: Marjorie Smith Mueller and Robert M. Gibson, "Age Differences in Health Care Spending, Fiscal Year 1974," *Social Security Bulletin,* June 1975, pp. 8 and 14.

[a] Preliminary.

Moreover, although the government paid 60 percent of the expenditures of the aged and less than 30 percent of the expenditures of the nonaged, both groups paid the same proportion of their bills directly (35 percent). On a per capita basis, older Americans paid $415 and younger Americans paid $117. Out-of-pocket payments by the elderly were substantial notwithstanding their Medicare benefits.

Medicare benefits, amounting to $11.3 billion in fiscal 1974, are concentrated in hospital care and physician services; for example, in fiscal 1974 three-fifths of hospital expenditure and one-half of the expenses for physician services were paid by Medicare.[10] The Medicare program does not cover medical checkups, nor does it pay for drugs, dental care, or eyeglasses. Also, Medicare payments for nursing-home care, a major health-care item for older Americans, are meager. Medicaid partly fills this gap by paying 46 percent of the costs of such long-term care. Thus, notwithstanding the public-sector support for the health care of the aged, the elderly still pay (directly or through supplementary private insurance) for almost all their dental services and drugs, half of the costs of their nursing-home care, two-fifths of all physician services and one-fifth of their hospital care.

The Medicare program consists of two parts. Part A covers institutional care: hospitals and skilled nursing homes. The premium for this care is paid by the working (nonaged) population. In addition, patients pay a flat deductible upon admission to any hospital and a share of the cost for each day in excess of a specified number of days per episode of illness; copayments begin on the 61st day and continue to the 90th day, and, should the need for further hospitalization arise, the patient can use his "lifetime reserve" which, over his lifetime, entitles him to an additional 60 days of Medicare payments. In nursing homes, there are no deductibles upon admission; copayments begin on the 21st day and continue to the 100th day. If any illness requires additional care in a hospital or a skilled nursing home, it is up to the patient to defray the cost.

Part B covers all physician services (in and out of the hospital), ambulatory X-rays and laboratory tests, ambulance services, and home health care. It requires each enrollee to pay a flat monthly payment (premium) that is subject to annual changes; this premium is matched by general-revenue funds. It also requires enrollees to pay a flat deductible amount over a period of 12 to 15 months, and to pay 20 percent of all allowable charges, i.e., charges that the Medicare program accepts for reimbursement. Thus, except for recipients of old-age assistance for whom Medicaid pays premiums and cost-sharing amounts, the aged have an open-ended commitment to pay their cost-sharing amounts and the difference between the level of their bills and the amounts accepted for reimbursement. More than half of all the elderly are enrolled in a private insurance program to help them pay for some of the costs of hospital care and surgical services.[11]

Concern has been expressed over the level of direct payments by the aged and its effect on the distribution of health-care services and Medicare benefits. The federal budget for Medicare is restrained by the upper limits set by the government on its reimbursements. These limits and the cost-sharing amounts are the same for all the elderly who do not receive public assistance. But with differences in income levels, such uniform payments are more restrictive on persons whose incomes are moderate than on persons who are comfortable or have supplementary private insurance.[12] As table 5.2 shows, the number of persons with reimbursable services under Medicare Part B increased consistently with income, as did the level of reimbursements per enrollee.

Medicaid. The Medicaid program, amounting to $11.2 billion in fiscal 1974, allocated most of its funds to institutional care (37 percent for hospitals and 32 percent for nursing homes);[13] but in contrast with Medicare, it paid not only for physician services, but also for prescription drugs and dental care. States are required to provide basic services but can add optional services with the federal government sharing in the cost. Required services include inpatient

Table 5.2 Medicare Reimbursements for Services Covered under the SMI [a] Program, 1968

Income ($)	Reimbursement Levels Per Enrollee ($)	Number of Persons Receiving Reimbursable Service (Per 1,000 Enrollees)
Under 5,000	79	432
5,000– 9,999	104	475
10,000–14,999	115	527
15,000 and Over	160	552
Ratio of Highest to Lowest Income Group	2.03	1.28

Source: Karen Davis and Roger Reynolds, "Medicare and the Utilization of Health Care Services by the Elderly," *The Journal of Human Resources,* 10 (Summer 1975), 361–77, table 1.

[a] SMI is Supplementary Medical Insurance of Medicare Part B. Services covered by this program are subject to an initial deductible ($50 in 1968) and a 20 percent coinsurance rate on all "allowable charges."

and outpatient hospital care, physician services, X-rays and laboratory tests, skilled nursing-home facilities and home health care for individuals over age 20, and for persons under age 21 periodic screening for diagnostic and treatment purposes. However, the states can set limits on the quantity of such benefits. Optional services include dental care, prescription drugs, optometrists' services, podiatrists' and chiropractors' services, prosthetic devices and other rehabilitative services, and family planning services. New York, California, and Massachusetts are examples of states that have had generous Medicaid programs.

Under federal regulations, all benefits within a state must be available uniformly to all public-assistance recipients. About half of the states provide Medicaid services to medically needy persons who would fall into welfare if they had to pay for medical care. A "spend down" provision permits coverage by Medicaid when income, after payment of medical bills, falls below 133.3 percent of the comparable public-assistance income level within a state. Beginning in January 1973, states had the option of requiring medically indigent persons to share the cost of services they were receiving under Medicaid.

The high cost of Medicaid and widespread discontent with the poor care for the poor have almost eclipsed some of its genuine achievements. Medicaid has greatly reduced the financial burden on its enrollees of paying for care and improved their access to medical facilities. However, poor persons not covered by Medicaid, or persons residing in states with only limited benefits, have had a double disadvantage. First, they either have not shared at all or have not shared fully in the benefits of Medicaid; and second, their expenditures for care have been affected by the rapidly rising prices for medical services attributable, at least in part, to Medicare and Medicaid. Table 5.3 permits comparison of physician services rendered to poor persons receiving no public assistance, poor persons who received aid, and the nonpoor.[14] After adjustment for differences in age and in health status (measured by the number of restricted-activity days per year and by chronic ill-health conditions), it appears that nonaged adult recipients of public assistance had at least the same number of physician visits as comparable middle-income persons. But similar poor who did not receive assistance lagged behind and reported fewer physician visits.

In summary, Medicaid eased financial constraints and reduced disparities in the use of services that might be attributed to differences in income. It relieved poor patients from the need to depend on charity and greatly eased their burden of paying for medical care. Yet Medicaid enrollees may still receive different care from middle-class Americans. Since physicians can refuse to accept the government-set Medicaid fees, they can, in effect, refuse to accept Medicaid patients. The poor, whether enrolled in Medicaid or

Table 5.3 Physician Visits by Family Income, Public-Assistance Status, and Age Group, 1969 [a]

Income ($)	Age Group			
	16 and Younger	17–44	45–64	65 and Older
(1) *Under 5,000*				
(2) No aid	3.0	4.1	3.9	6.1
(3) Aid	3.5	5.9	5.2	6.4
(4) 5,000– 9,999	3.9	4.5	5.2	6.8
(5) 10,000–14,999	4.2	4.6	5.1	7.5
(6) 15,000 and Over	4.5	4.8	5.5	10.4
Ratio of line (3) to line (2)	1.17	1.44	1.33	1.05
Ratio of line (6) to line (2)	1.50	1.17	1.41	1.70
Ratio of line (6) to line (3)	1.29	0.81	1.06	1.62

Source: Karen Davis and Roger Reynolds, "The Impact of Medicare and Medicaid on Access to Medical Care," in Richard Rosett, ed., *The Role of Insurance in the Health Services Sector* (a Universities-NBER Conference, volume forthcoming), table 2.

[a] Number of visits is adjusted for differences in health status.

not, may continue to receive care in crowded emergency rooms, subjected to long waits and to seeing a different physician on each visit.

Private Insurance Protection and Direct Payments by Patients. Medicare and Medicaid have constituted a major effort to close the gap in the protection provided by private insurance. Private insurance premiums are based on risk. For any given risk, the more extensive the protection, the higher the premium payments; and conversely, for any level of protection, the higher the risk, the more it costs to secure the covered benefits. Since premium levels are expected to be positively associated with income, private insurance benefits are also likely to increase with income. However, the relationship between risk and premium levels is not always obvious because the most prevalent form of private insurance is group insurance through employment. Premium levels for group insurance policies are lower than for comparable individual policies because the administrative costs per policyholder are smaller, and because the members of the group are often low-risk persons. In addition, persons who pay only part of their premiums directly may not realize that the employer's share in paying the premium is, in effect, part of their salary that is paid in kind.

The income relatedness of private insurance coverage is show in table 5.4. Since persons 65 years and older are covered by Medicare, HIS data are limited to younger persons. For persons between ages 25 and 64 in 1968, the proportion of those who had no insurance and stated that they could not afford to pay for it decreased steadily as income levels increased. Moreover, the federal government has been subsidizing health-insurance premiums, and the subsidy has been rising with income. Table 5.5 shows the extent of such subsidies, and how they constitute an increasing share of the insurance premium as income levels increase. The combination of the federal income-tax exemption for health-insurance premiums and the progressive tax schedule is responsible for this inequity; as income increases, so does the amount of federal income taxes that need not be paid.

Enrollment in private insurance plans is extensive. At the end of 1973, according to estimates by the Social Security Administration, about 77 percent of the population under age 65 had some protection against the cost of hospitalization, in-hospital physician services, ambulatory X-rays, and laboratory tests, while about 62 percent had some insurance to cover the cost of a private duty nurse and visiting-nurse services. Elderly persons, aged 65 and over, carried private insurance to supplement their Medicare benefits; more than half had insurance against the cost of hospitalization and surgical services, and two-fifths carried insurance against the cost of other medical services rendered in the hospital

Table 5.4 Number of Persons with No Health Insurance by Family Income and by Selected Age Groups, 1968

Income ($)	Total Population (in thousands) (1)	Uninsured Persons	
		Total, as Percent of Col. (1) (2)	Persons who cannot afford insurance,[a] as Percent of Col. (1) (3)
		Ages 25–44	
Under 3,000	2,694	67.3	37.2
3,000–4,999	4,266	41.0	19.1
5,000–6,999	8,889	18.0	6.1
7,000–9,999	12,009	8.5	2.2
10,000–14,999	10,985	5.8	0.8
15,000 and Over	4,916	5.2	—[c]
Total [b]	44,953	16.7	6.4
		Ages 45–64	
Under 3,000	4,589	55.0	28.0
3,000–4,999	4,840	31.5	13.2
5,000–6,999	7,056	15.4	4.9
7,000–9,999	7,930	8.3	2.3
10,000–14,999	7,640	6.7	1.2
15,000 and Over	5,269	5.5	—[c]
Total [b]	40,153	17.7	6.8

Source: U.S. Department of Health, Education, and Welfare, *Hospital and Surgical Insurance Coverage, United States, 1968,* Vital and Health Statistics, ser. 10, no. 66 (Washington, D.C., 1972), tables 3 and 17.

[a] Persons who *stated* that they could not afford to pay the insurance premium.

[b] Total exceeds sum of components because it includes persons whose family income is not known.

[c] Because of the smallness of this class in the sample, figure does not meet the standard of reliability.

Table 5.5 Subsidy for Health Insurance Premiums by Income Class, 1970

Adjusted Gross Income ($) [a]	Mean Insurance Premium ($) [b]	Subsidy [c] as Percent of the Premium
Under 1,000	152	0.4
1,000– 1,999	192	6.2
2,000– 2,999	177	9.5
3,000– 3,999	186	9.3
4,000– 5,999	184	9.8
6,000– 9,999	194–196	9.6–10.7
10,000– 14,999	195–198	11.1–13.6
15,000– 24,999	204–214	14.7–16.4
25,000– 99,999	224–243	20.6–25.6
100,000–999,999	241–253	23.5–24.5
1,000,000 and over	219	23.3

Source: Bridger M. Mitchell and Ronald J. Vogel, *Health and Taxes: An Assessment of the Medical Deduction,* The Rand Corporation, R-1222-OEO (Santa Monica, Calif., August 1973), table 4, p. 12.

[a] This is the definition of income used by the Internal Revenue Service.

[b] The mean insurance premium of taxpayers reporting personal expenses for insurance premiums.

[c] The subsidy is defined as the amount of unpaid income taxes due to the exemption of income from the federal income tax.

and against the cost of ambulatory X-rays and laboratory services.[15] Yet, private insurance paid for only 27 percent of all personal health-care expenditures in fiscal 1974, 37 percent of the hospital costs and physician services, and 7.5 percent of all other services.[16] It covered 34 percent of all personal medical expenditures of persons under age 65, but only 5 percent of the expenditure incurred by the aged (table 5.1).

Under the prevailing system, the patient is ultimately responsible for paying medical bills that are not reimbursed by private insurance or Medicare. In fiscal 1974, 35 percent of all personal health-care expenditures were paid directly by patients.[17] Such out-of-pocket expenses increase with income but at a slower pace than income and therefore constitute a decreasing share of income as income levels rise. For example, in 1970, all direct payments (excluding health-insurance premiums) increased 41 percent when income levels increased from under $3,000 to over $15,000; at the same time, premiums increased by only 16 percent. The average amounts of direct payments do not constitute an inordinate burden, but the distribution of payment levels may point out some hardship cases. The level of medical payments for persons above the 80th percentile may be quite high relative to their income levels; for example, 2 percent of the population reported direct payments (including insurance premiums) that exceeded $1,000, another 5.5 percent of the population had payments between $500 and $1,000, and an additional 14 percent paid between $250 and $500. Moreover, nearly 600,000 elderly persons had out-of-pocket expenses (excluding premiums) of $1,000, as did 2 million younger adults. And 2.1 million persons with incomes under $5,000 had medical payments in excess of $500.[18] Hence, though over any short timespan, relatively few persons are faced with large medical bills, most American families cannot be sure that they will not be subjected to financial hardships should one of their members be afflicted with a major health problem.

POLICY IMPLICATIONS

Health-care services are not expected to be equally distributed because health is not equally distributed. However, when market forces determine the allocation of scarce medical resources, persons who can afford to pay for services may secure them more easily than persons who cannot. Thus, an unequal distribution of income may be superimposed on the expected unequal distribution of medical services, widening the dispersion and reinforcing the inequality.

HIS data suggest that the lack of income is a restraining factor at the point of entry into the system, and in cases which require only few services. But the same data, though unadjusted for differences in health status, also suggest that income may not be a barrier to obtaining medical care when a health problem requires many services. However, income differences in such cases may be reflected through differences in the setting in which health-care services are provided.

Yet, if income does not appear to be a barrier to obtaining medical care when a health problem is serious, how are such services paid for? Most Americans are enrolled in programs which are expected to provide some protection against the cost of medical care. Of the total civilian population of 206 million at the end of 1972, at least 72 percent (under age 65) had some private insurance coverage for hospital care, [19] and 8 percent (under age 65) were enrolled in Medicaid.[20] Medicare Part A covered almost all individuals aged 65 years and older, amounting to 10 percent of the total civilian population. Hence, about 90 percent of the total civilian population appears to have been enrolled in some program that provided the benefits of third-party payments; the remaining 10 percent probably consisted of the poor who were not enrolled in Medicaid and other persons under age 65 whose employment status was tenuous, being either unemployed or employed part time. Students and other young adults who were not entitled to coverage under their parents' policies might have had no health-insurance protection, especially if they had no firm labor-market attachment; but they usually needed few health-care services. By contrast, older persons with no third-party protection were indeed vulnerable to the hardship of paying medical bills.[21]

It is not only the gap in enrollment but the paucity of benefits extended to those who are enrolled that has resulted in widespread dissatisfaction with the present insurance system. Many persons covered by private insurance policies do not know exactly the extent of the benefits to which they are entitled; and more often than not, they discover that their benefits are much more restricted than they have been led to believe. Hence, some families find themselves unexpectedly saddled with payment of bills that are large relative to income. Moreover, some types of medical expenditure are not covered at all by private insurance. Thus, when private insurance pays only 34 percent of all the personal health expenditures of persons under age 65 (table 5.1), there are likely to be many families with moderate and middle income for whom private insurance will pay very little or nothing at all.

Medicare, which covers the elderly, is a uniform federal program with limited benefits that pays only 38 percent of personal health-care costs (table 5.1). Copayment provisions and the ceiling on the government's liability for institutional care under Part A, cost-sharing provisions and the limits on reimbursements of fees under Part B, and the exclusion of such services as prescription drugs, dental care, and eyeglasses all suggest that older Americans who do not qualify for assistance have to pay a considerable share of their medical expenditures on their own. Medicaid's participation, 15 percent of the personal expenditures of the elderly in fiscal 1974 (table 5.1), was mostly allocated to paying for nursing-home care.

Uniform cost-sharing requirements and other payments for services covered under Medicare, applied to disparate economic fortunes of the elderly, have resulted in disparate distribution of benefits. The out-of-pocket amounts constitute a decreasing portion of income as income levels increase, and are, therefore, progressively less restrictive. Hence, persons with high incomes, who are less restricted in obtaining medical services, are more likely to pass the level of the initial deductible amount than similar persons with moderate incomes. Thus, although Medicare guarantees equal benefits for equal medical bills, it does not guarantee equal medical benefits for persons with different incomes. Proportionally a larger share of the benefits from the Medicare program are diverted to high-income persons at the expense of their low- and moderate- or even middle-income counterparts (table 5.2).

Medicaid, though it lowered financial barriers for the poor, has fallen into disrepute. Rapidly increasing costs which were not anticipated led alarmed legislators to restrict eligibility, to cut back benefits, and to require enrollees to share their bills. Also, as it is a federal-state program, standards of eligibility and the scope of benefits vary greatly among states. The likelihood of being covered by Medicaid and the extent of services covered depend on the fortune of residence. The poor who do not qualify for Medicaid are, in addition, faced with increasing prices partly attributable to Medicaid. And all Medicaid enrollees face a disadvantage in relation to middle- and upper-income Americans. Since physicians can refuse treatment to Medicaid patients, Medicaid enrollees often end up being served by different physicians and in a different setting than middle- or upper-income Americans. And thus, in effect, the federal and state governments have sanctioned a two-class system of medical care: one for the mainstream citizens, and another for their economically disadvantaged peers.

To sum up, although a large majority of Americans are enrolled in some program which provides them with some third-party benefits, a noticeable minority of Americans, who are economically vulnerable, do not have such protection. The exclusion of some medical services from insurance programs and the limitation of benefits in others require many Americans to pay medical bills that at times requisition a considerable share of their income, and at all times drive home the point that, should a major illness strike, it could plunge them into debt. And when Medicaid removes the financial barriers of access to care and eliminates the threat of financial disaster, it accomplishes this feat by creating a two-tier system of medical services. Thus, the burden of paying for health care, the haunting specter of financial hardship, and the inequality in the setting in which medical care is provided, all led to widespread voter dissatisfaction with the present arrangements, and to pressures for a different payment and delivery system. A national health-insurance program is one attempt to cope with the problem. Careful planning of scarce medical resources (specialized facilities and trained manpower) is another.

National Health-Insurance Programs

A national health-insurance program might be expected to provide an equitable solution to the payment problem. Specifically, it might be expected to protect Americans from unanticipated large bills and to accomplish this task without, in the process, creating a two-class system of medical care. Equity suggests that consumption of medical services by all Americans should be independent of their incomes, and the costs of such services should be distributed in line with their ability to pay. If properly structured, the national health-insurance system could be reasonably well within reach of this goal.

Insurance principles suggest that medical expenditure levels for a large group of persons can be predicted with fair accuracy. Hence, it is possible to spread the costs over all program participants by pooling revenues. Premium levels would be determined by the benefits that the program is expected to pay. This could entail all expenses above a predetermined upper expense limit. Such a ceiling on patients' direct outlays could be set as a fixed share of income, thus protecting all Americans from an inordinate burden of medical bills and basing actual payments on ability to pay.

The major bills that have come before the Congress express

a common denominator of agreement, but they also reflect sharp disagreements. They all specify some form of subsidized health insurance for the poor, and protection against large cost-sharing amounts for the entire population. But they differ on what is an adequate level of medical assistance, and what constitutes a catastrophic expense level. Moreover, they disagree on the population that would have to be covered by a national health-insurance plan, on the scope of benefits it should provide, and on its financing and administration. Since the bills proposed during the first session of the Ninety-fourth Congress are not likely to become the law of the land, the discussion here will not dwell on their specific provisions; rather, it will outline some of the issues that have been raised and the options for their resolution. Some of these resolutions would entail restructuring the health-care delivery system and would, therefore, involve entrenched economic and political interests. The conflicts among these interests have, thus far, impeded any meaningful action.

Any national health-insurance plan has to define who is entitled to what benefits, how these benefits will be financed, and how the plan will be administered. These three topics are often referred to under the headings of coverage, financing, and administration and management. They cover the following specific problems: (1) the population to be enrolled, the list of services to be covered by the plan, and the extent of benefits to be provided; (2) the mix of indirect (prepaid) and direct (cost-shared) financing; and (3) the composition and the authority of the program's management and administration.

COVERAGE

Any national health-insurance plan must specify who is entitled to what benefits. This decision entails a definition of the population that will be enrolled in the plan, the list of services to be covered, and the extent of benefits for each of these covered services. Enrollment can be either selective or universal, and it can be either voluntary or mandatory. Medicare Part B is an example of a selective and voluntary program, where the selection is by age, and all eligible persons are free not to join and not to pay the premiums required by the program. Some bills stipulate universal enrollment which is voluntary; all individuals and families can enroll but do not have to do so, and do not have to pay the insurance premium. This is the most acceptable model for a national health-insurance plan that assigns a major role to private insurance organizations. But bills which specify health insurance as a fringe benefit of employment do not permit the same freedom to employers; employers are required to offer an acceptable insurance program and pay part of the premiums directly (the Nixon bill introduced in the Ninety-third Congress is an example). Other legislative proposals specify universal and mandatory enrollment, which means that the entire population would be enrolled. Such bills assign a major financing role to the public authorities (the "Health Security Act" is a case in point).

The drawback of selective programs is that they limit enrollment and therefore may leave some population groups unprotected. Also, the criterion for selection often creates murky borderline problems, i.e., persons who would almost qualify but do not and, because they cannot enjoy the benefits of the program, are subject to greater hardships than the rest of the population. Such is the fate of the poor who do not qualify for public assistance or of the medically needy who have an income slightly above 133.3 percent of the public-assistance standard. The disadvantage of a voluntary program is that it will attract persons who anticipate large medical bills. Persons who do not expect to use the health-care system are not likely to volunteer payments for a plan that does not directly benefit them. Universal and mandatory enrollment guarantees coverage to the entire population. Nobody will fall between the gaps in coverage that can be created by a selective program. And because it is mandatory, the costs of the program will be widely diffused over the entire population.

The scope of services that are covered by the national health-insurance program is the basis for determining the benefits, which are, by definition, those services provided without direct payment by patients. Put differently, a national health-insurance plan has to specify which services are excluded and which are included, whether the included services are covered with or without quantitative limits, and with or without cost-sharing amounts. The level of copayments limits the benefits from services that are included in the program.

The bills that were introduced in the Ninety-fourth Congress recognized, in principle, that all enrollees are entitled to all covered services and benefits if they pay the required cost-sharing amounts. All bills are characterized by the "laundry list" approach, that is, the approach that names and specifies the quantities of covered services. Differences among the lists specified by different bills are not major. Broadly speaking, hospital inpatient and outpatient services, physician services, X-rays and laboratory services, and physical therapy are covered without any limits on quantity. Skilled nursing-home facilities and home health care are limited in quantity, as is the care for mental disorders. Vision and hearing tests (as well as eyeglasses and hearing aids) and dental care are provided for children only. Long-term care for the physically and mentally incapacitated is usually excluded from the program.

The exlusion of some services and the strict limits on the quantity of others have implications for the equity of the national health-insurance program. Health care is not really divisible. It cannot be confined to acute illness that can be treated in a short-term general hospital. Mental illness and physical paralysis, which require long-term care, are as much a medical problem as an acute disease; they have to be faced explicitly and not ignored implicitly. And because long-term care is expensive and beyond the means of many individuals who require such care, the issue of equity is pertinent; the national health-insurance system, which would spread the cost of therapy over the entire community, could greatly ease the financial burden that such care imposes on the patient and his family. In fact, the inclusion of long-term care in the program would not require much new funding because more than half the expenditure for such care is already being paid by the public sector.[22]

In addition, the scope of benefits is narrowed when covered services are subject to cost-sharing requirements. All proposed bills, except the "Health Security Act," specified a long list of copayments. Thus, the "Health Security Act," even if it has almost the same basket of covered services as other bills, provides more extensive benefits to patients. And curtailment of benefits through cost-sharing requirements not only affects the level of these benefits but also determines how they are distributed among different population groups. However, such direct payments serve as a convenient source of revenue supplementing the indirect payments that finance the national health-insurance program. The mix of direct (cost-shared) and indirect (prepaid) financing and its effects on equity in the distribution of benefits are more extensively discussed in the next section.

FINANCING

Direct participation by consumers of medical services in paying their bills has gained widespread acceptance. It can replace indirect payments as a source of revenue to defray the costs of such services, thus making an insurance plan more attractive to enrollees who do not anticipate heavy utilization of medical facilities. Cost sharing has several forms: initial full payments (deductibles), partial payments (coinsurance or copayments), and an upper limit on either the carrier's liability or the patient's responsibility for medical payments. All bills before the Ninety-fourth Congress proposed some upper limit on the cost-sharing amounts for covered services; but they differed in the method of setting the ceiling. Yet, in comparison with the situation under Medicare, where the patient's liability is open ended and that of the federal government is limited, any of the proposed provisions for an upper expense limit constitute a relief.

Cost-sharing amounts that are based either on the level of medical bills or on the number of service units consumed are independent of income. Such copayments, the same for different income levels, constitute a decreasing portion of income as income increases; their restraining effect gradually disappears as income levels rise. Hence, as can be inferred from the experience with Medicare, high-income persons are likely to pass the level of initial deductibles and to reach a fixed upper expense limit more often than persons who, because of their low or moderate income, are deterred or restricted by the copayment levels. A proportionally larger share of benefits from the national health-insurance program would therefore be diverted to high- and middle-income persons at the expense of their low- or moderate-income counterparts.

Mindful of this problem, and as a remedy for this situation, most bills propose to lower the cost-sharing amounts to be paid by the poor and low-income persons, i.e., to base copayments on income at least at the lower end of the income scale. Although appealing on paper, this solution is administratively complicated; it requires an income test to determine eligibility, and it creates a "notch" problem, or a situation where enrollees may want to keep their income below a certain level to avoid losing benefits.[23] Moreover, though these bills propose to subsidize the cost-sharing amounts of the poor and near-poor, they also permit an indirect subsidy through federal income-tax exemptions for the cost-sharing amounts paid by the affluent. And, while explicit subsidies, in the form of reduced copayments, are expected to fall off as income increases, implicit or tax-shelter subsidies actually increase with income.

This contradiction is even more striking when it is remembered that some proponents of a cost-sharing policy see in it not only a source of payment for medical care but also a rationing device. As such, it is designed to serve as a brake on utilization and to limit costs. Yet, the treatment of medical exemptions under the federal income tax counteracts the restraining effects that could be expected from positive cost sharing. And because the tax schedule specifies increasing marginal tax rates, the income-tax exemptions provide a greater subsidy for the copayments of the affluent. Moreover, the same bills that stipulate positive cost sharing also permit, or even encourage, supplementary private insurance against the personal outlays for the deductibles and coinsurance amounts; and this practice is unlikely to encourage restraint. Under these circumstances, if the cost-sharing policy restrains the use of medical services, it does so by restricting the consumption of health-care services by moderate- and lower-income persons more than the consumption of their middle- and high-income peers.

Indirect payments, if based on income, can equitably distribute the costs of health-care services. The issue of equity in indirect financing permeates every bill; though they may differ in specific provisions, bills can be classified into two groups with respect to the insurance base which they stipulate. One group requires premium levels to be proportional to income or earnings at least up to a specified income ceiling; the premiums are determined on a basis that applies equally to the entire population and collected by the federal government as a social-insurance tax. Another mandates that premiums are to be paid to private insurance organizations. The bills of the latter group specify what share of the premiums is paid directly by policyholders and what share is paid by them indirectly through their employers; the level of the premium is left to negotiation between employers and the insurance carriers. Enrollment in the private insurance plan is usually voluntary for the employee, but payment of premiums is obligatory for the employer. Individuals who are either self-employed or unemployed are entitled to purchase individual policies for which the premium levels are higher than those paid through group insurance. Thus, premium levels paid for private insurance protection do not reflect differences in income; instead they reflect differences in insurance risk (experience) and in employment status.

Private insurance premiums that are based on risk can be high relative to income. To counteract this effect, some bills specify direct and explicit subsidies that would depend on income, and for which eligibility would be determined by a means test. Moreover, as was stated earlier, though the national health-insurance bills propose to subsidize the premiums to be paid by low-income persons, they also permit an indirect subsidy through federal income-tax exemptions, and such subsidies constitute an increasingly larger share of the premiums as income levels increase (table 5.5). By contrast, premiums that are based on income and collected as social-insurance tax do not qualify for such tax exemptions.

The most prevalent form of private insurance is group insurance through employment, where the employer has the responsibility for negotiating the premium levels with the insurance organization and collecting premiums on its behalf. Premiums are determined according to insurance risk, based on the past experience of the group. Since an employer often pays a considerable proportion of the premiums, such an arrangement provides an incentive for the carrier and the employer to exclude high-risk persons from the insurance plan. If such exclusion is forbidden, there is a strong incentive to bar high-risk persons from employment altogether. Most bills specify that an individual who is not an employee can qualify for an individual policy or enroll in a government plan. But individual policyholders would have to pay much higher premiums than comparable members of a group plan.[24] Thus, depending on insurance risk and employment status, premium levels can be high relative to nonpoor income. Yet there is nothing inherent in a national health-insurance program that requires it to be tied to employment. Only through historical accident has health insurance become a fringe benefit of employment. In periods of unemployment, such a nexus creates additional hardships for unemployed persons, not only removing earnings, but also taking away their insurance protection or subjecting them to the much higher premiums of an individual policy.

If national health insurance is designed to protect consumers from facing large out-of-pocket payments in time of illness, then indirect financing through prepayment ought to constitute the major source of revenue for the program. Prepayment can serve to weaken the link between the distribution of income and the distribution of direct payments for medical services. The prepayment arrangements can be so structured as to spread the cost of medical care equitably across the entire population by basing prepayment levels on all incomes except public-assistance receipts and social-security benefits.[25] Moreover, these prepayment arrangements have to be "employment blind" and "risk blind." If they are not, then persons who have the "wrong" employment or risk status would be subject to a higher levy before they were entitled to the same benefits as their "right" counterparts.

Social insurance is blind to both employment and risk while private insurance is not. Social insurance can be sensitive to income [26] and private insurance cannot. Moreover, private insurance organizations are more likely to incur higher collection costs than the government would. The government, as an established tax collector, is well equipped to handle the collection of prepayment amounts at small marginal costs and without any of the marketing or advertising costs that are incurred by competing private organizations and passed on to policyholders. Thus, in the final analysis, the government can best secure an equitable distribution of the burden, and secure it at the least cost to the paying public.

ADMINISTRATION AND MANAGEMENT

The administration of national health insurance requires an organization which is in charge of collecting the indirect payments (premiums or taxes) and an organization that pays the benefits. Some bills assign a major role to the private insurance sector. For example, under the employer-employees plan, private insurance organizations sell policies and settle claims. Other bills, patterned on Medicare, specify that the federal government collects the health-insurance taxes and assigns the private insurance carriers the role of intermediaries or agents for the purpose of handling claims and making reimbursements. The Health Security Act relied solely on the public sector; the federal government would not only collect the health-insurance taxes and supplement them with funds from its general revenues, but it would also pay providers for the services that they would render to the entire population.

As was stated in the preceding section, the costs of collecting health-insurance premiums are likely to exceed the costs of collecting health-insurance taxes. Private organizations are likely to incur marketing costs in the process of competing against each other in an effort to secure the business; the federal government will not. The Internal Revenue Service (IRS) has the machinery to collect such taxes at a minimal additional cost. Moreover, since social-insurance taxes are based on income, they have a uniform tax base that applies to the entire population and a uniform pre-payment plan. And, when the setting of premium levels by the private sector requires a multitude of different arrangements, the cost of collecting such premiums is likely to rise. Thus, the multi-tier plans designed to subsidize the premium payments of the poor and the elderly are likely to be administratively complicated and costly. Similarly, when copayment levels are based on units of ser-vices or size of medical bills, they call for special arrangements to accommodate the indigent and the aged. A multi-tier system of paying cost-sharing amounts is likely to be administratively more expensive than a system which has no copayment requirements.

Equity considerations would suggest that national health in-surance cover the entire population for a broad range of health-care services, with indirect payments based on income and either with no copayments or with cost-sharing amounts that are linked to in-come for the entire population. Administrative efficiency would suggest a uniform financing plan instead of a multitude of different financial arrangements that adjust, in part, for differences in the economic fortunes of the enrolled population. But, legislators also weigh, in addition to the overall costs of a plan, their visibility in the budget; these considerations make it very likely that a health-in-surance law will stipulate some level of direct patient participation in paying medical bills.

For the purpose of avoiding too many complications and yet having cost-sharing amounts reflect income differences over the whole income range, it has been suggested that each family would be assured of a ceiling on its copayments, and that this upper limit would constitute a fixed share of income rather than a fixed level. The income-tax apparatus could be used to provide tax credits or refunds in order to offset any payments that exceeded the specified income share.[27] This policy would guarantee that the portion of income allocated to sharing the cost of covered services is the same across all income levels.

But, as the Medicare experience demonstrates, even when patients pay all the required cost-sharing amounts, they may still have to make additional payments to cover the difference between physician fees and the so-called allowable charges. In other words, since Medicare pays a predetermined reimbursement amount, and this is usually smaller than the physician fee, patients are obligated to pay the difference. Hence, bills which permit the same arrangements under national health insurance would require patients to pay more for the covered services than is specified by the cost-sharing amounts. In addition, some proposals exclude some costly services from coverage and strictly limit the quantity of others.

A case can therefore be made for setting an upper limit on the direct payments for *all* health-care services, and not only on copayments for covered services. This ceiling could be set at 10 percent of "adjusted gross income." As defined by the IRS, adjusted gross income excludes public-assistance and social-security transfers; hence, these cash transfers would not be counted in determining the base for computing the upper expense limit. Persons who depend solely on such transfers would have to make no payment for their health care; persons who have small incomes would pay very little for their medical services; and persons with large incomes are likely to pay for all their medical services.

Implementation of this policy would require that patients record all their medical payments on a special form; and if the total exceeded 10 percent of their adjusted gross income, they could claim a tax credit or a refund on their annual tax return. The additional cost to the federal government for checking the itemized medical bills would be relatively low since the IRS has the machinery required to check itemized deductions. However, such a system could obligate patients to pay out amounts that would be refunded or credited to their account only after a time lag of several months to a year, and this lag may cause hardships. Hence, it is suggested that a credit-card system to be set up, so that every enrollee would have a credit card to obtain services without immediate payment. The providers of services or an agency on their behalf could collect payments for services "charged" from patients or from the federal government.

Such a policy amounts to full payment (deductible) on all medical expenses up to the ceiling. In comparison with a system that specifies initially lower deductibles in combination with a layer of partial payments (coinsurance), this system would reduce the work load of both administrators and patients. Patients would not be turned into bookkeepers who maintain extensive records on deductibles and coinsurance amounts, a time-consuming chore currently required of persons who want to keep track of their reimbursements under Medicare. Yet, some proponents of positive cost sharing consider a layer of partial payments useful as a brake on utilization. Martin Feldstein argues that an expense limit which amounts to 10 percent of income should be extended over a considerably larger expenditure range by using partial payments together with an initial deductible.[28] However, since the physician and not the patient determines the use of medical facilities, the cost consciousness of patients is irrelevant; sick patients will only rarely refuse to follow their physicians' orders because of cost considerations.

A policy which guarantees that the upper limit on direct payments is set equitably does not necessarily remove inequitable financial restrictions below the ceiling; and such restrictions could discourage medically desirable (preventive) or necessary (early detection) utilization. While health-care administrators should restrict the use of the system for truly inconsequential health problems, they would not want to impose barriers on desirable and necessary services, especially if delay in obtaining them may prove to have grave and costly consequences. It is therefore suggested that preventive services such as immunization and family planning be exempted from all cost-sharing requirements, as should be all tests which screen possible diseases in population groups at risk. Since lack of time and competing claims on the family budget may cause delays in obtaining such services and undergoing tests, a national health-insurance system which removes financial barriers might avoid some unnecessary postponements.

It has been argued that a national health-insurance plan which covers the entire population for all health-care services is doomed to fail under the weight of its costs. Cost increases could be expected even without a national health-insurance system because of the rising number of older Americans and the ability of medicine to prolong the lives of more persons with chronic health problems. The Department of Health, Education, and Welfare (HEW) estimated the cost of the major programs introduced in the Ninety-third Congress.[29] Though the figures quoted may underestimate actual costs, their relationship to each other and to the level of health-care expenditures in the absence of national health insurance may be instructive. Without a national insurance plan, personal expenditures for health care were expected to rise 23 percent in two years to $103 billion in fiscal 1975; and the most expensive program, the Health Security Act, would have induced additional expenditures of about 13 percent. Moreover, some bills were more likely to be visible in the government's budget, especially if the federal administration rather than the private sector collected the revenues. Cost-sharing amounts requiring direct payments by patients are therefore likely to be an integral part of a national health-insurance system because they serve as a substitute for health-insurance taxes; hence, such copayments should be not only equitable but also administratively simple.

Although some cost increases may be unavoidable, there are areas in which savings could be made. The Health Security Act proposed that the country be divided into health-care areas, each with its own budget and administration and with the authority to allocate national health-insurance funds. The National Health Planning and Resources Development Act of 1974 (PL93-641) provided for a network of local Health Systems Agencies that are to report directly to the secretary of HEW and are empowered to oversee the spending of federal health-care funds in their respective areas. Such agencies as well as the state planning agencies may be able to reduce or eliminate underutilized facilities (e.g., hospital departments with low occupancy rates) and prevent duplication of expensive equipment. As suggested by Patricia Fishbein and Frank van Dyke,[30] a national health-insurance plan can impose sanctions or devise incentives for providers of health-care services to induce them to comply with the guidelines of the planning law. The reimbursement policies and procedures of the system could dovetail with the goals of national planning. The Health Security Act specified that the local administrative areas for the national health-insurance program should be the same as the Health Systems Agencies areas under the planning law. The administrators in each local area could be required to withhold national-health insurance funds from providers of services (institutions or individuals) who do not comply with the specific guidelines of the local planning agencies.

Moreover, since physicians, in fact, direct the health team, prescribing diagnostic tests and treatment procedures that can be costly, their activities should be subject to review and their fees subject to strict control. Steps in this direction have been taken since 1972 when Professional Standards Review Organizations were introduced to monitor, on a day-to-day basis, the quality and costs of health-care services prescribed for patients enrolled under Medicare and Medicaid. And, since medical care depends on decisions that are made by physicians, ready access to them is essential but not always forthcoming. In sparsely populated areas, patients have to travel long distances before they can find medical help; in central cities and other urban areas, the poor are often limited to obtaining medical care in crowded emergency rooms, and so are their more affluent peers at night, on weekends, and on holidays. Yet, without available manpower and facilities, the entitlement to a fair share in health care under a national health-insurance system would amount only to paper rights without much substance.

Physicians are not usually located in rural or otherwise remote areas. A study by Victor R. Fuchs and Marcia J. Kramer suggests that physicians tend to locate in places which have acceptable or good medical facilities in hospitals and medical schools.[31] When physicians are trained to regard medical cure rather than care as their most important function, employing hospital-based techniques for diagnosis and therapy, it is not surprising that they consider hospitals and biomedical research centers essential. Fuchs and Kramer also find that physicians are attracted to high-income urban locations for other than professional reasons. Thus there are large disparities among states in the ratio of active physicians and dentists to population. At the end of 1972, the District of Columbia led the nation in the ratio of active physicians and dentists to 100,000 persons in the civilian population (340 and 91 respectively); New York State came in second (197 and 68) and Massachusetts third (178 and 55). By comparison, Mississippi (75 physicians and 27 dentists), South Carolina (85 and 26), and South Dakota (72 and 34) had a shortage of such professional persons.[32]

The maldistribution of physicians and dentists manifests itself not only in location but also in specialties. States which have proportionally more physcans also have proportionally more specialists. This has led to an underutilization of highly skilled and expensively trained manpower (e.g., surgeons) [33] in metropolitan areas and to a shortage of such physicians in underserved areas. Yet, the cost of training a physician has only partly been paid by private tuition. Directly through capitation grants and indirectly through sponsored research and through tax exemptions for foundation grants and personal contributions, the federal government has been extensively supporting the education of physicians and dentists.[34] Hence, the Congress and the administration may be expected to use the power of the purse to change the distribution of professional manpower and to plan the training of specialists.

Conclusion

In his book *Who Shall Live?* [35] Victor R. Fuchs suggests that, given the current state of the art, medicine is unlikely to alleviate the major health problems of Americans by adding more physicians and hospital beds to the current supply. Potentially destructive lifestyles and hazardous jobs will continue to be detrimental to good health. R. M. Hartwell and Mark Perlman [36] point out that, historically, major gains in health, as measured by increased life expectancy, cannot be attributed to sophisticated medical care but rather to better nutrition and sanitary conditions. It may be argued, therefore, that the greatest potential for improving health is not in providing more medical care but in minimizing the health hazards of industrial pollution and emotional distress. In other words, scarce resources should be allocated to creating a safer and more relaxed environment rather than pouring additional funds into the seemingly bottomless pit of the medical-services industry.

Yet, when a disease strikes, Americans expect convenient access to health-care facilities and assurance that the best feasible diagnosis and therapy are provided without in the process depleting their economic resources. Private insurance and Medicare have not lived up to these expectations because they have not eliminated the threat of financial distress; Medicaid, which has removed financial restrictions for many of the needy, has done so at the price of poor medical care. A national health-insurance plan can provide an equitable solution to the payment problem without creating a two-class system of health care; yet the implementation of such a program would commit additional scarce resources to the medical-services sector of the economy. Careful planning and allocation of such resources would be required to eliminate the deficiencies of the prevailing maldistribution. Moreover, a reorganization of the delivery system is required in order to prevent the system from failing under the burden of inordinately high costs of administration and management.

HEW and Congress have been trying to improve the planning of health-care facilities and the distribution of health-care professionals. These efforts may provide a framework within which a national health-insurance system would be implemented. Delay in enacting health insurance may turn out to have been a blessing in disguise. With machinery in place to control the use of medical facilities and trained personnel, a framework could be established within which the health-care delivery system would accommodate the increased demand for medical services expected with the enactment of a national health-insurance law. And though the health-insurance system is primarily designed to solve the payment problem for patients, the funds that it will generate and its reimbursement procedures could induce providers to comply with nationwide planning goals. Equity and efficiency considerations would have to be balanced to guarantee a fair distribution of health-care services and payments in a system that is viable and that will not crumble under the load of administration and management costs.

The concern with equity calls for the following policy recommendations: (1) Enrollment of the population in a national health-insurance plan should be universal and mandatory. (2) Premiums on health insurance should be based on adjusted gross income across all income levels. (3) A ceiling on direct payments for *all* medical services should be set at a fixed percentage of adjusted gross income, and preventive services and screening tests should be exempted from any cost-sharing requirements.

Efficiency in the administration of national health insurance would call for the following institutional arrangements: (1) The IRS should collect the health-insurance taxes and provide tax credits or refunds for any direct payments that exceed the upper expense limit. (2) A credit-card system should be established to enable patients to obtain services without immediate payments; private insurance organizations might be given the task of acting as credit agencies for those consumers and providers of medical services who elect to join this system. (3) All direct payments should be full payments, and there should not be any additional layer of partial payments or coinsurance amounts.

Efficiency in managing the medical-services delivery system would mandate that service providers meet the following requirements in order to qualify for national health-insurance funds. (1) All institutions (hospitals, nursing homes, home health-care agencies, health-maintenance organizations, etc.) would have to obtain prior approval for their budgets, submit their expenditures to a strict audit, and open their financial records to the public. (2) Physicians and dentists would have to adhere to a strict fee schedule, periodically determined and publicly displayed; no physician or dentist would be allowed to charge any patient an amount that exceeded the fees set in the schedule. (3) Similarly, all providers of out-of-hospital ancillary services, supporting appliances, and prescription drugs would have to adhere to a price list set periodically and displayed in public. (4) Hospitals which have a training program for specialists would have to follow national guidelines with respect to training specialized manpower.

6

AFDC:
Symptom and Potential

WINIFRED BELL

In recent years public assistance has changed remarkably. The adult programs, Old Age Assistance (OAA), Aid to the Blind (AB), and Aid to the Permanently and Totally Disabled (APTD), graduated to a mini negative income tax called Supplementary Security Income (SSI), and new goals were grafted on the program for young families, Aid to Families with Dependent Children (AFDC). But the burdens on public welfare and its accomplishments still depend largely on what happens elsewhere—in the labor market, the housing market, the health-care system, tax policy, other cash transfers, family formation and breakdown rates, patterns of family support, population trends, and the state of the economy.

In the following pages, the shifting roles of public assistance are reviewed as a backdrop for discussing the performance and potentials of means-tested programs, especially AFDC, for distributing a larger share of income to the poor. This has never been an explicit goal of selective programs. They have simply shored up income modestly during periods of particular hardship in the lives of poor people. But growing awareness of persistent inequities in the economic structure has drawn attention to the need for income strategies that not only reduce poverty but also increase the share of national income that goes into poor homes. Does AFDC or any other means-tested approach have something to contribute to this effort? If so, what is the role and how can programs best be designed to achieve it?

The Evolution of Public Assistance

When the federal government joined the partnership of states and counties to finance public assistance during the 1930s, thereby creating a nationwide public-welfare system, the social context and program goals were very different from what they are today. The depression was primarily an experience in joblessness and plummeting community purchasing power. By 1935, the social insurances were blueprinted, but no benefits would be forthcoming until 1940. From the beginning it was recognized that benefits would have to be supplemented by private savings if most retired, aged, and unemployed citizens were to sustain even modest standards of living. This meant that during their productive years the supply of jobs had to be sufficient to go around. The federal government's chief answer to the cry for more jobs was the Works Progress Administration (WPA) which cost twice as much as public aid between 1935 and 1939 and almost equaled the national investment in public education. The program was designed primarily for able-bodied men, especially fathers.

But this still left a good many households without wage earners. Federal-state public-assistance grants-in-aid were designed to fill part of the gap. Three easily identified population groups were nominated for assistance: the aged, blind, and young fatherless families. All three were traditional objects of charity and compassion. All three were confronted with a relatively long risk of poverty. All three typically earned very low wages, if any. Without alternative income, though, some members of these groups might seek work in an already glutted labor market, thereby replacing able-bodied men and further depressing wages. So there were clear advantages to keeping them out of the labor market by providing modest, steady public aid. In doing so, federal planners apparently expected that when the nation recovered from the economic doldrums, states and localities would reassert their age-old interest in public welfare and organize statewide general-assistance programs to care for poor people excluded from other cash transfers and from the job market.

Within this context, federal involvement in public welfare was viewed as transitional, supplemental, and residual, pending a return to full employment and the maturing of the social insurances and state-local general-assistance programs. People even claimed that as these events came to pass, the federally aided public-assistance programs would "wither away." Almost forty years later, a few experts were surprised that the plan worked out so differently.[1] What they overlooked is that part of the blueprint was changed, part was delayed, and other parts were scuttled within the first decade.

As a matter of historical record, the OAA caseload grew until the mid-fifties, but even though it declined in the following years, by 1973, when with other adult public-assistance programs it was transformed into SSI and largely taken over by the federal government, the caseload still exceeded 1.5 million senior citizens. Why had OAA persisted so long? Two important reasons are that planned social-security benefit increases were sometimes delayed during the early years, and more than three decades elapsed before automatic cost-of-living adjustments were authorized. Even when OASDI benefits finally caught up with and exceeded OAA grants, since the former were wage related, the lowest-paid workers, who were least able to save for the future, ended with very low benefits. For this group, often the only answer was OAA supplementation. Other OASDI beneficiaries had also counted on private pensions, but not until 1974 did Congress take steps to protect their vesting, and so this group too often had no recourse but OAA supplementation. While performing these necessary functions, OAA could scarcely "wither away." Women's benefits (whether as former workers or as dependents) were well behind men's, and so it is not surprising that almost 70 percent of the OAA caseload in recent years has consisted of aged women.

The point is that public assistance, being income conditioned and individualized, is peculiarly dependent on what happens to other systems in its orbit, and this means any program, policy, or social or economic trend that has an impact on family poverty. Public assistance is the last defense against poverty, always relatively ready to compensate for the failure of other cash-transfer systems. This unique responsiveness and flexibility is an important virtue. It is seen in its purest form in OAA, where eligibility was relatively unconstrained by social controls and therefore more directly adaptive to financial need among the elderly. The quality is still apparent in AFDC even though efforts to enforce conformity to legitimacy norms and the work ethic periodically cause caseloads to rise or fall regardless of trends in family poverty.[2]

Even a cursory review of events that shaped AFDC gives clues to why the program, far from withering away, has grown remarkably in recent years. In the volatile manner of American politics, once World War II brought full employment, the need for a peacetime WPA was forgotten, and the program was repealed.

After the war, Congress formally rejected a genuine full-employment policy, falling back instead on a toothless assurance of efforts toward such a goal, which meant that there was no guarantee of sufficient jobs to go around. In similar spirit, states neglected unemployment compensation, permitting benefits to deteriorate in value while eligibility became riddled with constraints. One result is that less than half of all unemployed workers in 1975 received unemployment benefits. The notion of extending and improving general assistance also held little appeal to postwar state and local leaders and taxpayers. Many states refused to aid households with able-bodied adults, whether or not jobs were available, and some still do; and in no state is general assistance perceived, organized, or financed as a constructive family welfare program.[3] This role fell by default to AFDC, where for many reasons it could only be performed indifferently.

Designed essentially for fatherless families in a nation where policy planners assumed that most able-bodied men would either work or be insured during periods of unemployment, AFDC during the postwar years had to accommodate to very different circumstances. Family sociologists agree that the earning power of men has a great deal to do with family formation and marital stability, and in turn these variables influence the number of families who will need public aid. As babies, family breakdown, and unemployment surged after World War II, and unemployment rates gradually inched upward after each recession, it was inevitable that AFDC caseloads and costs would rise and that in time taxpayer tempers would become short indeed with the favored families that had at least some modicum of steady public support. By the same token, the existence of AFDC permitted leaders to postpone coming to grips with two basic problems: the need for more jobs at decent wages and the need for better unemployment insurance coverage. Only in 1961 when extreme and prolonged poverty in Appalachia convinced federal leadership to open the doors of AFDC to unemployed two-parent families was there a breakthrough for families with poor able-bodied fathers.

With this step came an interest in paid work as a desired goal for all AFDC families. As part of the War on Poverty and later in the 1967 public-welfare amendments to the Social Security Act, it became national policy to press AFDC mothers into the labor market or, if there were no suitable jobs, into vocational training, menial work relief, or public-service employment. Since AFDC is frequently, though incorrectly, perceived as a caseload of black families, these policies have serious racial overtones.[4] But that has not diverted reformers from insisting that the shift in goals is in the families' interest. What every family needs most is a wage earner, so the argument goes, and, implicitly, this role takes precedence over others like mothering or homemaking.[5] Birthed in economic theory, the argument reflects the bias that caring for one's own children and home is synonymous with leisure, the only productive use of time being paid employment. From this perspective, if poor mothers choose not to engage in paid work, logically they should pay a price, as they do in negative-income-tax plans with their heavy emphasis on low basic guarantees for nonworking families and relatively generous cash incentives for working families. But however neat and trim such welfare reforms appear to be, in the real world they produce some startling inequities and anomalies. Inevitably, welfare policies and proposals that reward some lucky mothers for being free to work and for finding jobs, that penalize others for not working (whether the decision is voluntary or involuntary), and that press women into the labor market irrespective of the labor demand in their communities have proved to be controversial and expensive. Until the controversies are resolved, no large-scale welfare reform is likely to occur.

How Much Money Does AFDC Redistribute?

Judging by the clamor over rising welfare costs and the complaints over fraud in AFDC, one might assume that a significant portion of personal income is now going into the pockets of welfare families. As a matter of record public-assistance income rose only from 0.8 percent to 1.1 percent of total personal income in the nation between 1960 and 1973. In 1960 the federally aided adult programs (for the aged, blind, and disabled) transferred 0.5 percent of personal income to poor adults, while AFDC transferred only 0.2 percent to young families. By 1973 the relationship was reversed, with AFDC responsible for redistributing 0.7 percent of personal income and the adult programs, 0.3 percent. This is a paltry share from any viewpoint. But the noteworthy trends are that OAA expenditures fell more rapidly as a percentage of personal income than the OAA caseload declined, and AFDC expenditures rose more sluggishly than the AFDC caseload increased, so that the share per person in both programs failed to keep pace with the growth in personal income. (When public-assistance programs are compared, it should be kept in mind that the aged dominate the adult programs, and for the majority of recipients, OAA supplements OASDI benefits. This is not at all the situation in the children's program. Only 33 percent of AFDC families had any nonwelfare income in 1973.) [6]

There are other ways of looking at this matter. Economists point out that means-tested programs like AFDC are more efficient economically and are therefore the preferred antipoverty investment. They refer to the fact that selective programs, being designed solely for poor people, channel cash transfers to poor households, while universal approaches such as social security or most veterans programs, for instance, distribute benefits to rich and poor alike. If the only goal is to shore up the income of poor families, however slightly, then AFDC could be viewed as an effective program. But if the goal is to prevent poverty, to move families out of poverty, or to redistribute income more equitably between affluent and poor people, then AFDC as presently constituted is accomplishing very little, as judged by some recent studies. When Irene Lurie measured the economic efficiency of various cash transfers in 1966, she found that 87 percent of AFDC households had incomes below the poverty threshold before the welfare check arrived, as contrasted with 84 percent in OAA, 63 percent in the other two adult public-assistance programs, 49 percent in OASDI, and a mere 9 percent in veterans' compensation.[7]

In 1973 part of this study was replicated and extended in the Center for Studies in Income Maintenance Policy at New York University. By then, about 92 percent of AFDC families were poor before the welfare check arrived, but fully 76 percent remained poor after the check was added to other family income.[8] Table 6.1 shows how pre-AFDC income for different types of families compares to the poverty threshold and what proportion of each group moved out of poverty with AFDC. Large and Spanish-surname families and those with parents of very limited education were most likely to be poor without the AFDC check, and American Indians were least likely to move out of poverty with the help of AFDC— the program treated even large families better. Whether families lived in urban or rural areas made little difference, but which region they lived in was very important. This difference was not just a matter of different welfare standards. Different wage levels in combination with welfare work incentives also contributed their share of inequity. In January 1973, average monthly earnings of fully employed AFDC mothers varied from $268 in the South to $353 in the north-central states, $385 in the Northeast, and $391 in the West.

Table 6.1 Poverty Status of AFDC Families before and after AFDC, January 1973 (Percent) [a]

| | Families below Poverty Threshold [b] | | |
	Before AFDC	After AFDC	Rate of Decrease
All families	92	76	17
Size of Family			
2 persons	91	71	22
3 persons	90	68	24
4 persons	93	79	15
5 persons	95	84	12
6 persons	97	84	13
7 persons	97	86	11
Race or Ethnicity			
White (excluding Spanish origin)	91	71	22
Spanish origin	97	79	19
Black	93	81	13
American Indian	95	86	9
Residence			
Inside SMSA	93	76	18
Outside SMSA	92	77	16
Education of Head			
Elementary	97	84	13
1–3 years high school	94	79	16
High-school graduate	87	69	21
College	87	67	23
Region			
Northeast	92	62	33
North Central	92	76	17
South	95	91	5
West	91	78	13

Source: U.S. Department of Health, Education, and Welfare, Social and Rehabilitation Service, National Center for Social Statistics, *AFDC Survey, 1973.* Derived in Center for Studies in Income Maintenance Policy.

[a] Estimate based on 65 percent sample of AFDC Survey schedules; excludes Puerto Rico, Virgin Islands, Guam, and Massachusetts.

[b] Poverty threshold as of 1972; families and income as recorded in welfare record January 1973. Monthly income annualized. The welfare definition of income includes cash value imputed to income in kind and a miscellaneous item, "other cash income," together consisting of less than 3 percent of total income.

The pitfalls of assigning responsibility for relieving family poverty to fifty-one states, with no national standards of need and few federal controls (except in the service of saving money), are illustrated by the variations in the incidence of poverty before and after AFDC. Restrictive welfare policies and low standards in California strongly influence the western rate, with the result that only 13 percent fewer families in the West were poor after the AFDC payment. But in the Northeast, the poverty roster dropped by 33 percent after the welfare check arrived. Even though southern states made remarkable economic gains in the past decade, welfare payments lagged behind. In 1973, they were still so low in most southern states that they served to reduce the poor AFDC population by only 5 percent.

But what does the overall picture convey about AFDC? For most families the program merely makes the difference between living in more or less poverty. Generalizing from the 1973 analysis, the poverty deficit, the difference between total family income and the poverty threshold, was reduced by 72 percent with the arrival of the AFDC check. This still left family income on the average almost $1,000 below the threshold. This is a grave deficit under any circumstance, but since 1959 the poverty threshold has fallen progressively behind median family income—a point referred to in chapter 1.[9] Had the threshold been fully adjusted each year to assure a similar relative definition of poverty from one year to the next, by 1973 it would have been at least 25 percent higher, or about $5,700 instead of $4,540 for an urban four-person family. Fewer than 7 percent of four-person AFDC families in January 1973 had incomes over $5,700, and the poorest three-quarters of the caseload averaged about $2,000 less.

In other words, when the poverty threshold is adjusted realistically, AFDC turns out to be useful primarily as a program to reduce family poverty, not to end it. In this sense, it falls short as

an antipoverty device, just as earlier it was shown to be a weak redistributive measure.

The Dynamics of AFDC and their
Implications for Income Redistribution

If cash-transfer programs are to play a significant role in redistributing income more equitably, they must have the capacity to grow
and thrive, gradually covering a larger share of poor people and
doing so more generously. Different programs have their unique
patterns of change depending on many factors, including political
popularity, method of financing, administrative auspices and style,
eligibility conditions and procedures, and method of fixing and
changing benefit levels. It is no accident that the life histories of the
social-security system and AFDC contrast so sharply. The former is
popular and well nurtured by powerful interest groups of senior citizens who are also voters. It is funded through federal taxes, earmarked for it, on virtually all workers and employers, and administered in a nice, clean, computerized fashion by the federal
government. Eligibility is defined precisely by statute and for the
largest group of beneficiaries turns entirely on the simple question
of age. Benefits are fixed by statute and are now protected with
cost-of-living adjustments.

AFDC is a very different program. Perhaps no public service suffers from such chronic political sniping or is more often the
object of censure by the public and the press. Caseload growth and
higher costs are virtually always regarded as major catastrophes in
spite of the number of poor children in the population or the absence of alternative sources of support. The program is financed by
two, sometimes three, levels of government, and since it is grant

aided, the final expenditures unfortunately depend not on the federal government with its broad tax base but on lesser jurisdictions.[10] Not only are decisions at all levels necessary to bring about system changes, but also, instead of one welfare standard, there are 55 standards. Within very broad limits, states define eligibility and administrative procedures, and local agencies, sometimes by plan, more often by default, have broad discretion in implementing the program. No jurisdiction does much to keep the system under control or to account for the expenditure of public funds, and rules are so numerous and complex as to give the impression of having been created to facilitate and obscure errors.[11]

These differences between OASDI and AFDC are well known, as is the fact that while the number of OASDI beneficiaries grows in relatively predictable strides, the AFDC caseload rises and wanes with little relationship to the prevalence of childhood poverty, employment or unemployment trends, or even the adoption of laws intended to stimulate or inhibit caseload growth. For instance, from 1960 to 1967, a period of declining unemployment, the caseload grew by 50 percent. The 1967 public-welfare amendments, designed to restrict caseload growth, heralded years of unprecedented growth: 17.3 percent increase between 1967 and 1968, 23.3 percent in the following year, and another 36.1 percent from 1969 to 1970. As the storm clouds of recession gathered, the rate of growth declined, plummeting to 1.1 percent in 1973. Then between mid-1973 and mid-1974, as the unemployment rate rose from 5.0 to 5.6 and was much higher in urban slums and for women, the caseload dropped by 100,000 children and adults, and federal welfare officials pointed with pride to the success of their new restrictive policies.[12] Their pleasure was premature: by late summer the upward climb had begun.

Piven and Cloward handed policy makers a tool for understanding cyclical welfare trends when they reviewed long sweeps of history and concluded that public welfare helps to stabilize social systems, expanding in times of civic disorder (often but not necessarily associated with widespread economic collapse), and contracting after law and order are reestablished and it is politic, once more, to use welfare programs to reinforce work norms.[13] These two scholars were closely involved with a movement designed in the 1960s to upset these seemingly ineluctable cycles. First, law students instructed the poor about their legal rights, and poverty lawyers challenged arbitrary policies and intake practices in a series of class-action suits, winning some resounding victories that opened the program to thousands of families.[14] Then the National Welfare Rights Organization, under the vigorous and brilliant leadership of George Wylie, undertook to destigmatize welfare, spread the word in urban slums about welfare rights, encourage families to apply for aid, and once on the rolls, to press for everything they had coming. This effort precipitated a flood of applications so that even after urban riots and ghetto fires were quelled and cooled, the restive lines at urban welfare agencies continued to grow.

Together, these developments spelled failure for the one drastic step taken by the federal government before 1970 to control caseload growth. In 1967, as part of a package of amendments, Congress passed what became known as the "absent parent freeze," thereby precipitating one of the more unassailable coalitions in recent public-welfare history. This provision set a ceiling on federal funding in behalf of "absent-parent families," the most rapidly growing sector of the caseloads. Henceforth, Congress declared, if this sector exceeded a defined share of each state's caseload, the cost of supporting the increment of families over the ceiling would not earn federal matching funds. The law did not permit states to exclude eligible families or to create waiting lists. It simply required states to pay the entire bill for maintaining families above the prescribed ceiling, thus increasing the burden on states and cities that were already crying for fiscal relief. So state and local leaders and welfare expansionists joined battle with congressional delegations, and soon the "freeze" thawed. A few years later it evaporated in the form of a little amendment tacked onto an excise-tax bill for chicory roots.[15]

But to earn a place in a family of cash transfers that can be counted on to redistribute a larger share of personal income to poor families, a program can scarcely depend for growth on exogenous forces, charismatic leadership, or unintended consequences. There must be an inner dynamic for growth and improvement, a forward momentum on the part of the system itself. In practical terms, this means that welfare caseloads should continue to grow while poor children are still uncovered by public cash transfers and that welfare grants should improve in all regions until they reach some reasonable standard.

In order to assess the growth dynamic of AFDC and to gain greater understanding of the conditions that promote or impede a forward thrust, we examined in detail four amendments to federal AFDC law during the 1960s. Three were deliberate efforts to increase the caseload by extending eligibility. The fourth was a package of work incentives that was intended eventually to reduce caseloads by helping families to become self-supporting. How did states respond to these amendments? Was their full potential realized, and if so, how soon? How much was thereby distributed to poor families? What types of families received the largest share, and why? Does the outcome suggest how lustier, healthier selective programs could be designed?

AFDC-UP

As noted earlier, prior to 1961, AFDC covered needy children only when a parent was dead, disabled, or absent from the home. But the 1957–59 recession and the long-term hardships suffered by families in Appalachia convinced the Kennedy Administration to recommend that eligibility be extended to children with unemployed parents. This was done on a temporary basis in 1961. For one year the federal government was to match the costs that states would incur if they liberalized their laws in this way. In 1962 there was a five-year extension, and finally in 1967 the provision became a permanet part of AFDC law. But in the process Congress cut back the definition of "unemployed parent" (UP). Only fathers with a relatively steady and recent attachment to the labor force could qualify. So jobless mothers and the hard-core unemployed whose plight inspired the amendment were excluded, and every state with an AFDC-UP program had to retrench.

Politically, it is much easier for states to add a new program or shift families from one program to another than it is to close down a program, thereby disqualifying a sizable group of families from public aid. It is not surprising, then, that states that promptly elected AFDC-UP in the early 1960s were chiefly those that saved money by doing so and had a program of their own in reserve if the federal one were discontinued. They were primarily industrial states where state-local general-assistance programs had long helped unemployed and underemployed families. Quite a share of the general-assistance caseload could be transferred outright to AFDC, with the result that as the AFDC-UP caseload grew, state-local general-assistance caseloads fell. Not until 1967 did they begin to climb again.[16]

In the early 1960s, AFDC budget standards were often higher than general-assistance standards, and so even though the new program served chiefly to conserve state and local funds rather than redistributing income to the poor, families also prospered somewhat. In 1968, though, general-assistance family payments shot ahead, and by 1974 they were half again as high as AFDC grants. So in some states the existence of AFDC-UP freed state and local funds for other poor families and for higher grants.

Jurisdictions with very limited general-assistance programs, as in most southern and border states, rarely extended public aid to families with able-bodied adults, and then chiefly in emergencies. They had nothing to gain financially from opting for AFDC-UP. They also had relatively poor unemployment-compensation programs and depressed wage structures. These were the very states that were needed in the fold to chalk up a good record of income redistribution for AFDC-UP, but most of them remained steadfastly opposed to the notion of public support for able-bodied fathers.

A brief review of state response to the amendment will clarify the issues. In 1961, 14 states amended their laws to approve AFDC-UP. Then the excitement dwindled. Only 3 followed suit in 1962, 1 more in 1963. During the balance of the decade, the number graduallly increased, although some states accepted very few families and often interrupted or discontinued the program. In 1970, more than three-quarters of the unemployed-father families lived in 7 states: California, Illinois, Massachusetts, New York, Oregon, Pennsylvania, and West Virginia. By that year, 29 jurisdictions had approved the program at one time or another.[17]

In 1971 the caseload peaked and states began instituting restrictions. New Jersey turned to a cheaper substitute, a Working Poor program with substantially lower benefits. Nationwide, despite worsening economic conditions and rising rates of unemployment, the AFDC-UP caseload dropped by 30 percent between December 1971 and December 1972. Part of the problem was that although welfare caseloads are flexible, welfare administration generally lags behind economic trends. As late as 1974, when stagflation was brooding over the land, federal officials were still trying to discourage people from applying for help. They proposed new WIN regulations requiring that parents not merely register for job training or employment but engage in as many "job searches" as state administrators chose to require before accepting applications for public aid.[18]

From 1961 through 1973, AFDC-UP was responsible for distributing some $2.7 billion to families, or about 6.4 percent of the total expenditures for AFDC payments ($42.7 billion). In March 1974, when there were only 102,627 AFDC-UP families, the Bureau of the Census estimated that the poverty roster included some 1.5 million male-headed families with children. Almost one-third of the fathers were unemployed part or all of 1973. Some could have qualified for AFDC whether or not they were unemployed because they were the only parent at home, but far more were excluded because of the restrictive definition of unemployment and the refusal of about half of the states to adopt AFDC-UP.

Second-Parent Amendment

The next amendment, effective in October 1962, and also optional, assured federal matching funds for the cost of including a second parent in the assistance budget when both parents were at home and one was disabled or unemployed. Until 1950, only the children's needs were considered in AFDC budgets.[19] Then federal matching funds were authorized for one "caretaking" adult. Beginning in 1962, disabled and unemployed fathers could have their financial needs taken into account.

In this provision too some states led the way. Before 1962 they had considered the needs of a second "essential person," usually an adult, and simply paid the cost themselves. So, to some extent, this new federal provision also redistributed income among levels of government rather than among income classes.

States responded in a livelier manner to this policy change: 25 signed up in 1962, 5 more in 1963, 8 in 1964. By the end of 1972, it was in effect in 49 jurisdictions, including the District of Columbia, the Virgin Islands, and Guam. Only Alaska, Minnesota, Mississippi, and Puerto Rico had no such provision in effect that year.

Inevitably, the impact of the second-parent policy depended on how many disabled- and unemployed-father families were accepted. In 1973, when about 16 percent of the AFDC caseload consisted of two-parent families, 13 percent of all families had two adults included in the assistance unit. From the inception of this amendment through 1973, it is estimated to have been responsible for distributing about $1.1 billion in AFDC funds, or about 2.5 percent of total AFDC payments.[20] (Since second parents in AFDC-UP families are included in the estimate of costs for both AFDC-UP and the second-parent amendment, the estimates for the two provisions are not additive.)

If the needs of another adult or an older child, not simply a second parent, could have been added to the family budget, as is currently done in some states at their own expense, the amendment would probably have fit the circumstances of AFDC family life much better. Quite a few out-of-school daughters over 18 years of age must be staying at home to help their mothers or fathers care for younger children or tending to sick or disabled parents. Grandmothers too old for paid employment and too young to qualify for SSI must live with some AFDC families. They probably help mothers a good deal, and families undoubtedly share whatever they have with them. In the end, not including them in the family budget distorts family needs and expenditures and exaggerates what the program provides for children.

18- to 21-Year-Old School Children

In October 1964 AFDC was extended to needy youth between 18 and 21 years of age if they attended vocational or high school. In the following year the provision was broadened to cover colleges and universities. These changes were adopted after President Kennedy's Back-to-School Drive in the summer of 1963 dramatized how many AFDC children dropped or were pushed out of school prematurely.[21] As teachers, social workers, and Peace Corps trainees were sent into homes to learn about the problems and invite youth back to school, records were collected on age and grade levels. It was soon apparent that many AFDC youngsters were two or more grades behind their age group, and that among other problems, becoming ineligible for program benefits on their eighteenth birthday made it difficult if not impossible to continue in school. Without a high-school diploma their job future could only be insecure. Prior to 1964, North Dakota and Wisconsin routinely used state funds to help older school children. The new amendments to federal law provided inducement for all states to do so.

States fairly promptly adopted one or the other of the amendments, which were in effect in 45 jurisdictions by 1968. But during the 1970s the tide began to shift. The extension of voting rights to 18-year-olds became the excuse for disqualifying them from AFDC. Legislation in Washington in 1971 lowered the eligible age to 18. Then Tennessee recognized 18-year-olds as adults and disqualified them for AFDC unless they were already parents and applied in their own right. Indiana dropped the age to 18 in September 1972. So once more, hopes were raised only to be dashed again.

In the spring of 1973 the Bureau of the Census estimated that about 954,000 poor children between 18 and 21 years old lived in their parental homes. Slightly under 187,000 turned up in the AFDC caseload in the January 1973 survey. This count excluded Massachusetts youth, since the state did not participate in the periodic survey, but even if the welfare agency there was unusually generous, approximately 750,000 children were not reached by the new amendments. The AFDC survey identified 17,000 out-of-school youth who were excluded from the family budget. Unfortunately, survey schedules included no questions about whether these youth were working or seeking work or helping in the home, whether they were in good health or poor. Perhaps AFDC is not the best answer for some out-of-school youth. Given their high rates of unemployment, a labor-market solution may be more to the point. But until an alternative remedy is available, inclusion in the AFDC budget would seem to be a minimum response to their needs.

Considering how few 18- to 21-year-olds were helped by these changes in AFDC law, it is fortunate that the policy had a sleeper. Occasionally, the fact that youth over 18 qualified kept parents eligible too. This happened when the child in question was the youngest in the assistance unit. In 1969 this was true in 1.5 percent of the families. This group received average monthly grants of $120, which suggests that most were mothers with one child. By 1973, the proportion had dropped to 1.1 percent and the typical grant had increased to $135. This represents little redistributional impact, but at least for a few mothers the eighteenth birthday of their youngest child was not the catastrophe it might have been.

Estimating how much money was expended because of this amendment is problematical, since no AFDC surveys were carried out between 1962 and 1967. In the latter year, children over 18 years of age comprised 1.2 percent of all recipients. If it is assumed that they represented 0.6 percent of the caseload in 1965, and that the percentage rose steadily in 1966 and between later survey years, it seems likely that about $754 million in AFDC funds (or 2.0 percent of assistance payments from 1965 through 1973) can be attributed to the policy. It would be helpful to know how many welfare agencies over the country informed school counselors and families of the amendment, and how many welfare workers offered to help in solving problems so that older children could remain in or return to school. This particular amendment might well have generated Back-to-School Alerts something akin to the Medicare and SSI Alerts with which the Social Security Administration filled the airwaves when those programs were initiated. But in AFDC the pressure is usually to restrict caseloads, not to increase them, and the most promising breakthroughs in welfare law can be, and often are, easily thwarted by a reluctant and politically sensitive welfare administration.

AFDC Work Incentives

By way of contrast, significant amounts of income were redistributed through the work-incentive policies. The policy package consisted of a series of administrative requirements and laws adopted during the 1960s to encourage AFDC families to work in the hope that they would soon become self-supporting.[22] Prior to 1962, welfare checks were supposed to be reduced $1 for every $1 families earned, an arrangement that obviously provided a strong work disincentive. To correct this incongruity, in 1962 welfare agencies were instructed to deduct work expenses. States had some leeway in defining appropriate items. In the beginning, some states made standard deductions while others paid actual costs. Deductions could include such items as income and social-security taxes, union dues, uniforms, transportation, lunches, and child day-care costs. In 1964, with the passage of the Economic Opportunity Act, the list increased to cover training allowances and stipends of various sorts. Then part of children's earnings were deducted on an optional basis. Except for the AFDC surveys, there were no reports submitted by states to show the impact of these requirements and options on family income, what percentage of wages was deducted, or even whether states were conforming to federal regulations. This meant, given the five-year gap between surveys, that in 1967 when Congress was under severe pressure from taxpayers to reduce caseloads and welfare costs and to encourage or force families to work, there was no information regarding the impact of existing work incentives. Nonetheless, Congress enacted new requirements for far more generous incentives. After July 1, 1969, states were to deduct all earnings of children who were full- or part-time students and for adults the first $30 of monthly earnings and one-third of the remainder. Since the wish was to lure people off welfare, not on, parents who had jobs when they applied for AFDC were not eligible for the new windfall, although their work expenses could be deducted.

When the 1967 AFDC survey was published in 1970, it became clear that the earlier incentives had relatively little effect on work behavior, were not systematically applied, and in some states were not in effect at all. Nonetheless, they helped to shore up the income of working families. About 49 percent of all nonwelfare income was deducted in 1967.[23] Had this been known at the time, lawmakers might have been more realistic about the handicaps of poor young AFDC mothers in the labor market. They tend to be unskilled, are often in poor health, and they have heavy home responsibilities for young children and disabled husbands, which adds up to the likelihood of inconsistent work performance, or so many employers might anticipate. Research into their work behavior over a span of time suggests that they move in and out of the labor market, with many working sometime during the year but few working full time year round. Even when they do so, economists estimate that over half earn too little to support their families.[24]

With this pattern, it may be a victory for the new incentives, in combination with heightened pressures to work and sanctions for refusing to work, that despite worsening economic conditions, between May 1969 (just before the new package became mandatory) and January 1973, the employment rate for AFDC mothers rose fromn13.5 to 16.4, and the full-time employment rate rose from 7.7 to 10.0. But many employed families, it turned out, rather than becoming self-supporting, stayed on public welfare for increasingly long periods. In 1967, families with working mothers comprised 6 percent of the families continuously on AFDC for three or more years. By 1973, they accounted for 11 percent. By then, almost half of all working mothers had held the same job for a year or more, and 20 percent had done so for more than three years. Increasing numbers clustered just below welfare ceilings, receiving very small AFDC checks but remaining eligible for food stamps, Medicaid, day care, homemakers, public housing, and other welfare-related services and in-kind benefits. If AFDC mothers had to compensate for the loss of these benefits, earnings would have to rise sharply, an unlikely event considering the barriers to promotion and high wages for even relatively well-educated and experienced women in the labor force.[25]

How much money have the work incentives transferred to working families? Because of the way deductions were reported in the periodic surveys prior to 1973, it is not possible to separate work-related from other deductions, but it is possible to distribute total deductions among working and nonworking families. In 1967, 56.8 percent of all deductions went to families with an employed member. With the increased emphasis on work thereafter, over 90 percent of total deductions (98.0 percent by 1973) was given to such families. If it is assumed that earnings and deductions increased in value steadily between survey years, the total value of the deductions in the seven-year span from 1967 to 1974 would be about $5.3 billion, or almost two-thirds more than was spent altogether on the AFDC-UP, second-parent, and older-school-children amendments in those years. Clearly, the overriding investment occasioned by these four amendments went toward reinforcing the work ethic and reaffirming the widespread belief that paid work is more highly prized than caring for children or homemaking.

What is far more important from a redistributive perspective is that while $5.3 billion of nonassistance income was disregarded, almost exclusively for working families which comprised less than one-fifth of the caseload, the total income of nonworking families, more than four-fifths of the total, lagged well behind increases in prices and community standards of living. Between 1969 and 1973, the consumer price index rose 21 percent, while the median income of four-person families rose 29 percent (from $10,623 to $13,710). In the same period the average estimated annual income of unemployed four-person AFDC families rose by only 14 percent, from $2,511 to $2,862. This means that in 1969, income of unemployed AFDC families averaged 23.6 percent of the median income of all four-person families, and by 1973 AFDC family income had droppped to only 20.9 percent of the median.[26]

The policy question is whether states might have improved standards for the very poor AFDC majority if they had not been required to allocate so much for work incentives to the better-off minority. Given the extreme poverty of many families, generous work incentives appear to be a luxury we can ill afford, especially when so many millions are unemployed and promise to be for some years to come. A reward to mothers for staying at home would appear to make more sense.

What insights does this brief review provide about how to design constructive welfare programs? First, if programs must be financed through grants-in-aid, equity will be elusive until there are national standards. Whenever amendments affect budget standards or eligibility, they should apply to every jurisdiction. This means that they should be mandatory, not optional. Second, when new provisions are adopted, they should be widely publicized so that all eligible families can apply if they wish to do so. When other institutions are involved, such as schools or employment offices, they should be encouraged to refer potentially eligible children and adults. Third, changes in law should be monitored carefully and promptly so that their impact is known by lawmakers before related changes are enacted. Fourth, and perhaps most important, lawmakers and top administrators should take the leadership they have been given by election or appointment to define clear and consistent goals for public programs. The proliferation of inconsistent goals in public welfare has contributed more than its share to the paralysis of the welfare system.

The Proliferation of Means-Tested Programs

Between 1968 and 1973 public expenditures for selective programs increased from $16.1 billion to $36.8 billion (see table 6.2) Health-care expenditures targeted toward the poor, especially through Medicaid, more than doubled, while the less expensive food-stamp program quadrupled. By February 1975, food stamps could be purchased in most counties in the nation and reached half again as many people as in 1973. With these developments, cash transfers (which families could spend freely for consumption items of most

value to them) took second place to more restrictive in-kind benefits and services. As this happened, it became increasingly clear
that if one means-tested program spells trouble, a potpourri of such
programs creates an administrative nightmare. With the fragmenta-
tion of decision making among congressional committees, the frag-
mentation of administration among agencies at all levels of government, and the push toward decentralization, means-tested programs
spawned different definitions of poverty, income, and resources.
They taxed family earnings differently. Some were available nationwide, others statewide (if they were in operation at all), and
still others, subject to local option, were scattered with no logical
relation to need. Different methods of financing, some capable of
generating far more funds than others, made programs more or less
accessible, adequate, and equitable. They tended to be organized
for select categories of people, leaving others who were equally
poor with nothing at all while admitting thousands of nonpoor.
About the one feature that income-conditioned programs had in
common was grossly inadequate reporting requirements which of-
fended every reasonable standard of public accountability. Their
impact severally and together could only be roughly approximated,
and then usually only through the medium of special surveys. Because so many provided in-kind benefits and services whose value
in terms of adding to or conserving family income was unknown,
even the annual ritual of counting the poor was thrown into dis-
array.

A closer examination of the sparse evidence about their impact will shed some light on the problem. Two questions are of particular interest: (1) To what extent have selective benefits and services helped to compensate for the inequitable distribution of
income? (2) How do proliferating work requirements and work incentives affect the redistributional thrust of selective programs, and
how can the issues they raise be resolved?

Table 6.2 Expenditures for Income-Conditioned Public Programs, Fiscal Years 1968 and 1973

| | Expenditures (Millions) | | | | | |
| | Total | | Federal | | State/Local | |
Programs, by Type	1968	1973	1968	1973	1968	1973
Cash [a]	$ 7,527.0	$13,872.0	$ 5,037.0	$ 8,575.0	$2,490.0	$ 5,297.0
Food [b]	893.0	3,855.0	893.0	3,855.0		
Health [c]	4,802.0	10,723.0	2,741.0	6,558.0	2,061.0	4,165.0
Housing [d]	783.0	3,358.0	783.0	3,358.0		
Education [e]	860.0	1,821.0	860.0	1,821.0		
Job and Training [f]	751.8	979.0	709.3	923.0	42.5	56.0
Social Services [g]	499.0	2,221.0	383.0	1,685.0	116.0	536.0
Total, all programs	16,115.8	36,829.0	11,406.3	26,775.0	4,709.5	10,054.0

Source: U.S. Congress, Joint Economic Committee, Subcommittee on Fiscal Policy, *Income Security for Americans: Recommendations of the Public Welfare Study*, 93d Cong., 2d sess., December 5, 1974, pp. 23–25.

[a] Includes AFDC, Emergency Assistance, Assistance to Cuban Refugees, general assistance to Indians, Pensions for Veterans, Dependents, and Survivors; state/local general assistance, Old Age Assistance, Aid to the Blind, Aid to the Permanently and Totally Disabled.

[b] Includes food stamps, food commodities, school lunch, school breakfast, special milk, special supplemental feeding programs for mothers and children, meals for the elderly.

[c] Includes Medicaid, veterans' care for non-service-connected disability, Comprehensive Health Services, Dental Health for Children, and other child and maternal care.

[d] Includes low-rent public housing, Section 235 homeownership assistance, Section 236 rental housing assistance, rent supplements, Section 502 rural housing loans, Section 204 rural housing loans, Section 516 farm labor housing grants, Section 523 rural self-help housing technical assistance, and Indian housing improvement grants.

[e] Includes Basic Educational Opportunity Grants, supplemental educational opportunity grants, college work-study, national direct student loans, interest on insured loans, nursing education, medical education, Head Start, vocational education, work study.

[f] Includes Neighborhood Youth Corps, Operation Mainstream, senior community service employment, job corps, work incentive projects, senior companions, foster grandparents, career opportunity grants.

[g] Includes legal services for the poor, social services to needy; aged, blind, and disabled, and social services to needy families.

THE QUESTION OF EQUITY

One important goal of public services in a democratic society is equitable distribution of benefits among the target population. But what does equity mean in this context? Does it suggest equal shares for all poor people? Or does it suggest varying shares sufficient to equalize the likelihood that all groups among the poor will end at some given age with about equal shares of income, good health, suitable housing, or sufficient education to earn a decent living? Is the relevant concept, in other words, absolute or relative and compensatory? If the latter, it is entirely appropriate that however eligibility is defined some people will receive more than others, since the ability to earn a living and the need for services vary. People with a higher incidence of health problems, like the aged, will need more health services than young and able-bodied people. Large families with difficulties in finding suitable housing at prices they can afford will need more subsidized housing. Also some crises in family life are complex, requiring a variety of services if problems are to be resolved, and in our fragmented service structure this means that several public benefits must be available simultaneously. If the distribution of benefits coincided perfectly or even approximately with need, in any given month of the year some families might receive none, others a dozen or more.

This is apparently what happens, according to a survey made by the General Accounting Office during 1973 in six low-income areas.[27] After an examination of the records of 100 federal, state, and local public programs, it was learned that 40 percent of the households received no public benefits at all, 20 percent received 1, 14 percent 2, and 9 percent 3. The proportion continued to descend as the numbers rose until only 1 percent received 8 or more benefits. Investigators did not presume to measure need, and so whether the distribution curve fit the need curve is still a mystery. Nonetheless, when the report was issued, informal claims were made that the survey proved how exploitative some poor families were. Further details about the distribution of benefits cast doubts on this complaint: the largest benefit shares went to households with aged heads, very large families, and fatherless families, while male-headed households received somewhat less than their share. In other words, the American habit of categorical programming naturally skews the distribution of benefits. It is not the mothers of poor children or the aged who should be blamed for receiving more than their share (although not necessarily enough), but the policy makers who chose to structure and finance programs in this way. Fortuitously, the groups receiving the most services are among the poorest in the nation, and so anyone who believes that equity is a relative or compensatory concept can rejoice in the outcome.

A later study, carried out for the Subcommittee on Fiscal Policy (the Griffiths Subcommittee) of the Joint Economic Committee, this time by the Chilton Research Services, investigated the distribution of public benefits to households participating in the food-stamp and food-distribution programs in 1973.[28] With everyone in the sample already receiving one benefit, the curve naturally differs from the one identified by the General Accounting Office. This time the typical household received 3 benefits while only 1 in the sample of 3,416 received 8 or more. This study was made primarily to estimate the impact of in-kind benefits on household income. For this purpose, beneficiaries of 1 universal and 7 selective in-kind programs were identified.[29] But researchers settled for such unsatisfactory methods of fixing the money value of in-kind benefits that the study is of little use except to illustrate pitfalls in surveys of this nature. For instance, in medical care, respondents' estimates of the costs defrayed by Medicare or Medicaid were used only if the respondents could recall them. Otherwise, national average payments were substituted, even though average payments differ drastically by age and location. This approach makes the impact of public medical services on family income dependent on the proportion and location of respondents with good memories or good records.

With public housing, total federal housing costs were prorated—$1,115 annually or $92.92 monthly—over relevant survey households. However, not only do the costs to families vary depending on household size, income, and location, but as Henry Aarons points out, public housing is not a gift.[30] Residents pay rent and if they fail to do so they are evicted. Since everyone has to live somewhere and each type of shelter carries a cost, the measurement task is to learn how much people save by living in public housing. To shed light on this aspect of the problem, data in the 1973 AFDC survey were analyzed in the Center for Studies in Income Maintenance Policy. It turned out that in January 1973, when only 14 percent of AFDC families lived in public housing, on the average they paid $27 a month less for shelter than families in private rentals, or about $791 less per year than was added to the income of public-housing residents in the study published by the Griffiths Subcommittee. Similar cost-allocation problems are reflected in estimating the impact of school breakfasts, lunches, and special milk programs.

Despite these frailties in the Griffiths Subcommittee study, it is more than likely, if history is a good guide, that the survey will be quoted repeatedly by critics of the poor and of programs in their behalf to prove that, after all the benefits are added up, there are no longer many poor people in our midst.

When we turn to more reliable evidence, it becomes clear that selective programs often deal inequitably with their target populations. In addition to helping some categories of poor people, they help people in some areas more than others. In 1973, only 17 percent of AFDC funds were distributed in southern states, where 46 percent of the nation's poor children lived. In June 1974, 15 million people purchased food stamps, but an estimated 50 million were eligible. The aged, disabled, and blind receiving SSI benefits were excluded from the program in California, Massachusetts, Nevada, New York, and Wisconsin. Rural families often found it difficult if not impossible to travel to food issuance and certification points, and experts report that unless transportation costs can be deducted or free transportation provided, relatively few will be able to participate in some parts of the country.[31]

In October 1973, 18,300 schools enrolling 5.3 million children, of whom 2 million were estimated to be poor, had no school lunch program. The school breakfast program reached fewer than 13 percent of the nation's low-income children. In reporting on the program, the National Nutrition Policy Study notes that ". . . (at its present rate of growth) it will take 190 years for 'breakfast' to reach the (inadequate) participation levels of today's school lunch program." [32]

There are many reasons why selective programs become skewed geographically. When federal laws leave the organization of services to state or local option, fiscal capacity and cultural attitudes determine where programs are sited. Maldistribution also reflects the habit of professionals to settle along the East or West Coast and in large cities, and the failure of government as it invests in programs to try to correct this pattern. Bureaucratic resistance explains some skewing. Nutrition experts, for instance, pointed for years to the resistance of the U.S. Department of Agriculture to extending food programs, and the fondness of officials for ending the year with surplus funds.[33]

But even if families manage to fall in the right categories and live in the right places, selective programs tend to be hedged with constraints that distort distribution and impede program growth. For instance, food stamps cannot be used to purchase restaurant meals, and so if people are too poor to afford cooking facilities, the program is irrelevant. Or if an otherwise eligible person takes in three boarders, the household is disqualified as a "boarding house," but with only two there is no obstacle, although everyone involved is very poor and the income from three boarders in some sections of the country falls well below that from two elsewhere.

Even for people who manage to qualify, different types of households are treated inequitably. Both in AFDC and in food stamps, large families come out with less than their fair share. In some 20 states, family ceilings are imposed on AFDC grants. Despite efforts to rid food stamps of similar problems, the regulations that became effective as recently as January 1975 are spotted with anomalies. It seems reasonable to suggest that larger low-income families should not pay a higher proportion of total income to purchase stamps than small families, since AFDC in many states and OASDI everywhere already discriminate against large families. But with monthly net income of $55, a single individual pays 14.5 percent of his net income for stamps, while a family of twelve is required to pay 22 percent. As net income rises to $160 monthly, the single householder pays 20 percent, and families of eight or more persons pay 28 percent. Families of the same size are also treated ambiguously. With net income of $55, a four-person family is required to spend 18 percent on stamps, while at $160, scarcely a munificent sum, the purchase price amounts to almost 26 percent of net income; but when income rises to $539, only 24 percent must be devoted to food stamps. How these variations are arrived at or justified is difficult to comprehend.

Nutrition experts claim that the high price of stamps is the single greatest factor in nonparticipation. In January 1973, the AFDC survey showed that in every region of the country, large AFDC families were remarkably less likely to purchase food stamps than small families. Over the nation, 78 percent of two-member families participated in areas with food stamps in operation. With each additional member, participation rates fell until they settled at 63 percent for families of eight or more.

On the other hand, the food-stamp bonus helps to compensate for variations in earnings, wage-related cash transfers, and state AFDC standards. Table 6.3 shows some of these compensatory effects in 1973. For participating families in the South, the food bonus was almost half the size of their total cash income, while in the Northeast, it was slightly more than one-tenth, and so the gap between family income in the two regions was closed somewhat. (Southern family income, as a percentage of northeastern family income, rose from 51 to 68 percent as the result of food stamps.) Less spectacular equalizing effects were noted for other groups, but the initial gap too was narrower. Thus, food bonuses decreased the differences in income between families that resided in standard metropolitan statistical areas and families that did not, families in which all children were legitimate and families where all were illegitimate, white and nonwhite families, and employed and unemployed families. But in this last instance, because food stamps too have work requirements and incentives, their equalizing effect was muted.

WORKS REQUIREMENTS AND WORK INCENTIVES

Work requirements and work incentives have become endemic in selective programs in recent years. Their impact on AFDC has already been discussed. But what happens when families receive food stamps, live in public housing, and receive SSI or AFDC, while their children are provided with reduced or free meals at school, and some member of the family needs Medicaid? How do benefits and incentives interact as earnings rise? How is the shining virtue

Table 6.3 Impact of Food-Stamp Bonus on Total Income of Four-Person AFDC Families Receiving Food Stamps, 1973 [a]

Families	Monthly Income [b] $	Monthly Income plus Food Bonus $	Increase %
Regions			
Northeast	318	354	11.3
North Central	247	304	23.1
South	162	241	48.8
West	269	323	20.1
S/NE	(50.9%)	(68.1%)	
Residence			
SMSA	293	344	17.4
Non-SMSA	249	309	24.1
Non-SMSA/SMSA	(85.0%)	(89.8%)	
Color			
White	299	351	17.4
Nonwhite	276	330	19.6
Nonwhite/White	(92.3%)	(94.0%)	
Legitimacy Status			
All legitimate children	296	348	17.6
All Illegitimate children	264	319	20.8
Illegitimate/Legitimate	(89.2%)	(91.7%)	
Employment Status			
Employed Adult	436	479	9.9
No employed Adult	254	309	21.7
Unemployed/Employed	(58.3%)	(64.5%)	

Source: U. S. Department of Health, Education, and Welfare, Social and Rehabilitation Service, National Center for Social Statistics. *AFDC Survey, 1973.* Derived in Center for Studies in Income Maintenance Policy.

[a] Estimate based on 65 percent sample of AFDC Survey schedules, 1973; excludes Massachusetts, Puerto Rico, Virgin Islands, and Guam. This sample of families includes all AFDC assistance units in which all members of the household were in the assistance unit. A small number had to be excluded because the value of the food-stamp bonus was not recorded.

[b] Total income equals total nonassistance income, AFDC payment, and general-assistance payment, if any. The welfare definition of income includes "income in kind" to which a cash value has been imputed and contributions from relatives.

of selective programs, their economic efficiency, affected when so many nonworking poor people continue to qualify as eligibility ceilings are pushed up by work incentives? And does a package of incentives reinforce or undermine the work ethic?

These questions have been exhaustively considered by experts and well summarized elsewhere.[34] Everyone agrees, theoretically, that work incentives in several programs operating simultaneously on a single household can turn into a strong work disincentive. The theory makes good sense. As the wage earner's pay goes up, his benefits in each program drop, and sometimes the total reduction exceeds his raise. Furthermore, if earnings exceed the income ceiling for welfare, he stands to lose not only the welfare check but eligibility for many other selective benefits. So at the very point where he might become self-supporting, he has the strongest incentive to level out work effort and resist further pay hikes or a transfer to a better job. What he has experienced in the package of selective programs, to put it in economic terms, is a very high marginal tax rate on earnings, so high as to make further work effort a very foolish choice.

Now, whether economic theory or econometric models tell the whole story is not at all clear. Certainly, as has been shown earlier, a small group of fully employed, relatively high-wage earners among AFDC mothers clusters just under the ceiling or break-even point for welfare benefits. Just as surely, if they earned enough to become ineligible, they would lose Medicaid, food stamps, subsidized day care, and public housing in most states, if not all. But are they clustered just below the ceiling because they refuse to earn more money, knowing these facts about public benefits, or because they cannot find better-paying jobs? It is possible that their present earnings represent the highest they can expect.

In any case, the very generous work incentives in AFDC have not materially changed the work behavior of AFDC families, most of whom are nowhere near the cutoff point for working families. While the incomes of virtually all AFDC families can only go up if they work, in any given month less than 20 percent do work. And this has always been true across the country unless states had such low standards and enforced work requirements so harshly that the choice was really one of work or starvation. So it seems likely that for fatherless families, at least, no amount of ingenuity in designing incentives for welfare or related programs will bring about any marked change in employment rates or work effort. For many reasons, paid work, homemaking, child supervision and nurture, and, for some, the care of invalid husbands is a combination that apparently proves too taxing. Also, welfare means a steady income while jobs come and go, and if mothers are laid off, the lengthy process of qualifying for welfare must begin again. This cannot help but discourage some mothers from taking the risk of trying to become independent in an uncertain labor market.

Much of the planning around work incentives in recent years has apparently been in anticipation of admitting able-bodied, two-parent families to an income-conditioned welfare system like the negative income tax. Do work requirements and incentives make more sense in this context? If they overlap and interact as present incentives do, their work disincentive feature would have far more serious consequences for a caseload chiefly consisting of working families. But if they were rationalized, would they make better sense for single men or two-parent families than for fatherless families? The experiments with negative income tax suggest otherwise. They demonstrate that a guaranteed income makes little difference in the work effort of men in their prime years, and virtually none at all for black workers of either sex.[35] Different guarantees and tax rates have been tested, always with similar results. Why, then, are they still a central feature of reform proposals? They cost a great deal of money. They are complex and expensive to administer. They demonstrably have little effect on work behavior, which makes their cost-benefit ratio as work incentives unattractive. If the tax rate on earnings is low, the number of eligibles rises drastically, and if we are to be able to afford the incentives, basic guarantees must be kept shamefully low. If the tax rate is high, there is no reason to expect any incentive effect. The larger the number of working poor in the caseload, the greater is the shift of the public investment in welfare from the poor to the nonpoor. These are the central dilemmas that must be kept in mind as reform packages of this type are considered.

A Blueprint for Welfare Reform

Instead of the largest possible income-conditioned welfare system, which seems to be the aim of most negative-income-tax proposals, the goal should be the smallest possible system. However, since the present welfare caseload cannot be reduced significantly unless other reforms occur first, these must be mentioned briefly:

1. The adoption of a full-employment policy that guarantees the right to work to all people who are able and wish to work. A sufficient supply of decently paid jobs is probably the best work incentive that could be devised, and a full-employment policy, effectively administered, is far more consistent with humanistic American values than gigantic welfare programs. The cost will be high, but the direct and indirect costs of joblessness and indecently low wages may well be higher.[36] In addition to enhancing self-respect, personal fulfillment, and economic productivity, a full-employment policy will increase tax revenues and bring about a notable redistribution of income to the groups that chronically suffer the highest rates of unemployment and underemployment.

2. Comprehensive tax reform including a universal tax credit that would be refundable to persons with income so low that they could not otherwise take advantage of the full credit. How much the welfare caseload is reduced by this approach depends on the size of the credit and the tax rate.

3. A national health service that offers comprehensive screening services and care for sick and disabled persons. Many alternatives have been proposed and debated in recent years. To the extent that we compromise these goals, part of the cost of sickness and disability is inevitably borne by other systems, notably the welfare and family systems.

4. Reform of the child-support system so that when parents separate or are divorced, laws on parental responsibility are enforced consistently and equitably at all income levels. Removing the responsibility for securing support from the family and turning it over to government will reduce the tensions and uncertainties that often pervade the support issue. The recent trend to strengthen efforts at collection from the fathers of welfare families seems to rest on the assumption that this group flouts its moral and legal responsibilities more than better-off parents, and on this score there is no convincing evidence. For many reasons, whatever is done with respect to one income group should apply to all, and a federal administrative agency can be expected to discharge this function more consistently and equitably than local courts.[37]

5. The qualifying conditions for disability insurance in the OASDI system should be broadened. At present the government is forced to devote much too much time and talent in litigating suits over its decisions regarding eligibility. The major impediments to qualifying people should be reviewed with the aim of redefining disability and the duration of the disabling condition so that far more of the occupationally disabled population will qualify.

With these reforms, part of the burden would be shifted from welfare to the systems whose present failures so aggravate the "welfare problem." But no discussion of welfare reform is complete without dealing with food stamps. Since the proliferation of means-tested programs has complicated life for poor people, for administrators, and for Congress in its role as the chief social-planning forum in the nation, consideration should be given to phasing out as many as possible of these programs promptly. The food-stamp program is a natural candidate for repeal. There is little public confidence in its administration or the administrative choice of income ceilings and work incentives, and it is an undue burden on families and the economy when employed recipients have to take time from work to be recertified at frequent intervals. Also, however important food is, if people are really poor what they need is more money, and they should not be forced into officially determined consumption patterns.

Assuming that the American penchant for incrementalism will prevail for a while longer, at the earliest possible moment the failure to achieve full employment should be charged entirely to an improved and extended unemployment-insurance system providing benefits for all unemployed full-time and involuntary part-time members of the labor force; universal health screening and care should be promptly assured to the young; and the child-support system should be reformed.

In this context a national welfare program with social services would be useful and manageable. It should provide: (1) long-term full and supplementary assistance to poor families with young children while parental disabilities, home responsibilities, age, or conditions in the labor market make full-time paid work an unconstructive or unrealistic expectation; (2) supplementary assistance to social-security beneficiaries who do not qualify for SSI and whose monthly benefits fall below the national welfare standard; and (3) short-term emergency help to all needy people with special crises requiring financial aid.

These recommendations assume that a complex society cannot function without programs that respond to special needs and compensate for bureaucratic errors and such vagaries as stolen or lost checks. In reserving the core program for families with no adult seeking or engaged in full-time work, the intent is to make a long-term commitment to the importance of consistent parental care and nurture of young children and the wisdom of constraining the number of mothers seeking full-time employment. Even if the nation moves to a full-employment policy soon, and invests in it generously, there will be more than sufficient challenge to guarantee jobs to all able-bodied youth and adults who want to work without also encouraging, let alone forcing, mothers (or fathers solely responsible for very young children) into paid work when they are needed at home. Whether mothers or fathers in one-parent families accept paid work is a decision that they should make freely from their own expert knowledge of their physical and emotional resources and the needs of their children. By the same token, though, when two able-bodied parents are in the home, one should be expected to join the labor force.

The grossest inequities in AFDC result from the different treatment of income and resources and the failure to establish national standards of assistance. These are also major reasons why the program has fallen short as a redistributive or an antipoverty instrument. The federal government should follow its own example with SSI and enact a basic guarantee for AFDC, this time taking into account the realistic differences in the cost of living between rural and urban areas and for children of different ages—adolescents are usually more costly than young tots. When the cash guarantees are set, it should be kept in mind that the program is an investment in children and is intended to provide an incentive to mothers to remain out of the labor force. This means that the guarantees should assure an adequate standard of living. The age-old concept of "less eligibility" only makes sense when public policy is bent on forcing adults to work and/or inhibiting the rise in wages at the bottom of the occupational structure. What standards are set will be negotiated in political forums, but it would be self-defeating to consider anything below a fully updated poverty level as the short-term goal. Any conflict created because welfare grants exceed low wages should be resolved in the labor market.

While poor mothers with young children are discouraged from joining the labor force on a full-time basis, consideration should be given ways to encourage them to continue their education and to work and engage in neighborhood and community activities on a part-time basis. Few people seem to grasp how very isolated and harrassed many AFDC mothers feel year after year, how little they know about how to improve their circumstances, and how ill-prepared they are to support themselves eventually. If a quid pro quo is needed in welfare, it would more constructively take the form of incentives for these women to engage in a wide variety of activities, including part-time work, that will bring them into the mainstream and help them to be more effective mothers and citizens. Free tuition, reasonable out-of-pocket expenses, and a flat-sum disregard (perhaps $40 or $50) of monthly earnings would have the virtue of legitimating, facilitating, and encouraging mothers to enlarge their horizons, develop new skills, and make new friends.

Federal financing, standards, and administration are recommended because the poverty of one-parent families is a serious and growing national problem, because there is no reason to expect present trends to be reversed, and because long experience confirms that too many states are unwilling or unable to support young able-bodied families at decent levels of living. Conversely, once states are freed of the cost of AFDC, they will be better equipped than the federal government to respond flexibly and promptly to individual and family crises requiring emergency aid. The quid pro quo for full federal funding of AFDC should be soundly financed, well-administered state programs providing emergency assistance.

An essential but separate task is to build a strong, responsive, national social-service system. For too long the social services have been poorly distributed, fragmented, uncoordinated, and of indifferent quality. It is often assumed that public services are poor services while services provided by voluntary agencies or purchased in the market are good services. This has yet to be proven. It is clear that some public services are so woefully underfinanced that they become symbols of community neglect. But by the same token, some of the most effective innovations in the service sector have been under public auspices, while the quality, coverage, and administration of many private agencies leaves a great deal to be desired. Defining the issue as public vs. private begs the question.

The search should be for comprehensive social services provided in a manner that builds on innate strengths, fosters dignity, focuses on prevention, and holds the service sector fully accountable for competent care, appropriate referral, and effective follow-up. The multipurpose neighborhood service centers launched with antipoverty funds in the 1960s, the family health-care demonstrations in North Carolina, and recent efforts on behalf of the mentally retarded, such as the Eleanor Roosevelt Developmental Services in New York, are steps in the right direction. All are organized to provide comprehensive and flexible services that aspire to give primary attention to prevention; all recruit and appeal to dedicated service-oriented professionals; all make excellent use of aides, technicians, and volunteers; and all have a lively interest in community development and more rational social policy. They should become the rule, not the exception.

In the meantime, the impediments to family formation and the pressures toward family breakdown continue to increase the pool of fatherless families, and our anachronistic institutional arrangements leave an increasing share of these families on the poverty roster. It is unrealistic to expect that most poor mothers can take on the wage-earning role, support their children at acceptable levels, and effectively discharge their homemaking and mothering roles simultaneously. This is certainly true unless the economy is booming and employers, faced with very tight labor markets, raise wages and either they or the government subsidize amenities and services that young families need. Whether a peacetime economy can be a thriving economy or whether a quickening interest in the quality of life will supersede materialistic and competitive goals remains to be seen. But children should not have to wait on the event.

7

The

Strategy and Hope

ALVIN L. SCHORR

We began with the observation that distribution of income depends on the distribution of wealth, the state of the economy, the structure of wages, tax and transfer policies, demographic changes, and more elusive considerations such as power and discrimination. We are far from satisfied with the way the distribution turns out. Unmanaged improvement in the economy does not reduce poverty to an equivalent degree, and shares seem to have an insidious story line of their own. With current shares, some individuals may escape from poverty but the nation will not escape from having poverty. Nor are inspirational and, indeed, necessary calls for unity and community matched by national action. In five chapters, we have surveyed the detailed policies that affect shares. In the next few pages, we note major recommendations before going on to comment.

Earnings and Taxes

Wages are central to income shares, accounting for more than three-fourths of all income. Low wages force working people into welfare, leading some analysts to seek a solution for low wages in welfare reform—an impossible task. More wage inequality places a greater burden on income transfers. Wages are themselves a vehicle for income transfers: social security goes only to those who have worked and relates to their wages. Those who have earned more and therefore had more opportunity to accumulate wealth receive more from income transfers as well.

We see that discrimination, whether by color, sex, or age, may be responsible for low wages. One might conclude that transfer policy is merely society's way of compensating for the discrimination it fosters or permits in wages. But we also perceive that discrimination is passed on to the transfer system. Routes to improving the distribution of wages are named in chapter 2—overall economic policy, proper minimum wages and coverage, programs for public-service employment, and the capacity of workers to bargain on their own behalf. A family of four with an adult member fully able to work should in no event find itself poor in the United States. The point was made by Paul H. Douglas in 1927; [1] the essential issue has not changed in fifty years.

Income transfers are financed by federal income and social-security taxes in particular and by other federal and state taxes as well. The impact of all taxation taken together is roughly proportional in the range from marginally poor to pretty well off ($5,700 to $35,500 a year). Thus, taxation contributes little to improving the share of those at the bottom. That is because the somewhat progressive effect of the federal income tax is counteracted by the regressive social-security tax and even more regressive state and local taxes. One sees more effect of transfers when government expenditures are introduced into the equation. People with incomes up to about $10,000 a year show a net benefit, on the average, from all taxes paid to and benefits received from the government. In other words, despite conventional wisdom, tax collection does not appear to be very redistributive, but the way collected funds are distributed somewhat improves the share of the bottom quintiles (for example, review table 1.2).

Taxation is a privileged preserve of technicians and those able to command them. The very definition of terms such as "income" and "deduction" creates results that can be less or more egalitarian. The complexities of tax policy lend themselves readily to a brand of Newspeak in which gains for the rich are justified by the needs of the poor. Thus, accelerated depreciation is justified in terms of job production but produces larger profits in the process. Or the tax on earned income rises no higher than 50 percent, in deference to income earned by "sweat of the brow." (One must have annual income well over $40,000 to profit from this courtesy.) A series of proposals for reordering the federal tax system are developed in the relevant chapter—a wider definition of income, treatment of capital gains and interest on state and local bonds as normal income (with accompanying changes to meet difficulties), and stringent death taxes. In place of the present income-tax exemption, a cashable tax credit is recommended. And so forth.

Transfer Payments

The social-insurance system comprises the bulk of cash transfers. Though not regarded as a set of poverty programs, it provides far more money to poor people than welfare. Though the system is somewhat redistributive in impact, that quality has not been improving for a variety of reasons. Benefits are tied to prior earnings, and recent improvement in benefit levels has been done in a manner that accentuates existing preferences. Cost-of-living increases designed as percentage increases add more for those who are getting more. Possibly unintended but real discrimination against minorities (who do not live as long to collect as much), against families with children (the maximum family benefit), and against women tends to limit the share of less-favored people. While attention has certainly focused on retirement, other programs such as unemployment and disability insurance have not improved in any way reasonably related to rising levels of wages and wealth.

The financing of "social insurance," like the term itself, is made up of two parts. One is a commitment by the government that rests on and is related to contributions from wages. It is recommended here that beneficiaries receive pensions based on that sum of money with compound interest. The other part of the financing of social insurance is a transfer from the working to the nonworking population. In social security in particular, that transfer, or subsidy, is very large indeed. As it is a transfer, the judgment about who should benefit most lies with the government or citizenry, and the recommendation here is that the payment should be a flat amount for all beneficiaries. Thus, the United States would come by a somewhat different route to the two-tier system widely used in the western world.

It is a fundamental problem in reforming our transfer system that it and our system of wages as well are seriously entangled over the issue of family size. If full-time, year-round work at minimum wages supports a family of four, a married worker with three children and minimum-wage income will find himself poor.[2] For that reason, some press for even higher minimum wages and find themselves resisted by the argument, among others, that overly high minimums will wipe out jobs. In the absence of higher minimum wages, of course, large numbers of employed families with children constitute the so-called working poor; some argue on grounds of equity that *they* should receive welfare. (Others reflect that equity would be as well served by reducing welfare benefits of the nonworking poor.) Unemployment insurance may provide modest though temporary support for a small family but is entirely inadequate for a family with three or four children. Therefore some states pay additional benefits for dependents; others do not. Social security's dilemma concerning maximum family benefits, that is, trying to provide for additional family members but limiting that provision to one or one and a half dependents, arises out of an attempt to adjust for family size without quite abandoning wage relatedness.

The solution we recommend to these dilemmas is that the United States should, like most industrial countries, in some measure separate the issue of support for dependents from wages and from the benefit structure of social insurances. A children's allowance would provide a transfer benefit for dependent children—a modest and at best partial adjustment for the additional cost of a child to the family. Even so, such a program could largely wipe out the problem of the working poor, and it would free transfer programs to develop a benefit structure without regard to size of family. A not inconsiderable advantage of such a development is that, as children's allowances would be payable without regard to income, they would not raise the question of incentive to work.

Children's allowances (described in chapter 4) represent an alternative to the proposal for a cashable credit in the income-tax system (chapter 3). Both would substitute a cash payment (or equivalent credit against taxes) for current income-tax exemptions. Since the exemption favors those with higher incomes, a uniform payment or credit in its place would favor those with lower incomes. The proposals diverge in that the children's allowance is limited to families with children while a cashable tax credit would be available to adults as well. For reasons rooted in the way children's allowances were introduced in Europe in the nineteenth century, they may be viewed as intended to encourage having children. Children's allowances appear not actually to have that effect, but the view remains a political liability which tax credits do not share. On the other hand, children's allowances would probably be even more redistributive—given a specified sum of money—than tax credits. As families with children tend to be poorer than other families, the limitation of allowances to such families itself selects poorer beneficiaries. Further, children's allowances may themselves be taxed as ordinary income—thus they are twice redistributive—while tax credits would not be taxed as income.

Apart from or in addition to such fundamental changes, much may be done in social insurance that would have redistributive effect. Benefit levels for dependent spouses may be converted from a percentage of the spouse's benefit to a flat amount. The maximum family benefit should be liberalized. The large number of people who retire before 65 should face a smaller reduction in benefit levels than law now provides. It should be easier to qualify for disability benefits, in terms of both required quarters of coverage and the definition of disability. Across-the-board increases in benefit levels should be replaced by or leavened with larger increases to those receiving the lowest payments. Proposals are also offered in the relevant chapter for reform of unemployment insurance and workmen's compensation and for the establishment of a nationwide program of temporary disability insurance.

The field of health is more complex, because it involves evaluation of the delivery of services rather than of cash and because one must examine an intermixture of governmental, profit-making, and philanthropic providers. Whether health services are the best or most efficient way to get good health is arguable, but this is not the central question here. The question here is whether health services that are provided are equitably divided. One has to conclude that the answer is no. "The major conclusion of [a study of Medicare] is that a uniform medical care financing plan has not been sufficient to guarantee equal access to medical care for all elderly persons." [3] The poor, blacks, and southerners suffer a sizable disparity in using medical services. Some poorer people are excluded from insurance and government programs; others are included only in a limited way. Cost sharing and tax deduction for medical care tend to discourage the poor from using services while encouraging those who are richer. The demonstrable effect is that those who are poorer, whether young or old, tend not to receive preventive care or treatment for less serious or not yet serious conditions.

A program of national health insurance, if we are to have one, must be carefully designed in terms that will promote equity. The chapter on health goes with great care into those terms— universal and mandatory coverage, financing through the government, a maximum payment by beneficiaries related to adjusted gross income, and no other cost sharing. Pains would have to be taken to specify the conditions under which providers might participate.

At the same time, it has to be acknowledged that the health-delivery system suffers from fundamental problems which health insurance may not adequately address. Considerable difficulties arise from the poor distribution of physicians geographically, from discriminatory practices by physicians, hospitals, and extended-care facilities, and from the pricing practices of physicians. For example, allowing physicians to collect payments from patients in addition to the Medicare charge (or forbidding the practice but failing to enforce the prohibition) shifts costs to the patient and discourages poorer patients from seeking care. More fundamentally, so long as patients must seek and pay for treatment by solo practitioners for illness as it occurs (as opposed to prepaid and group care), preventive care will receive relatively low priority and the disadvantaged will have difficulty in competing for attention.

In touching on these deeper issues in chapter 5, we addressed incentives and controls that might be attached to new financing mechanisms. However, financial incentives are remarkably susceptible to subversion and exploitation. Such was the experience with prepaid group care contracted out to private corporations in California.[4] New health planning and allocation systems have been undertaken in recent years, and given increased power. If they are not effective, presumably restructuring of the health-delivery system directly rather than through financing mechanisms will have to be undertaken.

Welfare is the last resort for those whom all these other work and transfer arrangements have failed. It has grown in costs and numbers because work has been less readily available and transfer programs have been providing less income relative to median income. As a redistributive mechanism, welfare has provided very little more over time to poor people. As an antipoverty device, welfare falls short of dealing with poverty by something between $1,000 and $2,000 per family, on the average, depending on how one measures the deficit. Of four program innovations since 1967, three had relatively trivial effect. The fourth innovation, meant to encourage work, increased the income of welfare families containing workers by $5.3 billion over an eight-year period. They were about a fifth of the caseload and, on the evidence, were not substantially induced to leave public assistance. It appears that jobs were not available at wages that would let them do that. As we have noted, the solution to providing work lies in the labor market, not in welfare. As for the other four-fifths of the caseload, their incomes lagged well behind rising cost-of-living and family-income averages.

Recommendations for reforming welfare lie, in the first place, everywhere outside welfare—a low unemployment rate, a tax credit or children's allowances, improved social security, health services, the kinds of proposals that have already been entertained. With such steps taken, welfare would become a program for a smaller group of people. It would deal with those whom other measures do not or cannot reach—chiefly mothers who remain outside the labor force and their children, and also a relatively few working-age adults who are in trouble for some special reason. Work-incentive provisions so laboriously inserted into welfare and so plainly not effective could be abandoned. More to the point would be social services intended to assure the nurture of dependent children and to help with the special problems of such a clientele.

Noncash Transfers

For a variety of reasons, including tradition, economic feasibility, the structure and power of provider groups, and the determination of legislatures to govern how beneficiaries conduct themselves, important transfers take the form of goods and services delivered rather than the money to purchase them. In discussing health services, we have dealt with one such program. Under other programs, an apartment may be provided in public housing or a builder subsidized to produce low-rent dwellings; stamps may be provided to exchange for food; or day care for a child or some other public social service may be provided. It may be supposed, at first thought, that these so-called in-kind or noncash transfers would tend to be self-limiting to people who are needy and therefore would be especially redistributive. A few words about each may suggest that managing their distributive effect is a very complex matter indeed.

The field of housing makes it clear, in the first place, that focusing on a particular in-kind program may mislead one about the distributive impact of overall policy in that field. While public housing, housing allowances, and in a sense public assistance are visibly housing programs, tax advantages to homeowners may escape attention. Careful analysis as far back as 1962 produced the conclusion that the federal government spent $820 million to subsidize housing for the poorest quintile of the population. For the uppermost quintile, the federal subsidy for housing (from federal tax benefits) was $1.7 billion.[5] The disparity has not disappeared in subsequent years. In 1969, the federal government spent (including 25 percent of the cost of public assistance) $2 billion on housing programs as social welfare,[6] but $4.5 billion on tax benefits for owner-occupied housing.[7]

Presenting even more difficulty as a distributive question is the fundamental issue of housing *production*. No nation, no matter how wealthy, or how egalitarian, maintains a decent distribution of housing unless it produces 10 new units per thousand of population annually.[8] Evidently, a minimum proportion of new housing is required to correct inequities as housing deteriorates and new families form. The problems here are of grand economic policy, and they are governing. In 1975 in the United States, new units of housing started constituted well under half of the necessary proportion. In that circumstance, political and economic pressures are such that equitable access to housing for poor people cannot be assured. Indeed, by 1976 subsidy programs to construct housing for lower-income people had virtually vanished, and relatively new programs of direct cash payment for rent were barely visible.

But even given satisfactory production of housing, close attention must be paid to program design and management. Providing income does not in itself assure fair shares in housing, nor do devices like cash housing allowances. The presumed link between supply and demand is disrupted by the gap of years between planning and building, by the operation of racial and economic discrimination, and by the fact that the housing market is heavily affected by developments unrelated to housing need. For example, the cost of credit, though it may govern the rate of new building, may be determined by general economic considerations that have little relation to housing need or cash in the hands of prospective tenants. Government or quasi-public housing does not do the trick either if the scale is small or the housing limited to poor people. The tendency in those circumstance is for housing to be overwhelmed by larger economic and social forces and to deteriorate or turn into ghettos. Housing provided under detailed regulation—payment to a tenant contingent on his prior housing and acceptable maintenance of his new housing—becomes in the end a vexing, impossible administrative problem.

Food stamps illustrate still other issues that develop in inkind programs. As there was widespread determination in the 1970s to keep welfare costs down, liberals concentrated on improving the food-stamp program. Liberalization combined with rising unemployment and inflation to balloon the program from 2 million participants in 1968 to 5 million in 1971 and 15 million in 1974. Yet that 15 million was only a third of the people thought actually to be entitled to food stamps. Why the failure in take-up? Staff of the Joint Economic Committee offered the following reasons: "(1) Purchase requirement of food stamps which compels households to give up a sizeable portion of income in order to participate; (2) stigma attached to food stamps; (3) insufficient outreach programs; (4) long lines at certification offices and complexity of applications; (5) inability to afford living quarters with cooking facilities; (6) or transient status, exemplified by a great number of potentially eligible migrant workers." [9]

In short, 15 million people were benefitting from a new transfer program but perhaps 30 million declined to participate. They did not have enough cash to participate, or the staging of the program in some manner discouraged them. One element of their problem is the food stamp itself, that is, its public visibility and its inflexibility (foods in specified quantity—period). The other element of their problem is that food stamps are income tested, an issue to which we will come shortly.

Finally, publicly provided social services—child welfare, vocational rehabilitation, activities directed to the aged, antipoverty and manpower programs, and so forth—are still a different form of in-kind provision. Although housing and food-stamp programs enter the private market at some point, in the public social services a client may deal with civil servants from beginning to end. For many reasons, including political payoffs and the fiscal needs of cities and states,[10] public social services have also expanded considerably in the past decade. By 1975, a little less than $8 billion a year was being spent on them, half from federal and half from state and local sources.[11]

It is difficult to assess these programs in general. Many provide poor care. Most public day care for children is custodial in nature, despite all the talk about quality. Juvenile and family courts widely provide social services to children who, if their families were wealthier, would not have been brought to court. (It is generally understood that not bringing them to court may be the most effective way to help children avoid subsequent delinquency.) Indeed, some programs are identified as social services that would hardly be acknowledged as such by their clients—for example, a federal program to force fathers to support their dependent children. On the other hand, quite different illustrations are available—fine day care for children, recreation centers and other services for the aged, mental-hygiene clinics. And it is a compelling argument that public programs such as AFDC that intrinsically deal with troubled people ought to include some provision for helping them.

Without going deeply into the problems of social-service programs, we may offer several generalizations. First, as with housing, the public social services do not represent the entire systems at issue. Those who are not poor prefer private rather than public care for their children. When necessary, they prefer boarding and military schools to public institutions.[12] Second, "there is a significant body of research about limited service utilization by the most disadvantaged, their high dropout and failure rates, and their general lack of access to the more sophisticated services." [13] That is, they do not use social services nearly in the degree that one supposes they need or might want them. And third, at least a substantial reason for poor service and poor access is that income-tested programs are designed and administered as much in response to public as to private (i.e., client) objectives. As a consequence, they may offer services that are not wanted by the clients, or offer services in limited quantities or in ways that discourage use. Quite naturally, therefore, use of services seems not to reflect presumed need.

We do not outline problems in these various in-kind programs in order to arrive at prescriptions for each. The correctives are different, and each program would require substantial consideration of its own. But it should be clear that, in establishing programs for food, or housing, or health service, or any special need, one should look beyond vouchers and service authorizations to how the market itself is structured and how these special demands will fit into it. That is particularly the case when, first, not cash but a service or product is being provided; second, the market in question is dominated by a well-organized and cohesive profession or group of providers or businesses; third, traditionally or intrinsically, the way the product is provided lends itself to discriminatory practices; fourth, most or all of the consumers are poor or otherwise disadvantaged and subject to exploitation; and fifth, the supply of the product is largely controlled by considerations other than purchasing power.

It will be perceived that in the real world many of these conditions occur together, and that can hardly be chance. For example, Medicaid beneficiaries are identifiably poor people, provided with an in-kind service by well-organized professional and provider groups. The supply of physicians and hospitals is, of course, barely if at all determined by need or purchasing power. In other words, in-kind programs may tend to operate within their own closed economies, insulated from or impervious to ordinary competitive considerations. As that is so, the decision to deliver an in-kind service must rest on a thorough understanding of the market and on carefully constructed safeguards. Otherwise, a program lends itself to poor service at best and exploitation of the beneficiary at worst, and in any case falls short of achieving a serious redistributive goal.

The issue of income testing overlaps with issues of noncash service, but it merits direct discussion.

Rationing and Income Testing

At least from the time of the depression in the 1930s, substantial sentiment looked to the government to control the more brutal manifestations of a free-market system. We expected the government to spend increasing sums and to provide expanding social services for the poor and otherwise disadvantaged. With a rapidly expanding economy after World War II, it even appeared that we might spend more for these purposes without reducing wages and profits. That appearance dulled the inevitable conflict between public and private demands; there was an undeclared moratorium in the struggle for shares. All the while, we took scant notice of what new benefit levels or new programs would cost when these innovations matured—that is, when everyone intended to be covered was covered, when staged benefit levels reached their peak, or when providers adjusted their prices to the new flood of money. Then quite suddenly, as it seemed, we found ourselves driven forth from Eden into a world where we could not count on continuous expansion of the economy or a "fiscal dividend" for government.

We operate with scarcities even in the best of times; so goods must be rationed. Our preferred method of rationing is pricing: Prices rise to a level where there is no more demand than goods, and the goods go to those who can afford them. Queuing, though we use it comparatively little, is another possible method. Instead of bidding against one another for a place in a day-care center or for elective surgery in a hospital, we might put our names on a list and wait our turn. Income testing is still another type of rationing device. It selects people under a specified income level, usually the poor; and usually the number of beneficiaries and the level of services are in relation to an overall amount we are willing to spend.

Now, it is possibly illuminating that income testing was expanding markedly as the moment of our loss of innocence approached. Between 1968 and 1973, the annual cost of social insurance and related programs increased by 77 percent.[14] But the annual cost of income-tested programs (see table 6.2) rose by 130 percent—from $16 to $37 billion. Yet income shares do not show a net responsive movement in favor of poor people.[15] We have touched on the reason in several chapters. If poorer people can be confined in terms of their benefits within a discrete and relatively small sector of the economy or the transfer system, though that small sector doubles and triples they will lose the larger prizes. Shortage of resources is an argument widely given in the United States and other western countries for moving to income testing. What is not usually made clear—is indeed concealed—is that widespread income testing, in the final outcome, saves money at the expense of the poorest people. Its published purpose may be efficient use of available funds for poor people but its ulterior purpose is rationing, and it is the poor who are restrained.

The United States is far from centrally planned and directed, and income testing would not be so damaging to the share of the lowest quintile if it were not intrinsically self-limiting. Some of the ways in which it is self-limiting have been referred to. First is the phenomenon of stigma, the feeling that income testing is associated with failure and consequent reluctance to apply for benefits or, on the officials' side, to provide benefits strictly in accordance with law. Failure in take-up is one consequence.

Second, it is well understood sociologically that programs with low-status clients have low-status professionals, and vice versa. Together, therefore, they tend to carry little weight politically, and are not an effective force in getting the programs improved. Low-status workers and clientele may take out their frustrations on one another, further undermining take-up and quality of services. More broadly, the quality and benefit levels of any program depend on the capacity of its constituency to monitor and improve it over the years. The constituency of income-tested programs is politically powerless, almost by definition. Thus, income-tested programs by their internal dynamics tend to support the implicit national purpose—giving the poor a strictly limited share.

We should not leave this matter without noting that, apart from its effect on shares, extensive income testing may have momentous social consequences. We referred in early chapters to warnings that a permanent underclass may be developing in the country. A broad move to income testing can only serve to reinforce this tendency. As the policy balance shifts heavily toward income-tested food, housing, medical care, day care, and higher education—not hypothetical examples—we move toward a duplex society. One portion of the population lives with a free market while the underclass lives in a world of welfare, public clinics, and housing administrators. It is not simply that their world is Dickensian, but the programs become impossible to administer and the relationship between the underclass and those who regard themselves as classless is fraught with danger to society.

The approach that contrasts with income testing, which we have pursued throughout without naming, is called universalism. The term is somewhat misleading, seeming to imply that everyone receives each benefit. Properly used, it means that everyone *within a designated population group* receives a benefit, without regard to income. Population groups can be large (children, the aged, the unemployed, those attending college) or very small indeed (everyone needing kidney transplant or dialysis.) Virtually all the proposals offered here are universal, in that sense, but a moment's thought will confirm that the proposals are nevertheless framed to favor those with lower income. Those non-income-tested measures, taken together, reflect what has been called a pluralistic strategy.

The Pluralistic Strategy

We have reviewed a large and disparate array of measures. Major emphases may be clear enough—high employment, tax reform, a cashable tax credit or children's allowance, two-tier social security, health insurance carefully designed for equity, welfare as a safety net rather than basic antipoverty program—but the details may be difficult to retain. Many of the elements of these proposals and recommendations are negotiable and changeable; the particular proposals are not the central point of the book. They merely illustrate the extent and versatility of redistributive measures available for a pluralistic strategy. The central point is that redistribution can be achieved in consonance with the way income is put together in the United States, that is, by dealing purposefully with the existing and developing assortment of national programs, laws, and regulations—congressional session by congressional session and fiscal year by fiscal year.

Those who require a schematic grand design or a single proposal that will do the whole job will not advance redistribution, for they do not understand the nature of the problem or of the American political process. Those who are impatient for a single political act that may bring the nation to social grace do not grasp that greed has more staying power. To be sure, the problem of a pluralistic strategy lies in its very complexity and in the variety of expertise it requires. Those who are wealthier or are advocates of the wealthy have so far seemed to have more patience for the task.

We began with the objective of shifting $55 to $60 billion from the highest two to the lowest two population quintiles. That might reasonably be expected to give the lowest fifth of the population a little more than one-tenth of national income. Because the proposals offered here are negotiable and not blocks of a grand design, they are not additive for purposes of pricing. Examples may make clear that the objective is achievable, but first a couple of caveats: Some proposals, like the cashable tax credit and children's allowance, are alternatives. Also, the framing of most proposals depends on what else is done. For example, benefits for dependents are not necessary in social security if we have tax credits or children's allowances. Therefore, the measures that are desirable may alter somewhat from year to year, as the trunk to which they are grafted grows and changes.

A cashable tax credit at $225 per person would cost about $20 billion a year. About 40 percent of the money would go to people with less than $5,000 a year income (the poverty level for a family of four), and 25 percent to people with incomes between $5,000 and $10,000. A program of children's allowances would have a net cost of about $34 billion (in 1974), of which about $10 billion would go to the bottom quintile of the population. We have noted that a public-service employment program would have a net cost (less recaptured taxes and savings in unemployment insurance and welfare) of $5 billion. Because of the wage levels envisioned (under $8,000 a year), the largest part of the $5 billion would go to the bottom quintile of the population and the remainder to the next higher quintile. As for the proposed two-tier system in social security, as presented it redistributes benefits within the existing total cost. In 1974, about 10 percent of benefits went to the bottom quintile of beneficiaries (not the same as but well within the bottom quintile of the population). It appears that the proposed two-tier system would have increased their share to 15 percent—a gain of about $3 billion. National health insurance might add $4 to $13 billion a year, depending on its form, to personal health-care expenditures. Obviously the distributive gains (or losses) to the lowest quintiles also depend on how the program is designed.

Of the $55 to $60 billion we are seeking to shift, $41 or $42 billion is required for the lowest quintile, and the remainder for the next quintile. Just three measures most readily evaluated—the tax credit, public-service employment, and two-tier social security—taken together, promise gains in benefits for the lowest quintile of at least $15 billion a year, and for the next quintile at least $5 or $6 billion. These three measures would shift a third of the necessary sum. They are an indication of the magnitude of what is possible if all feasible measures, large and small, were pressed over a number of years. Moreover, many of the provisions would have secondary effects. For example, public-service employment would tend to drive up wages at the lower levels, thus multiplying gains for the lower quintiles.

As for revenue, taxing capital gains at normal rates would provide about $9 billion. Dropping the property-tax deduction would net about $10 billion. Revision of death taxes might increase revenues by about $5 billion. Just these three measures would provide $24 billion and, as noted, some proposals are presented as revisions within *existing* revenues. It is worth bearing in mind also the constant pressure for tax reductions as increased national income brings more people into higher income brackets (see chapter 1). Revenue can be made available for redistribution by resisting the most unfair tax reductions.

After one settles for himself whether the objective is desirable, virtually the first question is whether the nation can afford redistribution of such magnitude. Part of the question is relatively straightforward: Will the government have the revenues that seem to be required? One shops for his answer at a counter that offers some range of choices. At the end of 1975, the Joint Economic Committee asserted that "by fiscal 1981, a full employment surplus of $66 billion will be available for division among new programs, tax reductions, and contributions to the actual budget surplus." [16] Only a small portion of that $66 billion a year, carefully directed, would achieve the redistributive objective in five to seven years. But properly understood, the pluralistic strategy is not an argument about new and expanded programs only. With much new spending, redistribution can (though even then it often does not) take place comparatively unnoticed. But with little new spending, the pluralistic strategy addresses the myriad changes that occur from year to year, and presses a gain for the poorer quintiles. The capacity to negotiate by increments toward fairer shares is an advantage of this strategy.

A more complex and difficult question is the relationship of redistribution to recession and inflation. We noted (chapter 1) that similar industrial countries, without adopting noticeably different economic or political forms, have a fairer distribution than we. In chapter 3, we argued that more equitable distribution of income may facilitate the development of human capital and itself promote economic growth—an argument comprehensively set forth by Gunnar Myrdal many years ago.[17] And beyond that, in chapter 2 we faced the questions brought on by the recent experience of inflation and recession and the failure of Keynesian economics to provide direct solutions. It appears that an incomes policy, which is to say wage and price controls, would be required to meet an objective of substantial redistribution if not to maintain full employment with price stability.[18] If an incomes policy is itself debatable, eminent economists from left to right have recognized the need to develop stronger instruments for national economic planning.[19] Such instruments should make plain distributional issues which have so far been treated as "classified." Stronger instruments are required for redistribution, if not for growth and stability.

The Prospect

It is written in Leviticus that every fiftieth year should be a year of Jubilee, proclaimed by the blast of trumpets throughout the land. In the year of Jubilee, fields were to be left uncultivated, debts forgiven, and Hebrew slaves set free. Lands and houses in open country that had been sold were to revert to former owners. There was redistribution! But that was a less complex and possibly more

God-fearing time. Nothing so drastic is likely to happen or to be proposed.

Distributive issues will be negotiated and fought out in this country over the next years. There is no question about that, and not much question that the distributive issues will now be more open. With the promise evaporating that everyone might gain without altering relative position, the struggle for shares sharpens. Every group thinks of its own interest—that is natural; along with that, all might agree on a measure of relative improvement for the poorer quintiles. That would be public policy, and would be pressed by sympathetic and hopefully sophisticated interest groups, and existing public institutions (the Council of Economic Advisers, the Department of Labor) and new ones.

The proposals here are incremental. They may fail to stir those with a more radical vision, but they are a great deal more than we have been committed to so far. And they are explicit and measurable, which are advantages not to be minimized. Those proposals are consonant with a tradition of liberal, negotiated progress and they address our income-transfer programs in the way in which they are, in fact, structured. Neater would be nicer, but we are not discussing housekeeping.

Social justice is at stake, but the urgency of dealing with the distributive issue should not be underestimated. The postwar reform movements have passed into history. They have had what effects they have had, but distributional problems remain acute. In the War against Poverty the United States mounted a struggle premised on the capacity of participatory democracy to achieve change. Whatever was gained from that struggle, many took from it the lesson that participatory processes are fruitless. Everyone experiences the sense of splintering sources of power, so that the lever to achieve a desired result may be out of reach—or there may be no lever. A generation is growing into middle years with a powerful sense that reform has been tried and has failed. Prominent legislators and administrators voluntarily vacate their seats, saying in one way or another that *they* find themselves powerless!

In other words, our technologies and bureaucracies may now be so diffuse and, in each of their parts, rigid that in most cases participatory processes will not reach the central issue of distribution of resources. If that is so, injustice can persist and increase to a point that endangers the political system we know and value. Futurists have written scenarios that explain how our system will be transformed without revolution or even visible change of scenery and symbols. The issue is acute because maldistribution and the sense of powerlessness are, quite naturally, accompanied by a loss of community. That is the way a society goes down, not in defeat but in recrimination.

Still, our society has the institutional framework for change. We require only assembling the will or policy to oppose our structure of privilege. We can match achievement to expectation somewhat more closely and knit real national effort to promises. Because the change required is modest, all stakes considered, and is in the enlightened interest of those who are or will be privileged, it still may be achieved.

Down that road, if we take it, we can approach the eradication of poverty; in the process we can gain community. The change would be heard in our land like the blast of trumpets.

11. Peter Barnes, "Earned vs. Unearned Income," *The New Republic*, 167, no. 13 (Oct. 7, 1972), 15–18.

12. Charles B. Markham, "Discrimination Held Main Cause of Income Inequality," quoted in *The New York Times*, February 25, 1970, p. 18.

13. H. J. Gilman, "Economic Discrimination and Unemployment," *American Economic Review*, 55 (December 1965), 1077–95.

14. Lester Thurow, "Occupational Distribution of Returns to Education and Experience for Whites and Negroes," *Proceedings, American Statistical Association*, 62 (1967), 233–43.

15. Theodore Cross, "Black and White Incomes: The Gap," *The New York Times*, July 26, 1975, p. 23.

16. Joseph Pechman, "The Rich, the Poor, and the Taxes They Pay," *The Public Interest*, no. 17 (Fall 1969), pp. 21–43; and Tibor Scitovsky, *Papers on Welfare and Growth* (Stanford: Stanford University Press, 1964).

17. George J. Stigler, "Director's Law of Public Income Redistribution," *The Journal of Law and Economics*, 13, no. 2 (October 1970), 1–10.

18. Henry Aaron, "Implicit Transfer to Homeowners in the Federal Budget," mimeographed (Washington, D.C.: The Association for the Study of Grants Economy, Dec. 26, 1969), p. 21.

19. Otto A. Davis and John E. Jackson, "Representative Assemblies and Demands for Redistribution: The Case of Senate Voting on the Family Assistance Plan," in Harold M. Hochman and George E. Peterson, eds., *Redistribution through Public Choice* (New York: Columbia University Press, 1974), pp. 261–88.

20. Robert L. Heilbroner, "Phase II of the Capitalist System," *The New York Times Magazine*, November 28, 1971, p. 85.

21. The President's Commission on Income Maintenance Programs, *Poverty amid Plenty: The American Paradox* (Washington, D.C.: Government Printing Office, 1969).

22. Irving Kristol, "Equality as an Ideal," *International Encyclopedia of the Social Sciences* (New York: Macmillan, 1968), p. 108.

23. John Rawls, *A Theory of Justice* (Cambridge: Harvard University Press, 1971), p. 62.

24. Hochman and Peterson, *Redistribution*, p. xvii. See also Jan Tinbergen, *Economic Policy: Principles and Design* (Amsterdam: North Holland Publishing Company, 1956); and Milton Viorst, "There is No Raymond Aron Cult, Talk With a Reasonable Man" *New York Times Magazine*, April 19, 1970.

25. See, for example, Arthur M. Okun, *Equality and Efficiency—The Big Tradeoff* (Washington, D.C.: The Brookings Institution, 1975); and James Tobin, "On Limiting the Domain of Inequality," *The Journal of Law and Economics*, 13, no. 2 (October 1970).

26. R. H. Tawney, *Equality* (London: Allen and Unwin, 1952), p. 113.

27. See, for example, Nathan Glazer, "Paradoxes of Health Care," *The*

Notes

1. Fair Shares

1. For an exploration of why this may be so, see Richard Goodwin, *The American Condition* (New York: Doubleday, 1974).

2. Irwin Garfinkel and Robert D. Plotnick, "Poverty, Unemployment, and the Current Recession," *Public Welfare,* 33, no. 3 (1975), 10–17.

3. Robert D. Plotnick and Felicity Skidmore, *Progress Against Poverty: A Review of the 1964–1974 Decade* (New York: Harcourt, Brace Jovanovich, 1975).

4. Robert J. Lampman, "What Does It Do for The Poor?—A New Test for National Policy," *The Public Interest,* no. 34 (Winter 1974), p. 71.

5. Alfred M. Skolnik and Sophie R. Dales, "Social Welfare Expenditures, 1971–72," *Social Security Bulletin,* December 1972, pp. 3 ff.

6. Robert J. Lampman, "Measured Inequality of Income: What Does it Mean and What Can It Tell Us?" *Annals of the American Academy of Political and Social Science,* 409 (September 1973), 81–91.

7. Ida C. Merriam, "Welfare and Its Measurement," in Eleanor Bernert Sheldon and Wilbert E. Moore, *Indicators of Social Change* (New York: Russell Sage Foundation, 1968), pp. 721–84; and Dorothy S. Brady, *Age and the Income Distribution,* Social Security Administration Research Report no. 8 (Washington, D.C.: Government Printing Office, 1965).

8. Benjamin Bridges, Jr., *Redistributive Effects of Transfer Payments among Age and Economic Status Groups,* Office of Research and Statistics, Social Security Administration, Staff Paper no. 10 (Washington, D.C., 1971).

9. Merriam, "Welfare and Its Measurement," p. 742.

10. Edwin Kuh, "The Robin Hood Syndrome," *The New York Times,* March 5, 1973, Op Ed page.

Public Interest, no. 22 (Winter 1971), pp. 62–77; and James Q. Wilson, "The Bureaucracy Problem," *The Public Interest,* no. 6 (Winter 1967), pp. 3–9.

28. Victor Fuchs, "Redefining Poverty," *The Public Interest,* no. 8 (Summer 1967), p. 89. See also Brady, *Age and the Income Distribution;* Lee Rainwater, "Economic Inequality and the Credit Income Tax," *Working Papers,* 1, no. 1 (Spring 1973), 50–62; and Alvin L. Schorr, *Poor Kids* (New York: Basic Books, 1966), pp. 87–91.

29. *Economic Report of the President, Together with the Annual Report of the Council of Economic Advisers* (Washington, D.C.: Government Printing Office, 1964).

30. Robert Hunter, *Poverty* (New York, 1904).

31. Economic Council of Canada, *Fifth Annual Review: The Challenge of Growth and Change* (Ottawa: Queen's Printer, 1968).

32. One perceives in all of this a law of halves. The poverty level has been half of median income, and the share of national income allocated to the poorest fifth has been half of that—that is, in the aggregate, one-quarter of its strictly proportional share.

33. W. G. Runciman, *Relative Deprivation and Social Justice* (London: Routledge and Kegan Paul, 1966).

34. National Commission on the Causes and Prevention of Violence, quoted in the *Washington Post,* November 29, 1969, editorial page.

35. Michael Lewis, *Urban America—Institution and Experience* (New York: Wiley, 1973), chapters 6, 7, and 8.

36. The first term was used by Gunnar Myrdal, in *Beyond the Welfare State* (New Haven: Yale University Press, 1960); the second term was used by Peter Townsend in *Sociology and Social Policy* (London: Allen Lane, 1975), p. 38.

37. Myrdal, *Beyond the Welfare State.*

38. Alvin L. Schorr, "The Duplex Society," *The New York Times,* June 4, 1972, p. 15.

39. Barbara Wootton, *The Social Foundations of Wage Policy* (London: Allen and Unwin, 1962); and John H. Goldthorpe, "Social Inequality and Social Integration in Modern Britain," in Dorothy Wedderburn, ed., *Poverty, Inequality, and Class Structure* (London: Cambridge University Press, 1974).

40. Ibid., p. 231.

41. United Nations, Department of Economic and Social Affairs, *Social Policy and the Distribution of Income in the Nation* (New York: United Nations, 1969), table 1, pp. 134–35.

42. John H. Chandler, "Perspectives on Poverty—An International Comparison," *Monthly Labor Review,* February 1969, p. 56.

43. See, for example, Herbert J. Gans, *More Equality* (New York: Pantheon Books, 1973), chapter 7, "Some Proposals for Research on Equality."

44. Joseph A. Pechman, Henry J. Aaron, and Michael K. Taussig, *Social*

Security, Perspectives for Reform (Washington: The Brookings Institution, 1968); U.S. Congress, Joint Economic Committee, *Income Security for Americans: Recommendations of the Public Welfare Study,* 93d Cong., 2d sess. (Washington, D.C.: Government Printing Office, 1974); Michael C. Barth, et al., *Toward an Effective Income Support System: Problems, Prospects, and Choices* (Madison, Wis.: Institute for Research on Poverty, 1974).

45. A negative income tax is in theory a highly simplified scheme of distributing money to people with incomes below specified levels, with an internal incentive for earning one's own income. It is usually proposed that administration be integrated with the federal income tax—thus, the name.

46. James Tobin, "Reflections on Recent History," Robert J. Lampman "The Role of Income-Conditioning in the American System of Transfers," and Alice M. Rivlin, "Discussion," in *Proceedings of the American Statistical Association, 1973* (Washington, D.C.: American Statistical Association, 1974).

47. President's Commission on Income Maintenance Programs, *Poverty amid Plenty.*

48. Among critiques of such restructuring, see Eveline M. Burns, "Welfare Reform and Income Security Policies," *The Social Welfare Forum 1970* (New York: Columbia University Press, 1970), pp. 46–60; Alvin L. Schorr, "The President's Welfare Program and Commission," *Public Welfare,* 28, no. 1 (1970), pp. 26–32.

49. U. S. Congress, Joint Economic Committee, *Handbook of Public Income Transfer Programs: 1975* (Washington, D.C.: Government Printing Office, 1974).

50. Three accounts of that legislative struggle are Vincent G. and Vee Burke, *Nixon's Good Deed—Welfare Reform* (New York: Columbia University Press, 1974); Daniel Patrick Moynihan, *The Politics of a Guaranteed Income* (New York: Random House, 1973); and M. Kenneth Bowler, *The Nixon Guaranteed Income Proposal* (Cambridge: Ballinger, 1974). See also Alvin L. Schorr, "Who Killed Cock Robin Hood?" *Harper's Magazine,* 246, no. 1477 (June 1973).

51. Norman Furniss, "The Welfare Debate in Great Britain: Implications for the United States," *Public Administration Review,* May–June 1975, p. 307.

2. Work and Shares

1. Peter Henle, "Exploring the Distribution of Earned Income," *Monthly Labor Review,* 95 (December 1972), 16–27.

2. U.S. Bureau of the Census, *Money Income in 1971 of Families and Persons in the United States,* Current Population Reports, P-60, no. 85 (Washington, D.C.: Government Printing Office, 1972).

3. Lester C. Thurow, "More Are Going To Be Poor," *The New Republic,* November 2, 1974, p. 26.

4. U.S. Bureau of the Census, *Statistical Abstract of the United States, 1974* (Washington, D.C.: Government Printing Office, 1974), pp. 386, 382.

5. From and derived from *Monthly Labor Review,* 97 (December 1974) table 3, p. 87.

6. Ibid.

7. Julius Shiskin, *Unemployment: Measurement Problems and Recent Trends,* U.S. Bureau of Labor Statistics, Report 445 (Washington, D.C., 1975), p. 6.

8. J. M. Cairnes, *Some Leading Principles of Political Economy Newly Expounded* (New York: A. M. Kelley, 1967), p. 65.

9. Peter Doeringer and Michael Piore, *Internal Labor Markets and Manpower Analysis* (Lexington, Mass.: D. C. Heath, 1971), chapter 8.

10. Ruth Fabricant Lowell, *Summary, The Labor Market in New York City: A Study of Jobs and Low-Income Area Workers in 1970* (City of New York, Human Resources Administration, Office of Research and Program Evaluation, released October 1975).

11. Karl Polanyi, *The Great Transformation: The Political and Economic Origins of Our Time* (Boston: Beacon Press, 1957), p. 177.

12. U.S. Bureau of the Census, *Statistical Abstract 1974,* pp. 352–56.

13. Ibid., pp. 346–49.

14. Ibid., p. 388.

15. U.S. Bureau of the Census, *Characteristics of the Low Income Population, 1972,* Current Population Reports, ser. P-60, no. 91 (Washington, D.C.: Government Printing Office, 1973), table 27, p. 94.

16. Howard Hayghe, *Labor Force Activity of Married Women,* Special Labor Force Report 153 (Washington, D.C.: Bureau of Labor Statistics, 1973), table 2, p. 33.

17. Howard Hayghe, *Marital and Family Characteristics of the Labor Force in March 1973,* Special Labor Force Report 164, printed in *Monthly Labor Review,* April 1974.

18. U.S. Bureau of the Census, *Statistical Abstract 1974,* p. 351.

19. Ibid., p. 339.

20. Howard Hayghe, *Job Tenure of Workers, January, 1973,* Special Labor Force Report 172 (Washington, D.C.: Bureau of Labor Statistics, 1975).

21. *Employment of School Age Youth, October, 1974,* Summary Special Labor Force Report (Washington, D.C.: Bureau of Labor Statistics, 1974).

22. U.S. Bureau of the Census, *Statistical Abstract 1974,* p. 338.

23. Derived from U.S. Bureau of the Census, *Income in 1967 of Families in the United States,* Current Population Reports, ser. P-60, no. 59 (Washington, D.C.: Government Printing Office, April 1969), table II, pp. 49–50; and *Money Income in*

1972 of Families and Persons in the United States, Current Population Reports, ser. P-60, no. 90 (Washington, D.C.: Government Printing Office, December 1973), table 4, pp. 132–33.

24. U.S. Bureau of the Census, *Statistical Abstract 1974,* pp. 352–56.

25. Ibid., p. 386.

26. These figures are derived from the two tables cited in note 23.

27. *New York Times,* November 29, 1975.

28. U.S. Bureau of the Census, *Statistical Abstract 1974,* p. 351.

29. U.S. Department of Health, Education, and Welfare, Social Security Administration, *Families with Disabled Parents under AFDC 1967–71,* Pub. no. (SSA) 74-11701, 20-1973 (Washington, D.C., December 20, 1973).

30. U.S. Department of Labor, *Annual Earnings of Household Heads in Production Jobs, 1973.* Summary Special Labor Force Report (Washington, D.C.: Bureau of Labor Statistics, March 1975).

31. U.S. Bureau of the Census, *The Social and Economic Status of the Black Population in the United States, 1972,* Current Population Reports, ser. P-23, no. 46 (Washington, D.C.: Government Printing Office, 1973), p. 49.

32. U.S. Congress, Joint Economic Committee, *Economic Problems of Women: Hearings,* Part 1, 93d Cong., 1st sess. (Washington, D.C.: Government Printing Office, 1973), p. 51.

33. Mary Huff Stevenson, "Wages, Education and Job Requirements in Women's Occupations" (paper presented at the First Annual Meeting of the Eastern Economic Association, Albany, New York, October 26, 1974), pp. 2–3.

34. See Hayghe, *Marital and Family Characteristics.*

35. *New York Times,* August 14, 1974.

36. U.S. Bureau of the Census, *Statistical Abstract 1974,* p. 351.

37. Henle, "Exploring the Distribution of Earned Income," pp. 23–24.

38. Data from independent work by Winifred Bell and Dennis Bushe, Center for Studies in Income Maintenance Policy, New York University.

39. *Employment and Earnings,* 19 (February 1973), table A-1, p. 27.

40. Robert M. Solow, "Inequality since the War," in Edward C. Budd, ed., *Inequality and Poverty* (New York: Norton, 1967), pp. 50–64.

41. Garth Mangum, *The Emergence of Manpower Policy* (New York: Holt, Rinehart, and Winston, 1969), p. 22.

42. Council of Economic Advisers, "The Employment Act: Twenty Years of Experience," in John A. Delehanty, ed., *Manpower Problems and Policies* (Scranton, Pa.: International Textbook, 1969), p. 5.

43. U.S. Bureau of the Census, *The Social and Economic Status of the Black Population in the United States, 1971,* Current Population Reports, ser. P-23, no. 42 (Washington, D.C.: Government Printing Office, 1973), table 38, p. 50. Data refer to Negro and other races.

44. See Hayghe, *Marital and Family Characteristics*. Half of white wives in the labor force were married to men with incomes less than $9,053 in 1972 and half of black wives were married to men with less than $7,246 in income. See ibid. table 2, p. 24. This relationship is complex and varies by color, age of children, and so forth.

45. U.S. Department of Labor, *Geographic Profile of Employment and Unemployment, 1973*, Bureau of Labor Statistics, Report 431 (Washington, D.C., 1974).

46. *Employment and Earnings*, 19 (February 1973), 186 and 189.

47. *Economic Report of the President*, transmitted to the Congress January 1973 (Washington, D.C.: Government Printing Office, 1973), p. 99.

48. U.S. Congress, Joint Economic Committee, *Economic Problems of Women, Hearings*, p. 52.

49. See U.S. Department of Labor, "The Employment Situation: December 1974," News Release, 75-1 (Washington, D.C., January 3, 1975), table A-2, p. 3.

50. U.S. Congress, Joint Economic Committee, Subcommittee on Fiscal Policy, *The Effectiveness of Manpower Training Programs: A Review of Research on the Impact of the Poor*, Studies in Public Welfare, paper no. 3 (staff study by Jon H. Goldstein), 92d Cong., 2d sess. (Washington, D.C.: Government Printing Office, 1972), p. 53.

51. From and derived from U.S. Department of Labor, *Manpower Report of the President, 1974* (Washington, D.C.: Government Printing Office, 1974), p. 132.

52. For a more detailed analysis of subemployment, see Helen Ginsburg, *Unemployment, Subemployment, and Public Policy* (New York: New York University School of Social Work, Center for Studies in Income Maintenance Policy, 1975), part 5. Later developments of subemployment measures are discussed in Mangum, *The Emergence of Manpower Policy*.

53. U.S. Bureau of the Census, *Characteristics of the Low Income Population, 1972*, table 30, pp. 97–98.

54. Ibid., table 4, pp. 26, 30, and 31.

55. Nancy H. Teeters, *Built-In Flexibility of Federal Expenditures*, Brookings Papers on Economic Activity, no. 3 (Washington, D.C.: The Brookings Institution, 1971), pp. 626–29.

56. Frank Furstenberg, "Work Experience and Family Life," cited in *Work in America*, Report of a Special Task Force to the Secretary of Health, Education, and Welfare (Washington, D.C., 1972), p. 22.

57. U.S. Department of Labor, *Manpower Report of the President, 1974*, p. 47.

58. Consumer Commission on the Accreditation of Health Services, *OSHA—A Means To Improve the Health of Americans*, Part 1 (Washington, D.C., 1974).

59. Controller General of the United States, Report to the Congress, *Impact of Federal Programs to Improve the Living Conditions of Migrant and Other Seasonal Farmworkers* (Washington, D.C., February 6, 1973).

60. Garth L. Mangum, "The Why, How and Whence of Manpower Programs," *Annals of the American Academy of Political and Social Science, Evaluating the War on Poverty,* September 1969, pp. 50–62.

61. Ibid.

62. John W. Dorsey, "The Mack Case: A Study in Unemployment," in Otto Eckstein, ed., *Studies in the Economics of Income Maintenance* (Washington, D.C.: The Brookings Institution, 1967), pp. 175–240.

63. MDTA, National Youth Corps, Job Corps, WIN, and JOBS.

64. Subcommittee on Fiscal Policy, *The Effectiveness of Manpower Training Programs.*

65. U.S. Congress, Joint Economic Committee, *Public Employment and Wage Subsidies (A Volume of Studies)* paper no. 19 (Washington, D.C., December 30, 1974).

66. Ibid., pp. 125, 126.

67. Sar A. Levitan and Robert Taggart, eds., *Emergency Employment Act: The PEP Generation* (Salt Lake City: Olympus, 1974), p. 12. This book provides an analysis of the public-employment-program experience.

68. Ibid., p. 26.

69. Ibid., pp. 31–32.

70. Ibid., pp. 31–32; and National Commission on Technology, Automation, and Economic Progress, *Technology and the American Economy* (Washington, D.C.: Government Printing Office, 1966), vol. 1, February 1966.

71. Harold L. Sheppard, "The Nature of the Job Problem and the Role of the New Public Service Employment," in Harold L. Sheppard, Bennett Harrison, and William J. Spring, eds., *The Political Economy of Public Service Employment* (Lexington, Mass.: D. C. Heath, 1972), p. 31.

72. U.S. Congress, Joint Economic Committee, *An Economic Evaluation of the Current Services Budget, Fiscal Year, 1977* (Washington, D.C.: Government Printing Office, 1975).

73. Polanyi, *The Great Transformation,* p. 177.

74. U.S. Bureau of the Census, *Statistical Abstract 1974,* p. 365.

75. Henle, "Exploring the Distribution of Earned Income," p. 17.

76. Ibid., p. 21.

77. Information provided by Jack Karlin, Employment Standards Administration, U.S. Department of Labor.

78. U.S. Department of Labor, Employment Standards Administration, "Estimated Number of Nonsupervisory Employees Paid Less than the Minimum Wage

Rates Specified in S. 2747 and Estimated Cost of Raising Their Wages to Those Rates on May 1, 1974.'' Table issued April 1, 1974.

79. U.S. Department of Labor, *Youth Unemployment and Minimum Wages,* Bureau of Labor Statistics, Bulletin no. 1657 (Washington, D.C.: Government Printing Office, 1970).

80. *Congressional Record,* House of Representatives, 93d Cong., 2d sess., vol. 120, no. 37, March 20, 1974, pp. H 1962 and 1967 (testimony and evidence of Representative Dent).

81. These conflicting interpretations are discussed by Donald E. Cullen, *Minimum Wage Laws* (Ithaca, N.Y.: New York State School of Industrial and Labor Relations, Cornell University, 1961).

82. U.S. Department of Labor, *Manpower Report of the President, 1971* (Washington, D.C.: Government Printing Office, 1971), p. 125.

83. Ibid.

84. Thomas Vietorisz, "We Need a $3.50 Minimum Wage," *Challenge,* May–June 1973, pp. 49–62, and Thomas Vietorisz, Robert Mier, and Bennett Harrison, "Full Employment at Living Wages," *Annals of the American Academy of Political and Social Science,* 418 (March 1975), 94–108.

85. Robert D. Plotnick, in *Poverty Report: A Decade Review* (Madison: Institute for Research on Poverty, University of Wisconsin, 1975).

86. Harry Johnson, "Unemployment and Poverty," in *Poverty and Affluence,* Leo Fishman, ed.

87. Plotnick, *Poverty Report.*

88. H.R. 50, entitled Equal Opportunity and Full Employment Act, January 14, 1975.

89. Robert Lekachman, "Managing Inflation in a Full Employment Society," *Annals of the American Academy of Political and Social Science,* 418 (March 1975), 85–93.

3. Taxation

1. Direct taxes are taxes levied on people such as the income tax. Indirect taxes are levied on commodities such as sale of cigarettes.

2. Other fiscal objectives which may conflict with these goals are growth in output and a favorable international balance of payments.

3. There are, of course, nonfiscal policy instruments for redistribution, for example, wage regulations.

4. For a view that espouses that the extent of distribution should be based on voluntarism and should be assigned locally, see: James M. Buchanan, "Who Should

Distribute What in a Federal System?'' in Harold M. Hochman and George E. Peterson, eds., *Redistribution through Public Choice* (New York and London: Columbia University Press, 1974).

5. Recent studies have indicated that the property tax is much less regressive than thought formerly. See, for example, Peter M. Mieszowski, "The Property Tax: An Excise Tax or a Profits Tax?'' *Journal of Public Economics,* April 1972, pp. 73–96.

6. There are, of course, methods for making sales and property taxes more progressive. For example, exempting food and clothing from taxation makes the sales tax more progressive. It is also possible to construct a consumption tax with progressive tax rates.

7. Other differences in need may be related to the health of the family, its age composition, and its location.

8. Benjamin Bridges, Jr., "Family Need Differences and Family Tax Burden Estimates," *National Tax Journal,* December 1971.

9. This analysis ignores benefits received by the nonpoor from government expenditures for programs which help poor people. Those benefits come from reduced crime rates and political unrest, for example. This is one basis for voluntary redistribution of income in society. For an interesting analysis of voluntary redistribution, see Buchanan, "Who Should Distribute What."

10. David H. Greenberg and Marvin Kosters, "Income Guarantees and the Working Poor" in Glen C. Cain and Harold W. Watts, *Income Maintenance and Labor Supply* (Chicago: Markham Books, 1973).

11. Michael J. Boskin, "The Economics of Labor Supply" in Cain and Watts, *Income Maintenance.*

12. Dale W. Jorgenson, "Capital Theory and Investment Behavior," *American Economic Review,* May 1963.

13. Robert M. Solow, "Technical Progress, Capital Formation and Economic Growth," *American Economic Review,* May 1962.

14. Arnold C. Harberger, "Taxation, Resource Allocation, and Welfare" in *The Role of Direct and Indirect Taxes in the Federal Revenue System* (A Conference Report of the National Bureau of Economic Research and the Brookings Institution; Princeton: Princeton University Press, 1969).

15. George Break, "The Incidence and Economic Effects of Taxation," in *The Economics of Public Finance* (Washington, D.C.: The Brookings Institution, 1974), p. 225.

16. Arnold C. Harberger, "Efficiency Effects of Taxes on Income from Capital," in Marian Kryzaniak, *The Effects of the Corporation Income Tax* (Detroit: Wayne State University Press, 1966), p. 116.

17. Richard Musgrave and Peggy Musgrave, *Public Finance in Theory and Practice* (New York: McGraw-Hill, 1973), pp. 459–60.

18. It is called adjusted gross income (AGI) by the IRS.

19. Musgrave and Musgrave, *Public Finance,* p. 268.

20. For a discussion of the merits and drawbacks of integration of the individual and corporation income taxes, see George Break and Joseph A. Pechman, "Relationship between the Corporation and Individual Income Taxes," *National Tax Journal,* September 1975.

21. Arnold C. Harberger, "The Incidence of the Corporation Income Tax," *Journal of Political Economy,* June 1962.

22. In addition there is a tax of 3.2 percent of earned income levied on employers to finance unemployment-insurance benefits.

23. There may have been a weakening in work effort due to benefits received. Joseph A. Pechman, Henry J. Aaron, and Michael K. Taussig, *Social Security: Perspectives for Reform,* (Washington, D.C.: The Brookings Institution, 1968), p. 120.

24. John A. Brittain, *The Payroll Tax for Social Security* (Washington, D.C.: The Brookings Institution, 1972), pp. 71 and 93.

25. Musgrave and Musgrave, *Public Finance,* p. 367; Bridges, "Family Need Differences."

26. A consumption tax can be tailored to individual circumstances. Exemptions and deductions can be incorporated into a consumption tax just as in an individual income tax. However, this is most easily accomplished by a uniform national sales tax, not state and local sales taxes.

27. A better way to make the tax less regressive is to give a tax credit to the poor against the individual income tax. For those whose income-tax liability is less than their credit, the credit may be returned in cash.

28. In a more sophisticated analysis the burden may actually be spread throughout the economy.

29. Henry M. Levin, "An Analysis of the Economic Effects of the New York City Sales Tax," in *Financing New York City Government* (New York: Graduate School of Public Administration, New York University, 1966), p. 662.

30. Musgrave and Musgrave, *Public Finance,* pp. 334–35.

31. Henry George, *Progress and Poverty* (New York: Appleton, 1882).

32. Naturally, whether a firm actually moves is dependent on many factors other than taxes and government service differentials between areas.

33. James M. Buchanan, *The Public Finances: An Introductory Textbook* (Homewood, Ill.: Irwin, 1970).

34. Raymond L. Richman, "The Incidence of Urban Real Estate Taxes under Conditions of Static and Dynamic Equilibrium," *Land Economics,* May 1967, p. 179.

35. Henry J. Aaron, *Who Pays the Property Tax?* (Washington, D.C.: The Brookings Institution,* 1975).

36. The Tax Reduction Act of 1975 generally lowered the tax benefits received from the depletion allowance.

4. Social Insurance and Redistribution

1. Social-insurance programs for income-maintenance purposes in the United States include: federal Old Age, Survivors, and Disability Insurance (OASDI); state unemployment insurance; state workmen's compensation; state temporary disability insurance; railroad retirement, railroad unemployment insurance, railroad disability insurance; and public retirement programs.

2. Alfred M. Skolnik and Sophie R. Dales, "Social Welfare Expenditures, Fiscal Year 1974," *Social Security Bulletin,* January 1975, p. 11.

3. Alfred M. Skolnik and Sophie R. Dales, "Social Welfare Expenditure, 1972–1973," *Social Security Bulletin,* January 1974, table 3, p. 11.

4. Max Horlick, *National Expenditures on Social Security in Selected Countries, 1968 and 1971,* Research and Statistics Note, no. 29-1974, Social Security Administration (Washington, D.C., Oct. 18, 1974).

5. Data for figures 1 and 2 were collected in March 1971 by the Social Security Administration, Office of Research and Statistics, with the cooperation of the Bureau of Census. See Dorothy S. Projector and Judith Bretz, "Measurement of Transfer Income in the Current Population Survey" in James D. Smith, ed., *The Personal Distribution of Income and Wealth,* vol. 39, *Studies in Income and Wealth* (New York: National Bureau of Economic Research, 1975), tables 1, 5, 6, and 7, pp. 380, 390–92, and 394–401.

6. Michael C. Barth, George J. Carcagno, and John L. Palmer, *Toward an Effective Income Support System: Problems, Prospects, and Choices* (Madison: University of Wisconsin, Institute for Research on Poverty, 1974), tables 5 and 6, pp. 26 and 28.

7. *Social Security Bulletin: Annual Statistical Supplement, 1971* (Washington, D.C.: Social Security Administration, 1971), table 8, p. 31.

8. Philip Frohlich, *Denied Disability Insurance Applicants: A Comparison with Beneficiaries and Nonapplicants,* The 1966 Survey of the Disabled, Report no. 11 (Washington, D.C.: Social Security Administration, Office of Research and Statistics, September 1970), table 11.

9. *Social Security Bulletin: Annual Statistical Supplement, 1972* (Washington, D.C.: Social Security Administration, 1972), table 56, p. 77.

10. Patience Lauriat and William Rabin, "Men Who Claim Benefits before Age 65: Findings from the Survey of New Beneficiaries, 1968," *Social Security Bulletin,* November 1970, table 5, p. 11.

11. Ibid., p. 17.

12. Ella J. Polinsky, "The Position of Women in the Social Security System," *Social Security Bulletin*, July 1969, table 8, pp. 6 and 10.

13. Ibid.

14. Luch B. Mallan, "Women Born in the Early 1900's: Employment, Earnings, and Benefit Levels," *Social Security Bulletin*, March 1974, p. 19.

15. *Social Security Bulletin Supplement 1972*, table 82, p. 103, and table 67, pp. 83–92.

16. See chapter 4 and, for example, James N. Morgan, et al., *Five Thousand American Families: Patterns of Economic Progress* (Ann Arbor: Survey Research Center, Institute for Social Research, The University of Michigan, 1974), vol. I, p. 129.

17. Leonard Rubin, "Economic Status of Black Persons: Findings from Survey of Newly Entitled Beneficiaries," *Social Security Bulletin*, September 1974, table 12, p. 27.

18. Lenore A. Epstein, "Workers Entitled to Minimum Retirement Benefits under OASDI," *Social Security Bulletin*, March 1967, table 2, p. 6; and Rubin, "Economic Status of Black Persons," tables 5, 9, and 10, pp. 21, 25, and 26.

19. Paula Franklin, "Earnings of Disabled-Worker Beneficiaries," *Social Security Bulletin*, June 1974, table 2, p. 19.

20. *Social Security Bulletin Supplement 1972*, tables 67 and 97, pp. 83–93 and 113–14.

21. Ibid.

22. Ibid., table 41, p. 64.

23. Unemployment-insurance contributions, expressed as percentages of total payroll in covered employment, were 2.6 percent in 1940, 1.2 percent in 1950, 1.2 percent in 1960, 0.7 percent in 1970, and 0.8 percent in 1972. See ibid., table 22, p. 48.

24. James R. O'Brien, "Unemployment Insurance: The Urgency for Reform," *The American Federationist*, April 1974, p. 23.

25. Ohio Bureau of Employment Service, Division of Research and Statistics, table RS 215.A-1 (3-6-74) and table RS 215.GI (5-14-73).

26. The analysis of the 1967 Survey of Economic Opportunity (SEO) data presented here is based on special tabulations prepared for the W. E. Upjohn Institute for Employment Research. These tabulations drew on information processed from the SEO interview questionnaires and edited and refined by the Brookings Institution. A subsequent editing and refinement was made at the University of Wisconsin and this version of the SEO is now more generally used for analysis.

27. U.S. Department of Labor, Manpower Administration, *Unemployment Insurance: State Laws and Experience*, (Washington, D.C. revised 1973), p. 8.

28. *Unemployment and Income Security: Goals for the 1970's* (Report of

the Committee on Unemployment Insurance Objectives Sponsored by the W. E. Upjohn Institute for Employment Research, July 1969), p. 11.

29. Data for all unemployment are from the Current Population Survey as reported monthly in *Employment and Earnings* (Bureau of Labor Statistics). Data for insured unemployment come from state employment security agency reports based on monthly surveys of recorded characteristics of claimants filing for benefits. The proportion of the unemployed who are insured for benefit, by sex, age, and race, presented here are averages for the fiscal year 1973, as published in *Unemployment Insurance Statistics,* June–July 1974, p. 21.

30. Joseph M. Becker, S. J., *The Adequacy of the Benefit Amount in Unemployment Insurance* (Washington, D.C.: The W. E. Upjohn Institute for Employment Research, May 1961), tables 3 and 4, pp. 37 and 41.

31. Idella G. Swisher, *Source and Size of Income of the Disabled,* The 1966 Survey of the Disabled, Report no. 16 (Washington, D.C., June 1971), table 3, pp. 34–36.

32. Idella G. Swisher, *Family Income of the Disabled,* The 1966 Survey of the Disabled, Report no. 13 (Washington, D.C., October 1970), table D, p. 9; and *The Poor in 1965 and Trends, 1959–65,* Research and Statistics Note no. 5-1967, Social Security Administration (Washington, D.C., February 16, 1967), table 2.

33. Data used for writing this section are from Alfred M. Skolnik and Daniel N. Price, "Workmen's Compensation under Scrutiny," *Social Security Bulletin,* October 1974, pp. 3–25.

34. Monroe Berkowitz, "Workmen's Compensation Income Benefits: Their Adequacy and Equity," *Supplemental Studies for the National Commission on State Workmen's Compensation Laws* (Washington, D.C.: Government Printing Office, 1973), vol. 1, pp. 181–274.

35. Daniel Price, "Cash Benefits for Short-Term Sickness, 1948–72," *Social Security Bulletin,* January 1974, p. 27.

36. Charles S. Wilder, *Time Loss for Work among the Currently Employed Population,* Vital and Health Statistics, ser. 10:71, National Center for Health Statistics (Washington, D.C.: Government Printing Office, 1972).

37. Swisher, *Family Income of the Disabled,* table D, p. 9; and Swisher, *Source and Size of Income of the Disabled,* table A.

38. Lawrence D. Haber, *Disability, Work, and Income Maintenance: Prevalence of Disabiity, 1966,* The 1966 Survey of the Disabled, Report no. 2 (Washington, D.C.: Social Security Administration, Office of Research and Statistics, May 1968), tables 3 and 4, pp. 5–6.

39. John R. Commons and John B. Andrews, *Principles of Labor Legislation,* 3d ed. (New York: Harper and Brothers, 1920), p. 382.

40. Robert J. Myers, *Social Insurance and Allied Government Programs* (Homewood, Ill.: Irwin, 1965), pp. 6 and 9–10.

41. I. M. Rubinow, *Social Insurance* (New York: Holt, 1913), p. 491.

42. U.S. Congress, Joint Economic Committee, Subcommittee on Fiscal Policy, *Income Security for Americans: Recommendations of the Public Welfare Study,* 93d Cong., 2d sess. (Washington, D.C.: Government Printing Office, 1974).

43. Joseph A. Pechman, Henry J. Aaron, and Michael K. Taussig, *Social Security: Perspectives for Reform* (Washington, D.C.: The Brookings Institution, 1968), p. 215.

44. U.S. Congress, Senate, *Future Direction in Social Security (Hearings before the Special Committee on Aging)*, 93d Cong., 1st sess., January 23, 1973, pp. 180–81.

45. Subcommittee on Fiscal Policy, *Income Security,* pp. 10–11.

46. U.S. Bureau of the Census, *Statistical Abstract of the United States, 1973* (Washington, D.C.: Government Printing Office, 1973), table 80, p. 58.

47. For more detailed discussion on the research methodology and policy implications of the study, see Martha N. Ozawa, "Individual Equity versus Social Adequacy in Federal Old-Age Insurance," *The Social Service Review*, 48, no. 1 (March 1974), 24–38.

48. Subcommittee on Fiscal Policy, *Income Security,* pp. 10–11.

49. The minimum primary insurance amounts were $40.00 and $84.50 in 1963 and 1972, respectively; the maximum were $68.50 and $266.10, respectively.

50. Calculations are based on *Social Security Bulletin Supplement 1972,* pp. 16 and 21, and table 34, p. 58. Also notice that, as a result of the 1972 amendments of Social Security Act, it is expected that the rate of benefit increase for future beneficiaries will be greater than for the currently retired. Under the amendments, not only will maximum taxable earnings be increased commensurate with the rise in wages and salaries but also the benefit formula itself is adjusted to account for the increase in the cost-of-living index. As a result, the future retiree will benefit from a double adjustment in benefit. Thus, it is expected that the disparity between the minimum benefit level and the maximum benefit level will increase and, at the same time, that the disparity between benefit levels of the currently retired and the future beneficiaries will also increase. However, it now appears that Congress recognizes the unexpected result of the 1972 amendments and is exploring possible alternatives to correct the situation.

51. U.S. Bureau of the Census, *Statistical Abstract, 1973,* table 80, p. 58.

52. Derived from Patience Lauriat, *Benefit Levels and Socio-Economic Characteristics: Findings from the 1968 Survey of the Aged,"* The 1968 Survey of the Aged, Report no. 2 (Washington, D.C.: Social Security Administration, Office of Research and Statistics, August 1970), tables 4 and A, pp. 10–11 and 16–17.

53. Richard E. Barfield and James N. Morgan, *Early Retirement: The Decision and the Experience and a Second Look* (Ann Arbor: The University of Michigan, Survey Research Center, Institute for Social Research, 1974), p. 3.

54. For more detailed discussion on the development of two-tier system, see Margaret S. Gordon, "The Case for Earnings-Related Social Security Benefits Restated" in U.S. Congress, Joint Economic Committee, *Old Age Income Assurance, Part II: The Aged Population and Retirement Income Programs* (Washington, D.C.: Government Printing Office, December 1967), pp. 312–39.

55. Some have recommended so-called indexation of taxable earnings. With indexation, the worker A who earns a given amount of wages, expressed in constant dollars, for a given number of years would receive the same social-security benefit as worker B who earns the same amount of wages, expressed in constant dollars, for the same number of years but at a different time. This is not currently the case. Indexation is offered as a method of eliminating the inequity in giving equal value, in deriving average monthly wages, to a dollar of earnings in 1951, say, and in 1976, despite deterioration in the value of the dollar. Computation of the investment value of contributions, in the fashion proposed above, implicitly adds credit for inflation and real growth and would have an effect similar to indexation.

56. The calculation of the basic benefit amount was based on the data supplied by "Summary Program Data: Old-Age, Survivors, Disability, and Health Insurance, and Supplementary Security Income," *Monthly Benefit Statistics,* no. 11-74 (December 10, 1974), table 1. In calculating the amount, it was assumed that two-thirds of OAI benefits for retired workers were financed by subsidies. Savings derived from the conversion of spouses' benefits into a flat benefit of $60 and from the elimination of children's benefits were used, together with the subsidized parts of OAI aggregate benefits for retired workers, to arrive at the basic benefit amount. For rationale behind the use of two-thirds of OAI benefits see Ozawa, "Individual Equity," pp. 28–30.

57. For further discussion on the subject, see Martha N. Ozawa, "Children's Right to Social Security," *Child Welfare,* 53, no. 10 (December 1974), 619–31.

58. "Summary Program Data: Old-Age, Survivors, Disability and Health Insurance and Supplementary Security Income," *Monthly Benefit Statistics,* no. 5-75 (June 10, 1975), table 1. Children include those of deceased workers, as well as retired workers and disabled workers.

59. In 1969, the ceiling in taxable earnings was 117 percent of the average earnings in the United States, compared with 161 percent in France, 165 percent in Austria, 174 percent in West Germany, and 227 percent in Sweden. See Max Herlick and Robert Lucas, "Role of the Contribution Ceiling in Social Security Programs: Comparison of Five Countries," *Social Security Bulletin,* February 1971, table 1, p. 23.

60. This figure is obtained based on estimated costs for a plan to combine workmen's compensation cash payments and a nationwide temporary disability insurance program which is similar to that presented here but is not to be administered by the federal government. A study estimates that such a combined program will cost

$5.4 billion in 1974, based on 88 claims per 1,000 covered workers, including work-related and non-work-related conditions, an average weekly benefit of $87, and an average duration of compensated incapacity of 8 weeks for nonoccupational illness and injury claims and 3 weeks for work-related injuries. The author subtracted, from the total estimate, $2.3 which was paid in 1973 for cash benefits under workmen's compensation. See Lawrence D. Haber, "Sickness and Injury Cash Benefits: A Proposal for Program Planning and Integration" (Unpublished paper, Division of Disability Studies, Office of Research and Statistics, Social Security Administration, May 10, 1974), pp. ii–ix; and Skolnik and Price, "Workmen's Compensation under Scrutiny," p. 9.

61. In 1966, among poor families, for example, discrepancy between the median income of a family of three and the poverty-line income for such a family was $1,000, compared with $1,560 for a family of six. See Mollie Orshansky, "Who Was Poor in 1966," in Eveline M. Burns, ed., *Children's Allowances and the Economic Welfare of Children* (New York: Citizens Committee for Children of New York City, 1968), pp. 32, 38, 43, and 57.

62. Ibid., p. 54.

63. Jame C. Vadakin, *Children, Poverty, and Family Allowances* (New York: Basic Books, 1968), p. 45.

64. James C. Vadakin, *Family Allowances* (Oxford, Ohio: University of Miami Press, 1958), p. 21.

65. Douglas's study in 1927 indicated that, in spite of expanded per capita children's allowances and wide coverage, the number of children per family in France remained unchanged, namely 1.66. See Paul H. Douglas, *Wages and Family* (Chicago: University of Chicago Press, 1927), p. 93. Another study reports that trends in birth rates in Canada and the United States have been quite similar despite the fact that Canada instituted children's allowances in 1945 and the United States did not. See Alvin L. Schorr, *Poor Kids* (New York: Basic Books, 1966), figure 5-1, p. 69.

66. "Summary Program Data: Old-Age, Survivors, Disability, and Health Insurance and Supplementary Security Income," *Monthly Benefit Statistics*, no. 8-74 (September 6, 1974), table 1.

67. Orshansky, "Who Was Poor in 1966," tables 2 and 6, pp. 32 and 38.

68. Data on the number of children (68.4 million) is from Current Population Reports, P-60, no. 86 (December 1972), table 20, p. 88; the costs of children's allowances are derived by updating data in Orshansky, "Who Was Poor in 1966," table 18, p. 54; data on savings in public assistance are based on data for April, 1974 multiplied by 12. See *Social Security Bulletin*, October 1974, tables M-11, M-12, and M-28, pp. 51–52 and 65.

5. Fair Share in Health Care

1. Some evidence for this can be found in a study of the disabled population. This study examines the relationship between income and medical care of disabled adults under 65 years of age. It found that income did not bar access to physician services except for the weakest economic group; and that once contact with the health-care delivery system was established, the lack of income did not affect the quantity of services rendered to the disabled but placed an inordinately heavy burden on the budgets of families with low or moderate income. See Rachel Florersheim Boaz, "The Burden of Medical Care," processed (New York: New York University School of Social Work, Center for Studies in the Income Maintenance Policy, August 1975).

2. Nancy L. Worthington, "National Health Expenditures, 1929–1974," *Social Security Bulletin,* February 1975, p. 9.

3. The estimates do not include the cost of training health-care professionals. Ibid., p. 8.

4. Since National Health Interview Survey data are not adjusted for differences in the health level of the population, this statement and the subsequent discussion are limited to the *direction of change* in medical services (rather than the difference in quantity of such services) associated with differences in income.

5. U.S. Department of Health, Education, and Welfare, *Persons Hospitalized by Number of Hospital Episodes and Days in a Year, United States, 1968,* Vital and Health Statistics, 10, no. 64 (Washington, D.C., 1971), table 17.

6. Idem., *Physician Visits, Volume and Interval since Last Visit, United States, 1969,* Vital and Health Statistics, ser. 10, no. 75 (Washington, D.C., 1972), table 21.

7. Idem. *Dental Visits, Volume and Interval since Last Visit, United States, 1969,* Vital and Health Statistics, ser. 10, no. 76 (Washington, D.C., 1972), table 11.

8. Worthington, *"National Health Expenditures,"* p. 16 and p. 19.

9. Ibid., pp. 10 12.

10. Marjorie Smith Mueller and Robert M. Gibson, "Age Differences in Health Care Spending, Fiscal Year 1974," *Social Security Bulletin,* June 1975, p. 10.

11. Marjorie Smith Mueller, "Private Health Insurance in 1973: A Review of Coverage, Enrollment, and Financial Experience," *Social Security Bulletin,* February 1975, table 4, p. 24.

12. Evelyn Peel and Jack Scharff, "Impact of Cost-Sharing on Use of Ambulatory Services under Medicare, 1969," *Social Security Bulletin,* October 1973, table 2, p. 8.

13. Worthington, "National Health Expenditures," table 3, p. 10.

14. Davis and Reynolds, in explaining table 5.3, point out that at the beginning of 1969, eleven states had no Medicaid programs, so that some public-assistance recipients were not enrolled in Medicaid; and other states had Medicaid programs for needy persons who were not on welfare. Yet the comparison between "aid" and "no aid," though imperfect, can still serve as a rough indicator for the difference in Medicaid coverage. See Karen Davis and Roger Reynolds, "The Impact of Medicare and Medicaid on Access to Medical Care," in Richard Rossett, ed., *The Role of Insurance in the Health Services Sector* (a Universities–National Bureau of Economic Research Conference held May 31–June 1, 1974; volume forthcoming.)

15. Mueller, "Private Health Insurance," table 3 and 4, p. 24.

16. U.S. Department of Health, Education, and Welfare, *Dental Visits, Volume and Interval since Last Visit, United States, 1969,* Vital and Health Statistics, ser. 10, no. 76 (Washington, D.C., 1972), table 11.

17. Ibid.

18. U.S. Department of Health, Education, and Welfare, *Personal Out-of-Pocket Health Expenses, United States, 1970,* Vital and Health Statistics, ser. 10, no. 91 (Washington, D.C., 1974), pp. 3–5 and tables 1, 2, 13, 15, 17, 19, 21, 23, and 25.

19. Marjorie Smith Mueller, "Private Health Insurance in 1972: Health Care Services, Enrollment, and Finances," *Social Security Bulletin,* February 1974, tables 3, p. 24.

20. According to data provided by the National Center for Social Statistics (in HEW), 19.4 million persons were enrolled in Medicaid on June 30, 1972, of whom 3.4 million were aged 65 or older and 16 million were under age 65. The aged persons were counted among Medicare enrollees as they were likely to have been "bought-in" by their state Medicaid programs. See U.S. Department of Health, Education, and Welfare, *Number of Recipients and Amounts of Payments Under Medicaid, 1972,* Pub. no. (SRS) 74-03153 (Washington, D.C., 1974), Introduction and table 10.

21. In mid-1975, the proportion of the population that had no third-party protection is likely to have been higher because of the higher unemployment level.

22. Mueller and Gibson, "Age Differences," table 1, p. 4.

23. The "notch" (or slight) increase in income can result in a "cliff" (or large) decrease in the subsidy. The notch problem results from an abrupt, instead of a smooth, change in the level of benefits at the boundary of each income class that is subsidized. An example taken from the Nixon Administration's proposal in 1974 can serve to illustrate this point. Suppose an individual who earns $5,200 pays $100 as a deductible; if his income increases to $5,300, his deductible increases to $150. Thus a $100 additional income gives rise to a $50 additional net payment; the net income at his disposal is $50. Individuals so affected may have an incentive to keep their income from rising.

24. The Department of Health, Education, and Welfare estimated that, under

the Nixon proposal, the average premium on an individual policy would amount to $900, compared to that for a group policy of $600 per family in 1975. At an annual income of $10,000, the premium on an individual policy would be 9 percent of income. See Saul Waldman's compilation, *National Health Insurance Proposals: Provisions of Bills Introduced in the 93rd Congress as of July, 1974,* Department of Health, Education, and Welfare pub. no. (SSA) 75-11920 (Washington, D.C., 1974).

25. A progressive scale, namely, where the marginal tax rate increases with income, may be more equitable than a proportional scale in terms of sharing the burden; but it creates other problems, among which is the "notch" problem, or the disincentive to earn higher incomes.

26. To base premiums on income and not only on earnings would require information on all the components of individual incomes. Only the government is legally entitled to such information, which it obtains because all taxpayers are required to file an annual income statement.

27. Karen Davis provides the following example: Suppose the upper expense limit is set at 10 percent of income, and a family incurs $4,000 in medical expenses. If annual income is $20,000, the family is entitled to a $2,000 tax credit; but if annual income is $40,000, the family is not entitled to any tax credit. See Edward R. Fried, Alice M. Rivlin, Charles L. Schultze, and Nancy H. Teeters, *Setting the National Priorities: The 1974 Budget* (Washington, D.C.: The Brookings Institution, 1973), pp. 118–19.

28. Feldstein considers coinsurance an improvement on his major-risk insurance plan, which requires setting a direct expense limit as a fixed percentage of income. The following example illustrates his point: Suppose the coinsurance rate is 25 percent; with no deductible and an expense limit that amounts to 10 percent of income, the range of expenditures over which a patient is cost conscious is exended to 40 percent of income. Put differently, with an income of $20,000, the direct expense limit is $2,000; but because of the partial payments, a $2,000 amount of direct medical payments will be accumulated when medical bills reach $8,000 (i.e., 40 percent of $20,000). A patient's sensitivity to the cost is stretched to the point where he consumes a level of $8,000 rather than $2,000 worth of medical bills. See Martin S. Feldstein, "A New Approach to National Health Insurance," *The Public Interest,* no. 23 (Spring 1971), pp. 93–105.

29. U.S. Department of Health, Education, and Welfare, "Estimated Health Expenditures under Selected National Health Insurance Bills," mimeographed (a report to Congress, July 1974).

30. Patricia Fishbein and Frank van Dyke, "Relationships of National Health Insurance to Other Federal Laws or Pending Legislation—Health Planning, Manpower, PRSO's and HMO's," processed (New York: Columbia University, School of Public Health, June 1975).

31. Victor R. Fuchs and Marcia J. Kramer, *Determinants of Expenditures for Physicians' Services in the United States, 1948–68,* NBER Occasional Paper 117 (New York: National Bureau of Economic Research, 1972), pp. 31–32 and pp. 37–41.

32. National Center for Health Statistics, *Health Resources Statistics, 1974,* U.S. Department of Health, Education and Welfare, pub. no. (HRA) 75-1509 (Washington, D.C., 1974), tables 39 and 49.

33. E. F. X. Hughes, V. R. Fuchs, J. E. Jacoby, and E. M. Levit, "Surgical Workloads in a Community Practice," *Surgery,* 71, no. 3 (March 1972), 315–27.

34. National Academy of Sciences, Institute of Medicine, *Costs of Education in the Health Professions, Parts I and II* (Washington, D.C., 1974), tables 9, 52, 53, 55, 56, 78, 85, 86, and 88.

35. Victor R. Fuchs, *Who Shall Live? Health, Economics, and Social Choice* (New York, Basic Books, 1974), chapter 2, pp. 30–55.

36. R. M. Hartwell, "The Economic History of Medical Care" and Mark Perlman, "Economic History and Health Care in Industrialized Nations," in Mark Perlman, ed., *The Economics of Health and Medical Care* (Proceedings of a conference held by the International Economic Association at Tokyo; London: Macmillan, 1974), pp. 1–32.

6. AFDC: Symptom and Potential

1. This notion appears repeatedly in congressional hearings on social-security amendments and the Economic Opportunity Act, but it is not clear whether responsible officials ever actually expected this outcome or simply found "withering away" a catchy slogan, equally useful in selling new legislation and in casting blame when past reforms failed to bring about promised results. However used, it kept alive the notion that the public goal was to reduce caseload size and expenditures, especially for AFDC, rather than to reduce poverty.

2. See, e.g., Frances Piven and Richard Cloward, *Regulating the Poor* (New York: Pantheon Books, 1971); Winifred Bell, *Aid to Dependent Children* (New York: Columbia University Press, 1965).

3. For the latest survey of these programs, see U.S. Department of Health, Education, and Welfare, Social and Rehabilitation Services, Assistance Payments Administration, *Characteristics of General Assistance in the United States,* Public Assistance Report no. 39, 1970 edition (Washington, D.C.: Government Printing Office, 1970).

4. Despite the much greater incidence of poverty among black children than

among white, since 1967 black families have comprised only about 46 percent of the caseload. All references in this chapter to AFDC caseload characteristics rely on reports of the periodic surveys carried out by National Center for Social Statistics of HEW. See *Findings of the AFDC Survey,* 1961, 1967, 1969, 1971, and 1973.

5. Congresswoman Martha Griffiths was a strong proponent of this view. See her comments and questions in U.S. Congress, Joint Economic Committee, Subcommittee on Fiscal Policy, *Problems in Administration of Public Welfare Program,* Hearings in Washington, D.C., pt. 1; Detroit, pt. 2; and Atlanta, pt. 3.

6. In January 1973, only 17 percent of AFDC families received another public cash benefit; 4 percent received OASDI benefits.

7. Irene Lurie, "The Distribution of Transfer Payments among Households," in President's Commission on Income Maintenance, *Poverty Amid Plenty* (Washington, D.C.: Government Printing Office, 1969), vol. 2, pp. 143–55.

8. Winifred Bell and Dennis M. Bushe, "The Economic Efficiency of AFDC," *The Social Service Review,* 29, no. 2 (June 1975), 175–90.

9. In 1969 the poverty threshold was not adjusted to reflect price changes for the expenditure patterns of poor households; instead, the consumer price index (reflecting average consumption patterns) was substituted. For yearly thresholds and methods of updating, see U.S. Bureau of the Census, *Characteristics of the Low Income Population,* Current Population Reports, ser. P-60, no. 98 (Washington, D.C.: Government Printing Office, 1973), pp. 159–62. For discussion of alternate definitions of poverty, see Eugene Smolensky, "Poverty, Propinquity, and Policy," *The Annals,* September 1973, pp. 120–25; U.S. Congress, Senate, Committee on Labor and Public Welfare, Subcommittee on Employment, Manpower, and Poverty, *Hearings on Comprehensive Manpower Reform,* pt. 5 (Washington, D.C.: Government Printing Office, 1972), pp. 2277–80; Lee Rainwater, *What Money Buys* (New York: Basic Books, 1974), chapter 7; and James N. Morgan, Martin H. David, Wilbur J. Cohen, and Harvey E. Brazer, *Income and Welfare in the United States* (New York: McGraw-Hill, 1962), pp. 88–196.

10. In about half of the states, those with local administration of welfare, local tax funds help to support the program. State equalizing funds and formulas now help to compensate for the difference in fiscal ability among localities.

11. Handler makes the intriguing point that the proliferation and confusion in policies and procedures has been a humanizing factor in welfare since they render the welfare system virtually unadministrable. Joel F. Handler, *Reforming the Poor* (New York: Basic Books, 1972), passim.

12. Martha Griffiths, "What Decline in AFDC?" *Congressional Record,* March 12, 1974, p. H-1753-1754. (HEW press release quoted.)

13. Piven and Cloward, *Regulating the Poor,* passim.

14. E.g., *King* v. *Smith* 392 U.S. 309 (1968), the so-called "man-in-the-

house" decision, modified policies excluding families from AFDC in some states if their homes were "unsuitable"; as a result, a conservative estimate of 500,000 children and adults became eligible for AFDC. Residence requirements were also overturned, making an estimated 25,000 to 50,000 more people eligible; subsequent state residency laws have begun to reverse this gain.

15. When this occurred in late June 1969, congressmen made a point of entering comments on the subject of the "freeze" in the *Congressional Record,* most of them testifying to their initial opposition to the amendment because of its implicit racism.

16. For eligibility conditions in general assistance, see Assistance Payments Administration, *Characteristics of General Assistance,* passim. For caseload and cost data, including breakdowns for general assistance, AFDC-UP, and AFDC, see *Public Assistance Statistics,* a monthly release of the National Center for Social Statistics.

17. U.S. Department of Health, Education, and Welfare, Social and Rehabilitation Services, Assistance Payments Administration, "States' Activities to Implement Subject Areas Affected by Administrative Actions and Amendments to the Public Assistance Titles of the Federal Social Security Act" (unpublished periodic report).

18. 39F.R., p. 3369 ff.

19. This is especially ironic since failure to take the mother's needs into consideration was apparently an oversight. See Grace Abbot, *Child and the State* (Chicago: University of Chicago Press, 1938), vol. 2, pp. 241–42.

20. The dates that each state adopted the amendment were provided by the National Center for Social Statistics. The number of families with a second adult in the assistance unit was reported in the 1967, 1969, 1971, and 1973 AFDC surveys. The number of second adults in alternate years was estimated by fitting a nonlinear trend line through the four survey points for each state with a policy in effect. For earlier years, the number of families with no adults was estimated by the same method, using 1961 and 1967 AFDC surveys to locate two points; after subtracting these families from the family count, children and one adult were subtracted from the recipient count, leaving a balance of second adults. Monthly reports on AFDC-UP were then used to subtract second-adult families in this sector, since the program tends to be in operation in states paying higher grants. Average payments were then calculated for second adults in AFDC-UP and in disabled-adult cases.

21. Winifred Bell and Raymond Clapp, *Public Welfare Demonstration Projects Focus on Education for AFDC Youth* (Washington, D.C.: Department of Health, Education, and Welfare, Welfare Administration, Bureau of Family Services, 1965).

22. For a detailed analysis of the impact of welfare work incentives, see

Winifred Bell and Dennis M. Bushe, *Neglecting the Many, Helping the Few: The Impact of the 1967 AFDC Work Incentives* (New York: Center for Studies in Income Maintenance Policy, New York University School of Social Work, 1975).

23. Old beliefs die hard. The literature published after 1970 is replete with measurements of the effect of a 67 percent tax on earnings, as though the only AFDC deduction is the $30 and one-third earnings deduction enacted in 1967.

24. Leonard Hausman, *The Potential for Work among Welfare Parents*, Manpower Research Monograph no. 12 (Washington, D.C.: U.S. Department of Labor, 1969).

25. Blanche Bernstein makes a similar point in her monograph, *Income-Tested Social Benefits in New York: Adequacy, Incentives, and Equity*, Subcommittee on Fiscal Policy Paper no. 8 (Washington, D.C.: Government Printing Office, 1973).

26. In July 1973, only 16 states met 100 percent of need. Department of Health, Education, and Welfare, Social and Rehabilitation Services, *Public Assistance Programs: Standards for Basic Needs, July 1973* (Washington, D.C.: National Center for Social Statistics, 1974).

27. Subcommittee on Fiscal Policy, *Problems in Administration of Public Welfare Program*, paper no. 6, March 26, 1973.

28. Ibid., paper no. 17, December 31, 1974.

29. The list included Medicare, Medicaid, public housing, School Breakfast, School Lunch, Special Milk Program, Supplementary Food Program. Since the samples were chosen from among users of food stamps and food commodities, the impact of nine in-kind benefits was measured.

30. Henry J. Aaron, *Shelter and Subsidies* (Washington, D.C.: The Brookings Institution, 1972), chapter 7.

31. U.S. Congress, Senate, Select Committee on Nutrition and Human Needs, *National Nutrition Policy Study: Reports and Recommendations—VII* (Washington, D.C.: Government Printing Office, June 1974), pp. 29–40.

32. Ibid., p. 108.

33. E.g., see Citizens' Board of Inquiry into Hunger and Malnutrition in the United States, *Hunger U.S.A. Revisited* (Atlanta: Southern Regional Council, 1972), passim.

34. See, e.g., Subcommittee on Fiscal Policy, *Problems in Administration of Public Welfare Program*, Papers 4, 5 (Part 3), 7, 8, 13, 14, and Report of the Subcommittee on Fiscal Policy, Dec. 5, 1974; Michael C. Barth, George J. Cargagno, and John L. Palmer, *Toward an Effective Income Support System: Problems, Prospects, and Choices* (Madison: University of Wisconsin, Institute for Research on Poverty, 1974); Glenn G. Cain and Harold Watts, eds., *Income Maintenance and Labor Supply* (Chicago: Markham, 1973).

35. For discussion of the implications of these experiments, see Barth, Car-

cagno, and Palmer, *Toward an Effective Income Support System,* chapter 3, and Joseph A. Pechman and P. Michael Timpane, eds., *Work Incentives and Income Guarantees* (Washington, D.C.: The Brookings Institution, 1975), passim.

36. Despite the emphasis in recent years on quantifying the impact of public antipoverty expenditures, there is still no systematic study of the costs and other consequences of poverty per se. Conceptually this is a far more difficult measurement task, but its accomplishment would make for far better-informed choices between doing something and doing nothing, deciding to continue to pour money into custodial and remedial services or to invest in prevention.

37. For a discussion of the issues, see Department of Health and Security, *Report of the Committee on One-Parent Families* (London: Her Majesty's Stationery Office, July 1974), vol. 1, pp. 64–240, 314–34.

7. The Strategy and Hope

1. Paul H. Douglas, *Wages and the Family* (Chicago: University of Chicago Press, 1927).

2. In 1974, 1.3 million more people were poor than in 1973. According to the Census Bureau, the increase was wholly accounted for by the inability of working people to improve their earnings in pace with an inflating poverty level.

3. Karen Davis, "Equal Treatment and Unequal Benefits; The Medicare Program," *The Milbank Memorial Fund Quarterly,* 53, no. 4 (Fall 1975), 480.

4. "California Issue on Health Widens," *The New York Times,* May 5, 1974; "Medi-Cal Reform—Favoritism and Shoddy Services," *Los Angeles Times,* May 23, 1974.

5. Alvin L. Schorr, *Explorations in Social Policy* (New York: Basic Books, 1968), chapter 18.

6. Alfred M. Skolnik and Sophie R. Dales, "Social Welfare Expenditures, 1968–69," *Social Security Bulletin,* December 1969.

7. Stanley S. Surrey, "Federal Income Tax Reform: The Varied Approaches Necessary to Replace Tax Expenditures with Direct Governmental Assistance," *Harvard Law Review,* 84 (1970). By fiscal 1976, tax benefits for owner-occupied housing had reached $8.2 billion. U.S. Congress, Senate, Committee on the Budget, *Tax Expenditures* (Committee print, Washington, D.C., August 1976).

8. Peter Townsend, ed., *The Concept of Poverty* (London: Heineman Education Books, 1970), chapter 6, "Housing Policy and Poverty."

9. U.S. Congress, Joint Economic Committee, Subcommittee on Fiscal Policy, *Handbook of Public Income Transfer Programs–1975* (Washington, D.C.: Government Printing Office, 1974), p. 277.

10. Martha Derthick, *Uncontrollable Spending for Social Service Grants* (Washington, D.C.: The Brookings Institution, 1975).

11. Alfred M. Skolnik and Sophie R. Dales, "Social Welfare Expenditures, 1950–75," *Social Security Bulletin,* January 1976.

12. Alvin L. Schorr, ed., *Children and Decent People* (New York: Basic Books, 1974).

13. Alfred J. Kahn, *Social Policy and Social Services* (New York: Random House, 1973), p. 93.

14. Skolnik and Dales, "Social Welfare Expenditures, 1968–69" and "Social Welfare Expenditures, 1950–1975."

15. It may also be interesting that social insurance is 100 percent federally financed, but states and localities shared very largely in the cost of income-tested programs. In a period when the rhetoric was quite otherwise, the balance of financing in these transfer payments was being shifted from the federal to state and local governments.

16. U.S. Congress, Joint Economic Committee, *An Economic Evaluation of the Current Services Budget, Fiscal Year 1977* (Washington, D.C.: Government Printing Office, 1975), p. 1.

17. Gunnar Myrdal, *Beyond the Welfare State* (New Haven: Yale University Press, 1960).

18. Robert Lekachman, "The Inevitability of Controls," *Challenge,* November–December 1974.

19. Robert L. Heilbroner, "The American Plan," *New York Times Magazine,* January 25, 1976. Heilbroner names John Kenneth Galbraith, Wassily Leontief, Felix Rohatyn, and Henry Ford as favoring the establishment of a national planning agency. See also James R. Crotty and Leonard A. Rapping, "The 1975 Report of the President's Council of Economic Advisors: A Radical Critique," *The American Economic Review,* 65, no. 5 (December 1975).

Index

Aaron, Henry J., 116
Ability-to-pay principle, 79, 114
Absent parent freeze, 233, 234
Accelerated depreciation, 97
Accidents, industrial, 46
Adjusted gross income, 102–3, 104
Aged, income of, 7
Aid to the Blind (AB), 221
Aid to Families with Dependent Children (AFDC), 221, 224–26; and redistribution of money, 227–31; and redistribution of income, 321–35; and unemployed parent, 234–37; and second-parent amendment, 237–38; and youth aged *18–21*, 239–41; and work incentives, 241–45, 253–57; and means-tested programs, 245–47; equity of, 247–53; and welfare reform, 257–63
Alaska, 238
Alienation, 18
Allocation of resources, 78
Anomie, 17, 18
Antipoverty instruments, 136–37, 160, 231, 272
Appalachia, 235

Barnes, Peter, 8
Benefits, 222; distribution of, 130–31;

welfare, 136–37; formulas for, 154–56; levels of, 156–57, 270; for dependents, 157–59; adequate minimum, 160–61; for children, 165, 170
Bergmann, Barbara, 39
Blacks: median family income, 6; earnings of, 9; unemployment rate of, 42–43; in work force, 60–61, 141–42
Bonds, interest from, 119
Boskin, Michael J., 95
Bridges, Benjamin, 91, 110
Buchanan, James M., 116
Bureau of Labor Statistics (BLS), 28, 29, 60, 62

Cairnes, J. M., 32
California, 230, 236, 272
Capital gains, 96, 102, 103, 105, 119
Census, Bureau of the, 4, 237
Child-care services, 54
Children: as beneficiaries, 142–44; dependent benefits for, 165, 170; *see also* Aid to Families with Dependent Children
Children's allowances, 172–76, 269, 270, 283
Civil Works Administration (CWA), 56

Cloward, Richard, 232
Coinsurance, 212
Commons, John R., 151
Community, sense of, 15–19
Comprehensive Employment and Training Act (CETA), 56, 57, 58
Consumption-leisure choice, 95
Consumption-savings choice, 95–97
Consumption taxes, 111
Corporation income tax, 81, 86, 99, 106–8, 118, 121
Corporate profits tax, 108–9
Council of Economic Advisers, 15, 43
Credit-card system for health care, 212, 218

Death taxes, 116–17, 121
Deductions, 120; itemized, 102, 104; standard, 105
Dependent benefits, 157–59
Depreciation, 69, 97
Differential tax rates, 81
Discrimination, 8–9, 33, 34, 57, 266, 268, 278
Disability, 38, 39
Disability insurance, 149–51, 161, 166, 268; temporary, 170–72
Disabled persons, 147–51
Disabled workers, 143
Disadvantaged persons, 138–51
Disease, occupational, 46, 47
District of Columbia, 238
Domestic workers, 62
Douglas, Paul H., 266
Dual labor-market theory, 33, 34
Duplex society, 17

Earned income, 103
Earnings: strategy, 27–48: race differential in, 37–38, and taxes, 266–67
Edelstein, Martin, 212

Education, 5, 34
Efficiency costs, 93–95
Emergency Employment Act of 1971, 56
Employment: goals, 28; continuity, 30–31; public-service, 54–59, 283
Employment Act of 1946, 41
Equal opportunity, 13, 14
Estate taxes, 121
Ethnic variations, in life expectancy, 158
Exemptions, 102

Fair Labor Standards Act (FLAS), 61, 63
Family budget, 29
Farmworkers, 47, 62, 69
Federal taxes, 5, 92–93; income, 9, 102
Female workers, 37, 61, 139–41
Fiscal federalism, 80–82
Fishbein, Patricia, 214
Food stamps, 3, 275, 276
France, 173
Fuchs, Victor R., 215, 216
Full Employment Bill of 1945, 41, 67, 71
Furniss, Norman, 23

George, Henry, 115
Gifts, and taxes, 116, 117, 121
Goldthorpe, John, 18
Great Britain, 162
Greenberg, David H., 95
Gross National Product (GNP), 75, 111, 126
Group insurance, 207
Guam, 238

Harberger, Arnold C., 97–98, 99
Harrison, Bennet, 64
Hartwell, R. M., 216
Hawkins-Reuss bill, 67
Health care, distribution of services and payments, 182–200
Health-delivery system, 271

Health, Education, and Welfare, Department of (HEW), 213, 217
Health insurance: premiums, 195; taxes, 209; national, 271, 283
Health-insurance programs, national, 200–1, 216–19; coverage, 200–4; financing, 204–9; administration and management, 209–16
Health Security Act, 204, 209, 213, 214
Health Systems Agencies, 214
Heilbroner, Robert, 11
Henle, Peter, 40
Housing programs, 274, 275
Hunter, Robert, 15

Illinois, 236
Income: shares, 1, 3, 5, 8; distribution, 2–7, 19, 36, 65, 71, 78; supplement, 22; and wages, 29; maintenance, 45–48; taxable, 101–3; earned, 103; low, 110; and medical services, 183–97; testing, 278–281; see also Corporate income tax, Individual income tax, Redistribution of income
Independent income tax, 109
Indians, American, 228
Individual income tax, 75, 80, 96, 100–1, 104, 106, 107, 118, 119, 120, 122
Industrial accidents, 46
Inequality, 30–45
Inflation, 38, 109
Inheritance tax, 117, 121
In-kind benefits, see Transfers, non-cash
Insurance: private and social compared, 152; premiums, 207; see also Private insurance; Unemployment insurance
Interest, from bonds, 119
Intergenerational transfers, 154, 158
Internal Revenue Service (IRS), 209, 211, 218
Investment, effects of taxation on, 97–98

Investment credit, 97
Itemized deductions, 102, 104

Job Corps, 51
Job Guarantee Office, 67
Job tenure, 37
Jobs, 33
Joint Economic Committee of Congress, 153, 157, 275, 284
Joint tax returns, 101
Jorgenson, Dale W., 97
Jubilee, 285

Koster, Marvin, 95
Kramer, Marcia J., 215

Labor force, 28
Labor Statistics, Bureau of, see Bureau of Labor Statistics
Leisure, 95
Lekachman, Robert, 67, 68
Life expectancy, ethnic variations in, 158
Local taxes, 86, 92
Low-wage earner, 29, 110, 138–39, 161
Lurie, Irene, 228

Mack Truck Co., 52
Macroeconomic policies, 49
Macroeconomy, 65–69, 71
Manpower Development and Training Act of 1962 (MDTA), 50–51
Manpower policy, 50–54
Marginal tax rate, 103, 105, 107
Massachusetts, 236
Means-tested programs, 245–47
Medicaid, 109, 186, 189–92, 197, 199, 217
Medical services, and income, 183–97
Medicare, 186–89, 190, 192, 193, 198, 211, 217, 271; Part A, 197; Part B, 202
Mier, Robert, 64

Migration policy, 70
Minimum wage, 59–65, 268
Minnesota, 238
Mississippi, 238
Musgrave, Richard and Peggy, 83, 86, 92, 99, 110, 118
Myrdal, Gunnar, 17, 285

National Commission on State Workmen's Compensation Laws, 148
National Commission on Technology, 58
National Commission on the Causes and Prevention of Violence, 17
National health insurance, 271, 283; see also Health insurance programs, national
National Health Insurance Survey, 184
National Health Planning and Resources Development Act of 1974, 214
National Welfare Rights Organization, 233
Negative income tax, 22, 23, 153, 226
New Jersey, 236
New York, 236

Occupational disease, 46, 47
Occupational Safety and Health Act of 1970, 47
Office of Economic Opportunity, 58
Okner, Benjamin A., 88, 89, 90
Old Age Assistance (OAA), 22, 223, 224, 227, 228
Old Age, Survivors, and Disability Insurance (OASDI), 46, 104, 126, 127, 144, 161, 167, 224, 228, 232
Oregon, 236
Orshansky, Mollie, 29

Patients, direct payments to, 192–96
Payroll tax, 109–11, 118
Pechman, Joseph A., 9, 88, 89, 90, 153

Pennsylvania, 236
Perlman, Mark, 216
Personal income taxes, see Individual income tax
Piven, Frances Fox, 232
Pluralistic strategy, 21–24, 281–85
Polanyi, Karl, 34
Policy options, for substandard wages, 48–71
Poverty, 15–19, 45–48, 159, 267, 268; threshold, 29, 35, 230; law, 233
Powerlessness, see Alienation; Anomie
Prepayment, 208
Preventive care, 272
Private insurance, 197, 217; and direct payments by patients, 192–96
Professional Standards Review Organizations, 214
Property tax, 75, 86, 113–16, 118, 120, 122
Public-aid programs, 123–24
Public assistance, 5, 8, 22, 23, 130, 133, 221; evolution of, 222–26
Public-service employment, 54–59, 283
Puerto Rico, 238

Queuing, 279

Race differential, in earnings, 37–38
Railroad retirement benefits, 130, 133
Rationing, 278–81
Rawls, John, 12
Real-property tax, 115–16; see also Property tax
Recessions, 41, 42
Redistribution of income, 25, 63–64, 73, 118, 281–85; through social insurance, 151–59, and AFDC, 231–34
Retired workers, 163, 164
Richman, Raymond L., 116
Rubinow, Isaac M., 152

Sales taxes, 75, 111–13, 120
Savings, 95, 96
School tax, 113
Scitovsky, Tibor, 9
Second-parent amendment, 237–38
Self-employed, 28
Social adequacy, 159
Social justice, 286; opposed, 14
Social security, 5, 11, 124, 133, 160, 161, 231, 268, 269; taxes, 5, 84–85, 86, 104, 109, 110; for disadvantaged persons, 138–44; disability insurance under, 150–51; income redistribution through, 153–58; as social adequacy, 159; proposals for reform in, 162–67; two-tier system of, 162, 163, 167, 171, 199, 283; see also Old Age, Survivors, and Disability Insurance
Social Security Act of 1935, 123, 144, 226
Social services, 276–77
Social welfare expenditures, 126–27
Solow, Robert M., 41
Stabilization of the economy, 78
Standard deduction, 105
Standby Job Corps, 67
State taxes, 86, 92
State temporary disability insurance, 149–50
Stevenson, Mary, 39
Subemployment, 28, 44–45
Substandard wages, and policy options, 48–71
Supplementary Security Income (SSI), 221, 223
Survey of the Disabled, 138, 147

Tax: benefits, 69, 274; burden, 82-93; characteristics, 99–100; individual income, 100–1, 106; credit, 104; corporate income, 106–8; corporate profit, 108–9; revisions (1975), 110; sales, 111-13; property, 113-16; death, 116-17; incidence of, 118; on commodities and luxuries, 119; cashable credit, 267, 270, 283
Tax rate: schedule, 101; marginal, 103, 105
Tax Reduction Act of 1975, 121
Taxable income, 101–3
Taxation, 117–22; for redistributing income, 73, 81; trends in, 74–77; reasons for, 78–79; effects of, 97–99; restructuring system of, 119; and earnings, 266–67
Taxpaying unit, 101
Tawney, R. H., 13
Training, 50–54, 72
Transfers: income, 2, 3, 21, 72, 123, 127, 231, 266; and policy, 3, 71; and payments, 5, 25, 71, 78, 81, 267–73; intergenerational, 154, 158; non-cash, 273–78
Trusts, and taxes, 116–17, 121
Two-tier system of social security, 162, 163, 167, 171, 199, 283

Underclass, undifferentiated, 17, 18
Unemployment: rates, 9, 37, 42–43; and low wages, 29; and inequality, 40–45; insurance, 46, 127, 128, 130, 160, 161, 168–69, 268, 269
Unions, labor, 59–61, 70

Van Dyke, Frank, 214
Veterans' compensation, 5
Vietorisz, Thomas, 64
Virgin Islands, 238

Wage: and income, 27; level, 30; system, 32; rates, 35; minimum, 59–65, 268;

Wage (*Continued*)
  see also Earnings, Low-wage earners,
  Substandard wages
War on Poverty, 226, 286
Wealth, 8
Welfare: reform 10, 12, 257–63; benefits,
  136–37; rights, 233; as redistributive
  mechanism, 272; *see also* Public assis-
  tance
West Virginia, 236
Who Shall Live?, 216
Wives, in labor force, 36
Wooton, Barbara, 18

Work, 31; attachment, 45–48; ethic, 48;
  incentives, 125, 273
Work Incentive Program (WIN), 44, 51,
  232
Working Poor program, 236
Workmen's compensation, 47, 127, 130,
  148–49, 161, 169–70
Works Progress Administration (WPA),
  56, 222
Wylie, George, 233

Youths: earnings of, 6–7; unemployment
  rates of, 42, 43